THE GREEKS

Paul Cartledge is Professor of Greek History, Chairman of the Faculty of Classics, and a Fellow of Clare College, at the University of Cambridge. Publications include most recently *The Greeks: Crucible of Civilization* (BBC Worldwide, 2001) and *Spartan Reflections* (Duckworth/University of California Press, 2001).

'Cartledge's *The Greeks* is bracingly enthusiastic with inter-disciplinary influences and interests.'

The Sunday Times

'the lively and succinct development of many ancient and modern arguments makes *The Greeks* a welcome and timely contribution to a number of continuing and important debates'   *Times Literary Supplement*

'it can be warmly recommended as a source of new insights and new approaches.'

Bryn Mawr Classical Review

'I know of no better book with which to introduce this "portrait of self and others" to students.'

Greece & Rome

'a study of the rise of a mentality, written in brilliant style, important, sometimes iconoclastic'

Il pensiero politico

To the St Paul's Schools, London, and
the Faculty of Classics, University
of Cambridge

The Greeks

A Portrait of Self and Others

SECOND EDITION

PAUL CARTLEDGE

OXFORD
UNIVERSITY PRESS

OXFORD
UNIVERSITY PRESS

Great Clarendon Street, Oxford OX2 6DP

Oxford University Press is a department of the University of Oxford.
It furthers the University's objective of excellence in research, scholarship,
and education by publishing worldwide in

Oxford New York

Auckland Bangkok Buenos Aires Cape Town Chennai
Dar es Salaam Delhi Hong Kong Istanbul Karachi Kolkata
Kuala Lumpur Madrid Melbourne Mexico City Mumbai Nairobi
São Paulo Shanghai Singapore Taipei Tokyo Toronto

with an associated company in Berlin

Oxford is a registered trade mark of Oxford University Press
in the UK and in certain other countries

Published in the United States
by Oxford University Press Inc., New York

British Library Cataloguing in Publication Data

Data available

Library of Congress Cataloging in Publication Data
Cartledge, Paul.
The Greeks: a portrait of self and others / Paul Cartledge.
Includes bibliographical references and index.
1. National characteristics, Greek. 2. Difference (Philosophy).
3. Greece—Civilization—To 146 B.C. I. Title.
938—dc20 DF78.C28 1993 92–45898

ISBN 0-19-280388-3

1 3 5 7 9 10 8 6 4 2

Printed in Great Britain by
Clays Ltd., St Ives plc

Acknowledgements

I HAVE to thank, first, the Oxford University Press, especially the academic editors of the OPUS series and its editorial director Ms Catherine Clarke, for the challenge they posed me by commissioning this book. Secondly, I am in the debt of David Konstan of Brown University, and Lene Rubinstein of Churchill College, Cambridge, who quite out of the line of normal duty subjected my penultimate and ultimate drafts respectively to the most searching and fruitful cross-examination. Thirdly, I have, I trust, profited from the observations of Oxford's peculiarly acute and assiduous anonymous reader. But above all this book is owed to the successive cohorts of Cambridge undergraduates who endured my 'The Greeks and "the Other"' lectures between 1989/90 and 1992/3, and to the friends and colleagues who helped me with the teaching of the course: Peter Garnsey, Penny Glare, Simon Goldhill, Edith Hall, Jonathan Hall, John Henderson, Geoffrey Lloyd, Paul Millett, Neville Morley, Sitta von Reden, Dorothy Thompson, and (by no means least) Jonathan Walters. It is to the Faculty which they represent or have represented that this book is dedicated, in a spirit not of alienation but of *homonoia*, like-minded identification; as it is also to the St Paul's Schools, my other principal educational preoccupation, in the same spirit.

P.A.C.

Trumpington
September 1992

Acknowledgements for Second Edition

Catherine Clarke has kindly kept a watchful maternal eye over the volume since it was first published eight years ago, but the idea for the second edition has come from a successor editor at the OUP, George Miller, to whom I am indebted also for much wise advice. My new colleague Robin Osborne, the Press's anonymous reader for the first edition, has compounded my debt by reading and advising on the new illustrated 'Entr'acte' below. I should also like to thank warmly the three translators of the revised English edition of *The Greeks* into respectively German and Japanese: their names will be found in the first note to the New Afterword.

Trumpington
October 2001

Contents

Hellas: The Greek World c.400 BCE

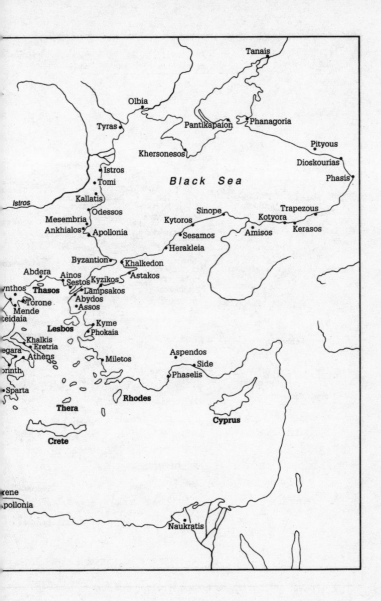

The Aegean Heartland

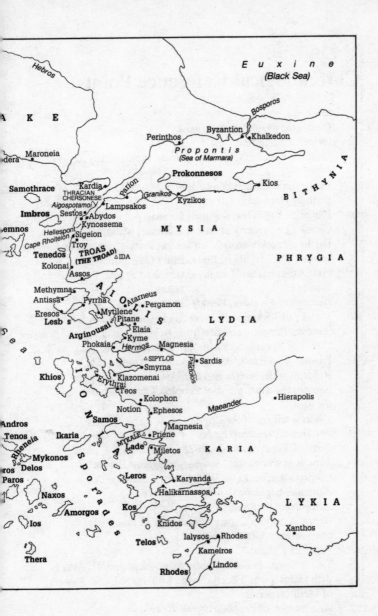

Chronological Reference Points

508/7	Democracy founded at Athens.
490	Battle of Marathon.
486	Death of Persian Great King Darius, succeeded by Xerxes (486–465).
	First competition in comic drama at Athens.
484?	Birth of Herodotus (d. 425?).
480–479	Expedition of Xerxes against Greece.
480	Greek naval victory at Salamis; Xerxes withdraws.
479	Further Greek victories, on land at Plataia, by land and sea at Cape Mykale in Ionia. End of 'Persian Wars'.
477	First Athenian Sea-League established against Persian threat.
472	Aeschylus' *Persians* (Perikles as impresario).
Early 460s	Victory of Kimon at Eurymedon in south-west Anatolia removes Persian presence from Aegean.
465	Death of Xerxes; accession of Artaxerxes I (to 424).
461–451	Further democratic developments at Athens.
461	Reforms of Ephialtes and Perikles (downgrading of Areiopagos, institution of People's Court with state-pay for jurors).
458	*Oresteia* trilogy of Aeschylus.
451/0	Perikles' Citizenship Law.
460?	Birth of Thucydides (d. 400?).
460–445	Athens at war against Sparta and against Persia.
460–457	Construction of 'Long Walls' from Athens to Peiraieus. Athenian hegemony in central Greece.
451	Armistice with Sparta.
449	Greek victory in Cyprus; Persia forced to abandon control over Asiatic Greeks.
448?	Peace of Kallias.
445	Thirty Years' Peace between Athens and Sparta. Athens, with Carthage and Persia, one of the three Great Powers of Mediterranean.
443–429	Ascendancy of Perikles.
	Akropolis building programme (Parthenon).

Cultural efflorescence centred on Athens (Herodotus, Protagoras, Anaxagoras, Hippodamos, Pheidias).

441?	*Antigone* of Sophocles.
431–404	Peloponnesian War.
430–429	Great Plague of Athens; death of Perikles.
428	Birth of Xenophon (d. 354?).
427	Birth of Plato (d. 347?).
424	Accession of Darius II.
421	Peace of Nikias.
415–413	Sicilian Expedition; Athenian disaster.
413–404	Dekeleian and Ionian Wars; Persia gives Sparta decisive financial aid.
411	*Lysistrata* of Aristophanes; oligarchic coup at Athens.
404	Fall of Athens; oligarchic junta (to 403).
404–371	Sparta succeeds to Athens's Great Power role.
405/4	Death of Darius II; accession of Artaxerxes II (404–359).
405–367	Dionysios I tyrant of Syracuse.
395–386	Corinthian War; King's Peace.
385?	Plato founds Academy.
384	Birth of Aristotle (d. 322).
371	Battle of Leuktra.
371–362	Ascendancy of Thebes.
362	Death of Epameinondas at Battle of Mantineia.
359	Accession of Philip II of Macedon (d. 336).
355–322	Career of Demosthenes (b. 384).
338	Battle of Khaironeia.
336	Graeco-Macedonian campaign against Persian Empire begins. Assassination of Philip, accession of Alexander the Great (to 323).
335?	Aristotle founds Lyceum research institute.
331	Battle of Gaugamela.
330	Alexander succeeds Darius III as Persian Great King.
322	Athenian democracy terminated by Macedon.

Abbreviations

ABSA	*Annual of the British School at Athens*
AC	*L'Antiquité classique*
AHR	*American Historical Review*
AJA	*American Journal of Archaeology*
AJP	*American Journal of Philology*
AncW	*Ancient World*
Annales (ESC)	*Annales (économies, sociétés, civilisations)*
ASNP	*Annuario della Scuola Normale di Pisa*
BCH	*Bulletin de correspondance hellénique*
BICS	*Bulletin of the (London) Institute of Classical Studies*
BM	British Museum
CA	*Classical Antiquity*
CAH	*Cambridge Ancient History*
CetM	*Classica et Mediaevalia*
CJ	*Classical Journal*
CP	*Classical Philology*
CQ	*Classical Quarterly*
CW	*Classical World*
DHA	*Dialogues d'histoire ancienne*
DHJ	*Durham Historical Journal*
EMC/CV	*Echos du monde classique/Classical Views*
G&R	*Greece & Rome*
GRBS	*Greek Roman and Byzantine Studies*
HPT	*History of Political Thought*
HSCP	*Harvard Studies in Classical Philology*
ICS	*Illinois Classical Studies*
JHI	*Journal of the History of Ideas*
JHS	*Journal of Hellenic Studies*
JWCI	*Journal of the Warburg and Courtauld Institutes*
LCM	*Liverpool Classical Monthly*
MH	*Museum Helveticum*
PBA	*Proceedings of the British Academy*
PCPS	*Proceedings of the Cambridge Philological Society*

PRIA	*Proceedings of the Royal Irish Academy*
QUCC	*Quaderni urbinati di cultura classica*
QS	*Quaderni di storia*
REG	*Revue des études grecques*
TAPA	*Transactions and Proceedings of the American Philological Association*
TLS	*Times Literary Supplement*
WA	*The World of Athens*, ed. P. V. Jones (Cambridge, 1984)

Illustrations

Plate 1 Myth v. History
The Parthenon frieze (detail)

Plate 2 Greeks v. Barbarians I
Athens, Nat Mus Inv. 9683 [*World of Athens* (*WA*) 7: 6 p. 298]
Heracles and King Busiris, *c*.470

Plate 3 Greeks v. Barbarians II
BM [Spivey 1997: fig. 141]
Bassae Amazonomachy

Plate 4 Men v. Women
BM, Inv. E 467 [*WA* 2: 5 p. 96]
Athene & Pandora

Plate 5 Citizens v. Aliens
BM E 532 [Bérard 1989a: fig. 192]
Satyr as citizen, Pelike *c*.430

Plate 6 Free v. Slave
Paris, Louvre 2587 [*WA* 4: 19 p. 185]
Thracian slave girl, Aigisthus Painter, *c*.475–50

Plate 7 Gods v. Mortals I
Brauron Mus Inv. 1153 (32 + 32a)
Sacrifice relief scene, 4 c.

Plate 8 Gods v. Mortals II
BM, Coins & Medals, Inv. 1871-11-7-1 [*WA* HI: 21 p. 50]
Gold Stater: Apollo (obv.) + Philip II (rev.)

Prologue

People who for years had been denied their pasts have begun searching for their own identities. . . . This revival of history ushers in a new era . . .

(President George Bush, addressing the United Nations General Assembly, 23 September 1991)

The Genesis of this Book

Unless President Bush was very much mistaken, identity—both group and personal—is one of the major engines of contemporary political and cultural change. What the late sociologist Norbert Elias called 'the cult of self-consciousness', and others label the 'politics of difference', seems to have reached a fever pitch both on the streets and in the study. As I wrote, a civil war raged in the ex-Yugoslav republic of Bosnia-Herzegovina, the majority of whose population see themselves as radically differentiated ethnically from the politically dominant Serbs. What is left of the former Soviet Union has become a not very cordial entente of competing republics and opposed ethnic groups—the 'unified team' that competed in another sense at the Barcelona Olympics did so for the first and almost certainly the last time. In the United States, Hispanics and Blacks and women struggle in their different ways, sometimes physically violent ones, to define a space for themselves within the contested arenas of a public culture that is no longer viewed in the relatively positive terms of a 'melting-pot'. Here, finally, on the mean streets of a decayed post-industrial Britain poor, unemployed youths riot partly in order to demonstrate that they too have a social identity and a life to live that are no less valuable to them for having been marginalized by the 'free market'. There is no reason to suppose that these specific examples, only a small selection of those available, will not be replaced or supplemented by more of the same for the foreseeable future.

Academics tend to express their views in less physical, if not always less violent, ways. Of late, group identity—whether based on gender, class, ethnicity, race, religion, or sexual preference—has appropriately preoccupied a wide range of social science, historical, and literary-cultural disciplines, generating many theoretical and empirical disagreements. Among all these, the concept of alterity has nevertheless found a large measure of favour. This is by no means a new word in English (though 'otherness' does appear to be neologistic), but it owes its current popularity chiefly to the inspiration of Emmanuel Levinas, a Lithuanian Jew by origin who along with many other oppressed European Jewish intellectuals migrated to Paris ('Vilna on the Seine') between the two World Wars.

As redefined and reconstituted by Levinas, alterity has come to mean in particular the condition of difference and exclusion suffered by an 'out' group against which a dominant group and its individual members define themselves negatively in ideally polarized opposition. It is perhaps no surprise that this redefinition should have been the achievement of a Jew, a representative of Europe's longest-established 'other' group. 'Jew', indeed, encapsulates alterity in the fullest sense, in that together with its antonym 'gentile' it constitutes a logical polarity. The two terms of the opposition, that is, are not only mutually exclusive but jointly exhaustive, since all human beings are by definition, from this point of view, either Jews or gentiles (though the term 'gentile' no longer carries its original etymological sense of 'having a nation'). It is with such binary polarities of Classical Greek thought and culture that the present study will be principally concerned.

Shortly after the last War Simone de Beauvoir gave Levinas's *altérité* a wider currency in her now classic *Le Deuxième Sexe* (1949). But in English at least it remained a sufficiently alien import for de Beauvoir's English translator (1953) to feel the need to apologize for using the seemingly outlandish term 'alterity'. Thus it was that the conception and construction of 'woman' as 'other'—that is, not merely different in terms of sexual biology, a fact of 'nature', but deemed categorically opposite and inferior in terms of gender, a fact (or factoid?) of 'culture'—entered the mainstream of English-language social thought. It was also by this route that the concept of 'alterity' eventually penetrated my own consciousness, there to lie dormant for many years until I was approached to contribute a volume on the ancient Greek world to the OPUS series.

By then the emphasis of my historical interests and researches had opportunely shifted away from the material (social and economic) and the political (broadly interpreted) to the intellectual or social-psychological. In common with many of my peers, and under the particular influence of structuralist social anthropology and cultural history, I had become especially concerned to interpret and understand the mindset or mentality of the Greeks, the underlying and often unconscious spiritual and cultural mechanisms that made them 'tick'.

'The Greeks', however, is an abstraction, and, at times, an inconvenient one. Herodotus may have thought that he could usefully define *to Hellēnikon*, literally 'the Greek thing' or 'Greekness', in terms of common blood, language, religion, and mores (see Chapter 3). But not only did he have to omit political institutions or structures from his definition in order to do so, when there were well over a thousand separate Greek political communities who could never form more than local, shortlived, and usually imposed interstate ties. He also had to create the fiction of genetic homogeneity and gloss over important differences of dialect, religion, and mores within the broadly 'Hellenic' world. In other words, *to Hellēnikon* was no less of an ideological construct than, say, Christendom was in the Middle Ages or 'the Arab world' is today.

On the other hand, it was no more of an artificial construct than those, either. 'Greekness', that is to say, had at least enough purchase on reality to allow of a definition that was not purely wishful thinking. Even if it had relatively little tangible impact in the sphere of practical politics, it certainly was enormously influential in the cultural arena within which Herodotus himself introduced it, the domain of historiography.

The writing of history, arguably, was a distinctively Greek form of intellectual activity, if not a Greek invention (Chapter 2). Not the least of its effects from Herodotus onwards, irrespective of its openly announced aims, was to forge or underpin a properly 'Greek' self-consciousness among its audience or readers. It was this social-psychological function that put me on the track of the governing idea of this book. Why not pursue and examine what made the Greeks 'tick' by exploring how they represented themselves, and others, to themselves in works of history, the stuff of which was supposedly objective factual knowledge?

Further reflection, however, made it plain that this approach would not take me nearly far enough along the right track. For was not 'history' itself a problematic notion in its ancient Greek context, in relation to, say, 'myth' (Chapter 2)? And whose history was it that we should be studying, history for whom as well as of whom? Here, surely, was a much more promising line. For the ideal ancient reader of Herodotus and his Greek historian successors, the reader whose values they regularly assumed or invoked was the citizen, the fully paid-up member of the club the Greeks called the *polis*. In the Classical fifth and fourth centuries BCE that club was virtually closed to free, adult, male Greeks distributed according to ethnic assumptions among the hundreds of *poleis* (Chapter 5). This in turn brought me back to alterity, othering, and polarity. For the characteristically 'Greek' way of defining the citizen was precisely by negative polar opposition to a whole series of 'others'—the unfree, minors, females, and non-Greeks, not to mention those omnipresent and omnipotent superhumans, the gods. Hence there arose the undergraduate lecture course at Cambridge (1989–93) on which the present, much abbreviated, text is based: 'The Greeks and the "Other" in the Writing of History'.

The Greeks and 'Us'

My lecture course began and ended with reflections on the Greek heritage or legacy, the Greeks and 'Us'. These were prompted by such remarks as the following, included in an essay on 'The Freedom of Oedipus', by a leading expert on ancient Hellenic culture: 'Both of these extremes [suppression of freedom and anarchy] are of course repugnant to the human spirit and especially to that of the West, which is that of the Greeks' (Knox 1990*a*: 55). Similar views have been expressed in two recent general books on the same subject of freedom, by Jacqueline de Romilly (1989) and Orlando Patterson (1991). In all three writings there are to be found the implicit assumption and even the explicit assertion that freedom, one of the West's most cherished ideal values, was invented or discovered by the Greeks in pretty much the same form or forms in which it is cherished by 'us' today. Knox and Patterson, to be fair, do not suppress or palliate the fact of slavery in ancient Greece. But neither do they doubt that there is a continuum, or at any rate an evolutionary progression, from the Greeks to us in 'our' shared positive evaluation of freedom. My own reading of the Greek historians, and of other privileged cultural texts from Classical Greece such as the surviving Athenian tragic and comic dramas, has persuaded me otherwise, indeed almost diametrically so (Chapter 6). For me, as a modern commentator on Greek tragedy once put it, the ancient Greeks are in crucial cultural respects, ideological no less than institutional, 'desperately foreign' (Jones 1962; see further our Epilogue).

The Savage Greeks

Let us stay briefly with ideas of freedom. Benjamin Constant, reacting violently in 1819 against some French Revolutionaries' attempted appropriation of ancient Greece, distinguished sharply—perhaps too sharply, but still in my view rightly—between 'the liberty of the Ancients' and 'the liberty of the Moderns' (Constant 1988: 307–28); the distinction he drew depended on their incommensurably different constructions and evaluations of the individual's status and function in relation to the community or State. From Constant through Fustel de Coulanges, Emile Durkheim, and Louis Gernet, and thence on to J.-P. Vernant and his 'Paris School', there is traceable in French scholarship on the Greeks an unbroken line of thought that stresses the Greeks' essential difference, even 'otherness', from 'us' in crucial areas of awareness and representation of Self.

That line of thought has intersected, fruitfully in my view, with the 'anthropologization' approach inaugurated a century earlier than Constant by the Jesuit missionary J.-F. Lafitau in 1724. Briefly stated, the anthropologizers suggested that, if the Greeks were not merely earlier versions of themselves, with (most obviously) an immeasurably less sophisticated technological toolkit, then perhaps they were more usefully to be compared to and interpreted in the light of the so-called primitive peoples targeted by European colonial expansion. The fact that the Classical Greeks were polytheists and practised animal sacrifice as a central ritual of their religion was a great encouragement towards such relativistic anthropologization. So too, more recently, has been Claude Lévi-Strauss's 'structural' anthropology. The binary oppositions he detects in, and uses as a key to explaining, the myths of contemporary Amazonian or North-west Pacific Coast Indians bear an uncanny resemblance to the 'polarity' that informed Classical Greek social and political thought (see Chapter 1).

On the other hand, there are or should be limits to the 'othering' of the Greeks. The case of Athenian tragic and comic theatre marks them out rather nicely (Epilogue). No doubt, the DWEMs ('Dead White European Males') like Aeschylus & Co. who have provided us with the bulk of our extant evidence for Classical Greek culture ought not to have a monopoly claim on our attention; but it is hard simply to ignore or even consciously to marginalize them. One alternative strategy is to stress the racially or ethnically distinct inputs that went into the making of Classical Greek culture, especially those from the Semitic East and the Negroid South. But though superficially attractive, politically speaking, this runs up against insuperable obstacles on empirical grounds (Chapters 3 and 7). My aim therefore will be, in Edward Gibbon's phrase, to 'hold the balance with a steady and equal hand'.

Legacy for Whom?

But not with a dead hand. For although, and indeed especially because, the Greeks are not in fact 'like us', their legacy, what we have chosen to inherit or see ourselves as having inherited from them, is still in active process and requires constant scrutiny and re-evaluation. Supposing then that the non-specialist readers for whom this book is particularly intended were to demand some justification of this lavish expenditure of energy, time, and money on the Classical Greeks, I might respond as follows.

Consider our current vocabulary of politics. It is no secret that almost all of it—including 'politics' itself—is Greek in derivation. But what, then, does and should it mean to us that 'democracy' was a Greek invention (celebrating its 2,500th anniversary in 1993/4), when our democracy is so different from theirs, both institutionally and ideologically? Or, to put that question more brutally and with closer reference to our immediate concerns, how was it that it was 'okay' for the Greeks to find the idea and practice of democracy perfectly compatible not only with the disfranchisement of women (Chapter 4), which was of course true of all democracies until the present century, but also with the outright enslavement of many thousands of human beings (including their fellow-Greeks) (Chapter 6), whereas for us today that combination is not at all 'okay' on principle?

Or take, finally, a historiographical illustration. As I shall try to show in my second chapter, Herodotus and Thucydides were children of their time and in no useful sense our 'colleagues'. Yet they are also simultaneously the joint fathers of 'History' in some broadly acceptable current sense of that term.

The Greeks, in sum, were 'other', but at the same time they are a part, and not a negligible one, of 'Us' too. Their language may be dead, but their legacy is a live, indeed a searingly vital, issue. Our identity, quite as much as theirs, is at stake in the terms in which this book has been conceived and written.

I

Significant Others

Us v. Them

And how can one imagine oneself among them
I do not know;
It was all so unimaginably different
And all so long ago

(Louis MacNeice, *Autumn Journal* sect. 9)

Black and larger than life, it held one hand, the left,
hidden behind its back

(Elias Canetti, *The Play of the Eyes*)

A Comparativist Perspective

My approach to the ancient Greeks is informed by that
'comparativist perspective' without which

students of Greek antiquity will easily mistake, indeed can hardly fail
to mistake, what may be distinctive, and what may be said to be in no
way exceptional, either in the intellectual products of the society they
study or in the circumstances and manner of their production.

This clarion call to comparativism occurs in the preface to a
collection of essays on Greek science (G. E. R. Lloyd 1991*a*:
p. xii), what the Greeks called 'the enquiry into nature' (*hē
peri phuseōs historia*). But the study of nature is of the essence
of our present project in the history and historiography of
Classical Greek culture too; and Lloyd's prescription applies
to the study of Greek culture generally no less than to that of
Greek science in particular. For 'to study what passes for
science in a society is to go to the centre of the values of that
society' (p. 353). Besides, our word 'history' comes ultimately
from the ancient Greek word for 'enquiry' (cf. Chapter 2).

Greece: Problems of Generalization

'Society', however, is a problematic term for us in a special way, since 'Greece', meaning Classical Greece between about 500 and 300 BCE, was not a single society. Arguably, though, it was a single culture, and a crucial component of an argument for Greek cultural homogeneity is the figure of Aristotle (384–322). A northerner by origin, he was born and brought up on the fringes of the Hellenic heartland, where his father was court physician to a king of not quite entirely Greek nor yet wholly 'barbarian' Macedon. But he passed most of his adult life in the Greek south, as a resident alien in the city of Athens that his mentor Plato had dubbed 'the City Hall of Wisdom' (*Protagoras* 337d). It could be claimed that Aristotle was primarily a scientist, especially a zoologist and biologist; certainly, the teleological method he applied to his empirical researches into the nature of non-human animals informed equally his classification and analysis of what he considered to be the human community *par excellence*, the Greek *polis* (Chapter 4). But what counts here is that Aristotle, at any rate, felt it was legitimate and justifiable to talk in general and generalized terms about 'Greeks' and what was 'Greek'. Being both an insider and an outsider himself, his own views and his reportage of those held by others deserve particular attention and respect.

Nor does Aristotle's Hellenism exhaust his peculiar utility for our present purposes. Apart from the extensiveness and comprehensiveness of his surviving writings, his special advantage springs from his method of grounding his 'political' theorizing (which embraced the ethical, social, and cultural as well as the narrowly constitutional) in what he took to be common cultural perceptions, received and reputable opinions about what was and what ought to be the case. For it is precisely such general Greek attitudes and beliefs, such a Greek mindset or 'mentality' (if that term may be permitted), that I am here seeking to excavate and, if possible, explain in all its often contradictory complexity. Aristotle's *Politics* was somehow based on a vast mass of empirical research conducted by the pupils at his Lyceum institute into over 150 separate Greek communities. It combines what we might want to call value-free political science with consciously ethical and educative political theory. It will thus constitute for me a privileged text, although for that very reason it will have to be read and reread with especial sensitivity and care. Aristotle for all his proclaimed methodological subservience to received and reputable beliefs was by no means a 'typical' Classical Greek, let alone a representative specimen of the chimerical—because in fact heterogeneously composite—'Greek mind'.

I have therefore exploited a variety of other sources—written and non-written, highly polished and unpolished, dramatic, philosophical, historiographical—to correct or balance what may be peculiarly Aristotelian biases. In particular, I have made special use of what came to be seen by later scholars (but should not necessarily be so viewed by us) as the canonical historical writings of Herodotus, Thucydides, and Xenophon. Historiography, in the sense of the study of historians' texts, is something of a Cinderella or stepchild in classical studies. Few scholars now take the study of historiography as a primary focus of their teaching or research. Few, therefore, have been specifically concerned, as I shall be, with the emergence of historiography as a recognizably distinct intellectual and literary practice in the latter part of the fifth century BCE. In order to set this intellectual advance in context, while at the same time emphasizing its inbuilt limitations, I shall discuss it under the partly ancient, partly modern, polarized rubric of 'History v. Myth' (Chapter 2).

For in the major Classical Greek historians we have at our disposal gifted storytellers, who operated at a level somewhere between pure entertainment and high philosophical theorizing, and who had to appeal to and hold the attention of a live, physically present audience. All literature, in fact, in the basically oral societies of Greece was typically heard not read. Yet it was an essential part of their self-perception and self-presentation as narrators and commentators that the historians were not 'mere' storytellers, making it up as they went along. Rather, they purported to be telling it 'how it actually was' in the Greek and non-Greek past (from *c*.550 to 350 BCE, from Italy to Iraq) in a manner and according to assumptions that were generally shared by their audiences or readerships. Provided that full allowance is made for the artifices of rhetoric with which they adorned their often far from plain tales, as well as the multiplicity of subtextual allusions and the constraints of generic and intellectual context, there is every reason to expect these writers to yield a peculiarly rich harvest of information on the most basic Greek cultural concerns.

Who Were the Greeks?

No concern, perhaps, was (and is) more basic than that of identity, whether collective or individual, ethnic, tribal, political, or whatever. Beginning at the highest level of generality, the Classical Greeks divided all humankind into two mutually exclusive and antithetical categories: Us and Them, or, as they put it, Greeks and barbarians (Chapter 3). In fact, the Greek–barbarian antithesis is a strictly polar dichotomy, being not just contradictory but jointly exhaustive and mutually exclusive. Greeks + barbarians = all humankind. Not that the Greeks are unique in so distinguishing themselves from others: compare the division and opposition between Jews and *goyim* (gentiles), for example, or Europeans and Orientals. But for the Classical Greeks the Greek–barbarian polarity was but one instance of the ideological habit of polarization that was a hallmark of their mentality and culture. Moreover, they pressed polarization to its (ideo)logical limits. Thus whereas Greeks were ideally seen as not-barbarians, barbarians were equally envisaged as being precisely what Greeks were not.

The ideological quality of the Greeks' polarized logic is even more starkly apparent in their representation of sexual difference—or rather gender-difference, if by sex we mean biology or anatomy, and by gender the Greeks' variously motivated and grounded ideological construction of male nature as not just different from but opposed (and hierarchically superior) to female nature. For whereas the very word 'barbarian' lent itself to what we might call negative polarization, that is, denigration of the category defined as opposite, the male–female dichotomy need not in and of itself have been construed in a hierarchical and derogatory manner. Roughly half of all barbarians were, after all, male, so maleness was not intrinsically something by which male Greeks could claim to be specially or uniquely privileged. Nor, given the fact that half of all Greeks were female, was there any reason in strict logic why the Greeks—that is, articulate male Greeks—should have defined the female as not only opposite to but categorically inferior to the male. Yet, as we shall see, the Greeks were nevertheless radical constructionists in this sense, Aristotle being by no means the least determined among them. 'Female' was considered categorically inferior to 'male', and it was an essential part of Greek heterology that male barbarians should have been construed as naturally effeminate (Chapters 3 and 4).

In the Greeks' construction of the male–female dichotomy, to put it in other words, culture overrode nature. Yet their polarization of gender was ultimately based on objective and irreconcilable empirical differences. That, however, was not the case with the three other dualities through which I have chosen to explore Classical Greek mentality and culture. There was nothing in nature that straightforwardly determined whether an inhabitant of Classical Greece was or was not, or was or was not capable in principle of becoming, a citizen (Chapter 5) or a legally free person (Chapter 6), as opposed to a non-citizen or a slave. Even less straightforwardly did something in nature give rise to the dichotomy between men (in the sense of mortal human beings, whatever their gender, ethnic affiliation, or political or legal status) and the sort of gods in which they believed (Chapter 7).

In other words, there is a sliding scale here from the wholly or largely 'natural', albeit culturally overdetermined, to the largely or wholly 'cultural'. Yet to the Greeks—and this is my basic point—all five of these pairings (Greek–barbarian, men–women, citizen–alien, free–slave, gods–mortals) were construed equally as polarities. Never could the twain of any of these disjunctive dichotomies meet. The Greeks thus in various ways constructed their identities negatively, by means of a series of polarized oppositions of themselves to what they were not.

Polarity in History

On the other hand, it would be quite misleading to suggest that these polarities did not themselves have a history, specifically a culturally determined, discursive history. This implication is of course built into the very terms of the contested distinction between myth and history: one person's 'history' was another's 'myth'. But even the seemingly transparent polarity of Greeks and barbarians did not make its appearance before the fifth century, becoming firmly embedded only after the Greeks' (or rather some Greeks') victory in the Persian Wars of 480–479 (Chapter 3). Not once is 'barbarian' used as either a substantive or an adjective in all the many thousand lines of Homer, the foundational text of Classical Greek culture, even though the plot of the *Iliad* is premissed upon the confrontation between a more or less united Greek world and a coalition of non-Greek foreigners. Moreover, when 'barbarian' did make its first appearance in surviving Greek literature, it carried few or none of the pejorative, especially 'orientalist', connotations with which the term became charged in the Classical era. There are, in other words, polarities and polarities, and it is with the pejorative, derogatory, morally loaded kind that this book is concerned: with polarities the two terms of which are not conceived as opposite but equal, or mutually complementary, but as asymmetrical, hierarchically ordered, and antagonistic.

It was one of the less celebrated but none the less essential aspects of 'the Greek achievement' to take this process of negative polarization to extremes. Such extremism was a likely consequence of the agonistic, public, face-to-face way in which Greeks defined their argumentative positions in open debate. But no less Hellenic was the ability of some Greeks to reflect upon even their most basic and ingrained habits of thought and categories of social classification. Aristotle, indeed, gave the first formal analysis of the logic of opposition as such (of which polarity is but one species). To illustrate his discussion,

TABLE I. *Pythagorean Principles*

Opposites	
unlimited	limited
even	odd
plurality	one
left	right
female	male
in motion	at rest
crooked	straight
darkness	light
evil	good
oblong	square

he cited a list or table of opposites (*sustoikhia*) that was considered normative within a branch of the Pythagorean school of philosophy (*Metaphysics* 986[a]; see Table I). It must be stressed that this table was not merely a theoretical construct, since Pythagoreanism was a way of life and not only an academic movement or exercise. For us, however, it also serves graphically to highlight the arbitrary and variable character of Greek binary cultural classification—and indeed of binary classification as a cultural key altogether (below). Only a tiny minority of Greeks were paid-up Pythagoreans (or members of any other such exclusive and prescriptive sect), so there was plenty of room for dispute as to what should be opposed to what, and on what side of the line each supposedly polarized quality should be placed.

The Greeks all agreed, for example, as have many otherwise disparate cultures, that right was good and left was bad. Two of the Greek words for 'left' were blatant euphemisms (*aristeros*, 'better'; *euōnumos*, 'of good name'). But they were not all agreed as to precisely what values or qualities right connoted, nor whether such qualities and values as might be lined up on the right side of any table of opposites were also mutually correlated in a relationship of homology rather than merely by analogy. Consider, for example, the following two polarities (as deployed by Aristotle in the first book of the *Politics*): male–female, and master–slave. Does lining up male and master imply that the male was by his nature masterly, and the female naturally servile, or was it merely by culturally determined analogy that male seemed to be to female as master was to slave? Aristotle had his own unequivocal, positive answer, which he derived from the premisses of his philosophical system (Chapter 6). But—happily, as it might seem to most of us today—neither his premisses nor his conclusions were universally shared.

All such theoretical-cum-pragmatic cultural problems were given a Sophistic spin in the latter part of the fifth century. The hypothetical opposition between custom or convention (*nomos*) and nature (*phusis*) was the special contribution of the so-called Sophists to Greek cultural debate as a whole. Was it a matter of mere arbitrary convention that barbarians were as they were generally supposed by Greeks to be, that is, not merely culturally inferior (a matter of accident and dictated by custom) but also intrinsically servile (a matter of unalterable nature)? Were women's natures, though biologically different, still morally and psychologically equal to men's? Was belief in the existence and efficaciousness of the gods merely a conventional and socially convenient fiction rather than a due recognition of a fact of nature? Heterodox proponents of the affirmative answers to these and other likewise fundamental cultural questions could be found in the general movement of thought associated with these astute professional teachers. So high was the Sophists' profile at Athens, indeed, that Aristophanes had a crack at them in his *Clouds* of 423 BCE, casting Socrates as a typical specimen—a public image with which he was thereafter stuck, and thanks to which, in part, he came fatally unstuck a quarter-century later at his trial for impiety in 399. It was above all against a variety of Sophistic readings of the culture–nature polarity that Aristotle pitted his own constructions, which supposedly were grounded in the best *communis opinio*.

The problem of dual symbolic classification, however, does

not only have an ancient history. It is no less a matter for dispute within contemporary cultural or cognitive anthropology. (A professional in-joke has it that there are two kinds of anthropologists, those who believe in the heuristic and explanatory power of binary classification, and those who do not.) What is seriously at issue here is whether, as some versions of Lévi-Strauss's structuralism appear to hold, all cultures operate at their deepest levels in a dualist way. The narrating of myths, for example, is famously seen by Lévi-Strauss as a method of mediating contradictions between deeply structured binary polarities such as men v. women and mortals v. gods. On the contrary, there are those who contend that supposedly dualistic belief systems are better analysed as triadic or yet more complex structures of thought.

My own more modest view is that, regardless of the truth of the claim to universality made by hardline Lévi-Straussians, the hypothesis of structural dualism does at any rate have a peculiar purchase on the culture of the ancient Greeks (the ultimate intellectual source, one may suspect, of the Lévi-Straussian theory). However, as has been rightly stressed with regard to the seminal work in ancient Greek cultural studies of the French structuralist J.-P. Vernant, it is not 'a static system of polarities' that we have to deal with, but 'overlapping sets of dynamic interrelations, complex transformations and shifting tensions, viewed in the context of history, social institutions, ritual and political life' (Segal 1982: 232).

Interpretative Charity

Finally, however, it should in all fairness be added that there may be a further, yet more daunting, methodological obstacle in the way of applying any theory of interpretation to the culture of the ancient Greeks. This is the notion that it is literally impossible to get inside the skin or mind of any other— let alone an 'Other'—society. The ancient Greeks, it is argued on 'anthropologizing' lines (see Prologue), were irreducibly alien or desperately foreign to us in their culture, in something like the same way that contemporary 'primitive' peoples are alleged to be. Their language, besides, is now a dead one, and their visual repertoire of images is either impenetrable or at any rate not certainly translatable into our terms.

I have much sympathy with the impulse behind this interpretative strategy. Its laudable intention is to defamiliarize the ancient Greeks and so to knock them off the pedestal on which our Roman, Renaissance, Enlightenment, or Romantic forebears once placed them as being essentially like us, only earlier, and thus anticipating and legitimating fundamental characteristics of our culture, in contradistinction to other contemporary ancient peoples (the Phoenicians, for example, or the Egyptians). Perhaps, too, such a move is particularly helpful in sensitizing us to the underlying assumptions of what must otherwise strike us as repellent features of Greek mentality and culture: how, for instance, could a giant thinker like Aristotle, founder of western logic and political sociology, entertain for a moment the considered views he did in fact hold on the nature of women (Chapter 4) and slaves (Chapter 6)? At all events, generous dollops of what is known to philosophers and intellectual historians as interpretative charity must certainly be applied to make sense of such seeming paradoxes.

On the other hand, in its most extreme, logically couched, version, this defamiliarizing strategy seems to me to be mistaken. Are not the Victorian English (say) alien or foreign to us in culturally fundamental respects? But we do not treat their culture as a closed book on principle. In short, although it is not the case, as too many Classicists appear to wish to believe, that 'we are all ancient Greeks' (or Athenians), and although Classical Greek culture is both as a whole and in fundamental details deeply alien, it is nevertheless possible for us to gain a sympathetic understanding of it (see further Epilogue). If, moreover, the exploration of alien modes of thought is an essential part of the historian's task, then polarity provides a useful map and compass for exploring the culture and mentality of the Classical Greeks. But in the spirit of Herodotean *historia* we should strive to go beyond mere exploration, to explanation. Discussion of the dynamic tension between myth and history in Herodotus and Thucydides should set us on the right road.

2

Inventing the Past

History v. Myth

> Blessed is the man endowed with the learning that comes from enquiry (*historia*)
>
> (Euripides, fragment 910, ed. Nauck)

> The ancient historians gave us delightful fiction in the form of fact; the modern novelist presents us with dull facts under the guise of fiction
>
> (Oscar Wilde, *The Decay of Lying*)

History v. Fiction

Among the many achievements for which the Classical Greeks are hailed as privileged cultural ancestors, the invention of history holds an honoured place. In echo of Cicero, Herodotus is dubbed the 'Father of History', while Thucydides' status as Klio's favourite son has been endorsed by Renaissance and later historians as different as the Florentine Guicciardini, Macaulay, Leopold von Ranke, and Sir Ronald Syme. What is meant by 'history' in this context can vary, but conventionally it connotes a shared, almost sacred, ideal of veracity, in pursuit of which the criteria of evidence, argument, objectivity, and accuracy are fought over and the narratives of history are subjected to rigorous validation and criticism. Historical truth, that is to say, by convention is and ought only to be the polar antithesis of fiction in the sense of consciously false assertion.

Since I am one of those who do not see the matter in quite these black and white terms, I must briefly explain why, by returning to the fountainhead, to the source of our current if problematic discourse of truth, fiction, and history. That means returning to Greece, and more particularly to the city of Athens, in the second half of the fifth century BCE. There is, I shall argue, some virtue in the standard view of Greek historiographical ancestry, but the issue is far more complex than any simple truth:fiction antithesis would suggest. In particular, if we wish to read the Classical Greek historians as mediators of the truth about Greek self-perceptions and identifications, we have to grapple first with a series of variations on the opposition between history and fiction or, as we say following the Greeks, between history and myth—an opposition which itself has a history.

Definitions

Both 'history' and 'myth' are, at best, ambiguous terms. In the case of 'myth', the possibilities for persuasive definition easily exceed just two. But the ambiguity of 'history' can be pinned down at its simplest to the distinction between, on the one hand, 'the past' and, on the other, 'the systematic study of and writing about the past', the latter sometimes called historiography precisely to make that distinction explicit. The trouble is that, although that distinction is explicit and clear enough in principle, it is not in practice absolute. What actually happened in the past, and how, cannot ever be captured or re-produced *in toto* either in the imagination or on paper; and it would not in any case be worth the effort to attempt to do so, since not all past facts are equal. There are, bluntly, facts—such as my writing of this book—and what are judged by historians and their addressees to be historically significant facts.

In short, partly for sheer practical, physical reasons, and partly because not all past facts are born equal, historians do not write history in the sense that they reproduce the past, all of it. Rather, they each create their own, selective, and often very different pasts. To that extent I am at one with Hayden White's conception of 'the historical text as literary artifact' (White 1978), and I endorse the view that historical representations are by their nature essentially provisional and contingent. That, however, need not mean that there is not a distinction to be drawn in principle between a true history and fiction. For aside from an inescapable element of authorial intervention and subjectivity, a history that is as critical (including self-critical), disinterested, accurate, and persuasively explanatory as its conditions of production allow may fairly be called true. I find it preferable, therefore, to regard the 'boundary between history and fiction' as an 'open' one (Gearhart 1984), often difficult and for some purposes positively harmful to delineate precisely.

The problem of defining myth, of deciding which stories, or tales, or narratives (or types of stories, etc.) are or are not mythical, is vexed. Walter Burkert's definition affords a useful starting-point: 'a myth is a traditional tale with secondary, partial reference to something of collective importance' (Burkert 1979: 23). 'Traditional' does not exclude invention in the telling, indeed a constant process of invention and reinvention; but the basic plot-line or theme of a properly mythical tale has to be sufficiently stable and significant to become common or communal property and perform some collective purpose or function, whether aetiological, justificatory, monitory, exemplary, or symbolic. Almost anything or anyone, though, may be mythified or mythicized, provided only that they have some collective significance and some enduring social relevance or interest. For whatever else myths may do or mean, they 'anchor the present in the past' (P. S. Cohen 1969). Thus, either because of what they stand for, or because of their subject-matter, human or divine, myths are traditional tales that are capable of becoming overlaid with countless other and often paradoxical meanings.

So far as Classical Greece is concerned, it is perhaps a moot point whether it is legitimate or useful to distinguish a popular or mass culture from an élite or high culture: the Parthenon and Aeschylus' *Oresteia*, for instance, which were certainly purveyors of myth, were surely also vehicles of both popular and élite culture simultaneously. However, the myths that we have access to from Classical Greece are to be found either in written works characterized by a more or less single-minded pursuit of literary excellence or in visual media that are literally or metaphorically highly polished. This must be kept firmly in mind even or especially in the case of Herodotus. For his art of the performed narrative (one of several meanings of the Greek word *logos*), which received its initial 'publication' through oral recitation, was precisely the kind of art that conceals art.

Myth as History

So much then for matters of definition, eternally controversial. I shall now consider some of the possible permutations of the relationship between these ambiguous terms under three headings: myth as history; myth in history; and myth versus history. There is a logic behind this progression, as I shall hope to show, but no simple linear evolution. The writings of Herodotus and Thucydides will provide the focus, and Athens the point of reference. For although fifth-century Athens was in many ways a remarkably untypical Greek *polis*, its myths and mythology seem to have been, on the contrary, hugely typical. But that only makes all the more amazing—and problematic—the eventual emergence of something that might be called 'history' from within the matrix of Greek 'myth'. What is surprising and cries out for explanation, in other words, is not that it took the Greeks so long to invent history, but rather that—given the overwhelming presence and authority of myth in Greek culture high and low, sacred and secular—they ever invented it at all.

'The atmosphere in which the Fathers of History set to work was saturated with myth. Without myth, indeed, they could never have begun their work' (Finley 1986c: 13). Finley had specifically in mind orally transmitted tales of the kind involving Prometheus, Herakles, and other divine or semi-divine culture-heroes, the myths of the Trojan War, and so forth, those 'historical' myths that enabled the Greeks to select from the uncountable data of the past those 'facts' to which they could give a usable meaning in the present. But Finley's point may be enlarged by observing that myths, in the broad sense of oral traditions (Greek *muthoi*), were virtually all that Herodotus could possibly have used to recount and account for the origins, development, and outcome of his chosen subject, the Persian

Wars. Even Thucydides, who witnessed the growth of public documentation associated with the development of radical democracy at Athens, was still reliant essentially upon oral traditions and testimonies.

Herodotus described his method—and just once, possibly, the result of his method (7. 96)—as *historiē*, 'enquiry', a term with a special conceptual charge (see below, 'Myth versus History'). What he enquired into were various kinds of oral testimony, the plurality of traditions presented to him in various ways by different sorts of informants. Of course, the Greeks had had an alphabet since at least the mid-eighth century and had begun to inscribe 'documents' in permanent form from about 650. But, notwithstanding the thesis of Goody and Watt (1962/3, modified 1968)—that the achievement of alphabetic literacy had as a necessary consequence the development of a critical attitude to the past and a concern to fix it in authentic, immutable, and incontrovertible documentary form—the ancient Greek world down to and indeed beyond the fifth century remained essentially a world of oral discourse.

Oral historiography, meaning the study of oral traditions with a view to writing history, has become something of a growth industry in the last couple of decades, not only among Africanists but also among historians of, for instance, London's East End. However, after initial excitement about its seeming possibilities—for correcting or supplementing 'official' records or even yielding up the authentic and verifiable 'facts' of an illiterate or semi-literate community's past—some painful truths have been learned by modern oral historians. Or rather, they have had to be relearned, since they were already perfectly clear more than a century ago to the pioneer modern historian of ancient Greece, George Grote. 'With what consistency', Grote (1873: 87) rightly demanded, 'can you require that a community which either does not command the means, or has not learned the necessity, of registering the phenomena of its present, should possess any knowledge of the phenomena of the past?' The contrary, rather, was likely to be the case. For social-psychological factors, such as the desire to 'be in the know', unwillingness to face up to ignorance, and an inclination to believe whatever accorded with the prevalent religious, political, or aesthetic feelings of the group, could and did lead to an easy acceptance of sheer fiction. The latter, in turn, would become intermingled with both accurate and exaggerated matter of fact in such a way that not even the most skilled native participant, let alone an outside critic, however professional, could possibly disentangle them.

A couple of passages in book 6 of Herodotus, not coincidentally placed close together, give an inkling of the sort of non-supernatural myths about the Athenian past that originated in the Archaic period (seventh and sixth centuries) and were transmitted to Herodotus in the Classical fifth century. First, there is his famous digression on the Alkmaionids (6. 125–131), too long to quote in full here, occasioned by his equally famous—or notorious—defence of this noble lineage against an accusation of treachery at the time of the Battle of Marathon in 490 BCE. I am not here interested in the truth of this accusation or in the identity of Herodotus' informants, but in the nature and function of the tales that lay behind Herodotus' brilliantly polished versions. For these myths of the Alkmaionids are illuminatingly multifunctional—partly aetiological, partly justificatory, partly exemplary, partly symbolic—and thus capable of manipulation and differential emphasis in accordance with the narrator's needs.

They are, first, aetiological, because the ostensible function of the digression as a whole is to explain how and why the Alkmaionids became so famous an Athenian house. They are justificatory, because Alkmaionids or men with close Alkmaionid ties included such great contemporary or near-contemporary figures as Kleisthenes, who in Herodotus' phrase 'set up the democracy' at Athens (in 508/7), and Perikles, son of an Alkmaionid mother. They are exemplary, morally, socially, and politically. In about 575 the hand of Agariste, daughter of a dictator, was made the prize of a competition in aristocratic excellence staged over an entire year by her father. It was considered right and proper that powerful men should use marriageable women as political counters, and right that men should compete to marry them. The prize was won by

Kleisthenes' father, however, partly by moral default: his main rival (also Athenian) displayed a regrettable lack of public decorum and self-restraint, thereby abusing his host's magnificent hospitality (shades of Homer's Paris and of the suitors of Penelope). The myths are symbolic, finally, because the way in which the eponymous Alkmaion had supposedly become super-rich (by cramming every last inch and orifice of his body as well as his clothing with King Croesus' Lydian gold-dust) was emblematic of Greek *mētis* ('cunning intelligence') exercised at the expense of an oriental barbarian monarch.

Here we touch on the Greek–barbarian polarity that is further explored in my second Herodotean instance of myth as history (6. 137–40). At one level this is a classic example of what the anthropologist Bronislaw Malinowski dubbed a 'charter-myth'. For Herodotus is here giving a version of the tale that provided the Athenians with a charter to legitimate their forcible occupation of the island of Lemnos (maintained for most of the fifth and fourth centuries, since they considered the island of vital importance to them as a site for the settlement of excess Athenian population, as a source of grain in its own right, and as a strategic way-station along the grain-route from south Russia to the Peiraieus). But the tale also speaks to other Athenian concerns, in particular those with which we shall be dealing in the next two chapters, the construction of ethnic and gender identity respectively.

Herodotus' story begins in the timeless past, with the expulsion of some non-Greek Pelasgians from Attica. For this, Herodotus is able to present two contradictory accounts—that of 'the Athenians' and that of the anti-Athenian proto-historian Hekataios (to whom we shall return in connection with the move from myth as history to myth versus history). The scene then shifts to Lemnos, and Herodotus describes one of the proverbial 'Lemnian deeds', a crime committed by the Pelasgian men who had once lived in Attica but had been expelled. These men had first returned from Lemnos to Attica and abducted some Athenian women from Brauron under cover of the women-only Brauronia festival. They had then killed both the sons of these unions and the Athenian mothers themselves.

In consequence of this impious slaughter of the innocents, Lemnos suffered natural disaster: no crops would grow, and their cattle ceased to reproduce. So the Pelasgians consulted the Delphic oracle, which advised them to pay to the Athenians in reparation whatever compensation they should demand. This advice the Pelasgians felt unable to follow—hardly surprisingly, since what the Athenians demanded was nothing less than the entire island of Lemnos. Therefore, Miltiades was perfectly justified in seizing the island for the Athenians in the 490s, and the Athenians were equally justified in keeping hold of it subsequently.

Interwoven with this are several other strands which bear more directly on Athenian (that is, male citizen Athenian) perceptions—and doubts—about their own place and social arrangements at home in Classical Attica. In other written accounts Pelasgians are the aboriginal inhabitants of Greece, and it is clear from Herodotus' confusions and contortions on the Pelasgians' ethnic and linguistic affiliations elsewhere in his work (e.g. 1. 56–7) that he was perfectly well aware of this widespread view. But the Athenians too crucially identified themselves as a political community in terms of their aboriginality, or rather autochthony—the claim that the aboriginal Athenians had been born of the soil of Attica. So to conform to the demands of Athenian mythopoeia, these Attic Pelasgians had to have been originally invited to live in Attica—a plot-elaboration that enabled the Athenian mythmakers to illustrate another civic quality on which the Classical Athenians peculiarly piqued themselves, their magnanimous hospitality towards strangers (whom, conversely, they rigorously debarred from acquiring Athenian citizenship: Chapter 5).

A third, equally important, strand of the myth teases out relations between the sexes, with regard to both division of labour and legitimacy of children. For the reason why the Pelasgians had been expelled from Attica, according to the Athenian version, was that they had the ungrateful and barbarous habit of raping Athenian daughters, which they had the opportunity to indulge since in those days free women performed the (now) servile function of fetching water from wells (and, it did not need to be spelt out, because Athenian females were not as closely guarded within the home as they ideally were now).

Once settled on Lemnos the expelled Pelasgians, as we saw, returned to Attica and violated the sanctity of a women-only religious festival, the Brauronia. But the Athenian women who had been abducted to Lemnos as forced concubines got their own back with a vengeance: with truly Greek *mētis* they brought up their Pelasgo-Athenian sons to behave like Athenians, to speak Attic Greek and thereby (because, it would be understood, all Athenians, including the women, were cleverer than non-Greek Pelasgian men) to threaten to usurp the birthright of legitimate all-Pelasgian boys. It is, I suggest, the passage of Perikles' citizenship law of 451/0, which required the mothers of future citizens as well as their fathers to be Athenian, that gives special political point to the Greek–barbarian antagonism and the men–women role-reversal in this story. Indeed, this wholly favourable portrayal of Athenian women in a myth is so exceptional that some such extraordinary and political explanation seems inescapable (see further Chapter 4).

Here, then, in Herodotus' Lemnian tale we have a particularly good example of a myth that combines tradition and innovation, that attempts both to reinforce ethnic solidarity through polarization and to mediate contradictions over civic status and gender-role differentiation, and at the same time serves the overall political function of providing a legitimating charter for the seizure and retention of vital foreign territory. Whether it is true or not in terms of actual historical fact is beside the point.

Myth in History

So if the atmosphere in which Herodotus set to work was saturated with myth of that sort, the prognosis for the birth of 'History' in something like a modern professional sense— critical, disinterested, objective, accurate, and explanatory— was not exactly favourable, even if we stress (as I would) the open-boundedness as opposed to the supposed scientificity of all history-writing. Nevertheless, something that some of us anyway would want to call at least 'proto-history' did emerge. How and why, I shall return to discuss in the final section. First, though, let us consider myth in history, by way of three occasions on which attempts were made to influence the course of genuinely historical events by appeal to the discourse of myth. Not all the attempts were successful, but it is the naturalness of the resort to the language and ideology of myth that is significant, rather than its success. For it confirms the atmospheric saturation achieved by myth in the thoughtworld in which Herodotus and Thucydides were implicated, and thus the immense difficulty of the breakthrough from myth as or in history to myth as opposed to history that they and their public achieved.

Two of the three occasions involved the same myth, another in the rich Alkmaionid tradition. In 508 and again in 432 Sparta invoked 'the curse of the Alkmaionids', prompting both Herodotus (5. 70–1) and Thucydides (1. 126–7) to recount what they understood to be the historical origins of the hereditary religious curse, with Thucydides providing some detailed corrections of his predecessor. In fact, the true origins of the curse were unknowable after two hundred years, but Thucydides' corrections of Herodotus do imply the development of a 'scientific' historiography which distinguished sharply between (romantic and fictional) myth and (true) history. However, most telling of all is that in historical actuality the Spartans twice employed myth as a weapon of propaganda and persuasion in interstate relations with Athens. For that has an obvious bearing on this book's principal theme of Classical Greek mentality.

In 508 the ploy had worked, and the 'accursed' Kleisthenes and his relatives and supporters had been expelled (if only briefly). This will no doubt have encouraged the conservative Spartans to try it again three-quarters of a century later. But in 432, according to Thucydides, the reason the Spartans gave for invoking the curse was simply their pious wish to honour the gods. Thucydides scorns this, despite the Spartans' well-known and surely genuine religiosity, and substitutes his own,

characteristically secular and rationalistic, explanation—the
Spartans merely wanted to make Perikles unpopular. But even
if that was the Spartans' true aim, the implied authorizing logic
of their demand that the Athenians 'expel the accursed' was
the biblical view that the sins of the fathers are visited upon
the sons. This view was certainly held by Herodotus himself
(e.g. 7. 137), so it was very likely also held by most ordinary Athenians. We should not therefore underestimate, as
Thucydides does, the psychological impetus that the Spartans'
mythopoeic invocation of the Alkmaionid curse will have
given to the growing chorus of criticism of the Alkmaionid
Perikles for having started the Peloponnesian War (see further
Chapter 4).

My other example of myth in history is the dispute over
precedence between Athens and Tegea on the battlefield of
Plataia in 479 (Herodotus 9. 26–8), which will serve also as a
bridge from myth in history to myth versus history. Now, there
is nothing intrinsically implausible in the story that, in order to
demonstrate the priority of their respective claims to the extreme
left-wing position in the Greek battleline, both the Athenians
and the Tegeans cited, as matters of fact, precedents couched
in the terms of myth. That, after all, was still standard procedure
in fourth-century Athenian oratory. On the other hand,
Herodotus' invented speeches are hardly to be considered
authentic in all their details. Not only has he anachronistically
retrojected into this earlier context rhetorical topoi and tropes
from genres of public oratory such as the Athenian *epitaphios*
(public funeral speech) that were only formalized after 479,
but he has included in the Athenians' set speech a feature
which unmistakably betrays its origins in his own historical
consciousness.

For the past exploits on which Herodotus' Athenian speakers
rest their claim to precedence are not all equally historical.
Rather, the Athenians are made to draw a sharp contrast
between the dim and distant past (when Athenians heroically
fended off invading Amazons and fought in the Trojan War)
and the present (*ex hypothesi* 479), on the grounds that people
who were once brave in that time might easily by now, in this

time, have become morally inferior; though naturally they
hasten to add that, in this instance, the Athenians have not so
degenerated—witness their victory at Marathon just eleven
years before. An apparently similar contrast is drawn by
Herodotus' model, Homer, between the men of yore and the
(degenerate) men of today, but that was entirely within a
single continuum of heroic time. The contrast that Herodotus'
Athenians are implying, however, is between the time of heroes,
on the one hand, the *spatium mythicum*, and the time of men,
the *spatium historicum*, on the other. That contrast had been
made explicit earlier on by Herodotus himself, speaking *in
propria persona*. For at 3. 122 he marks off the legendary
Cretan ruler Minos and any predecessors of his who may have
ruled the sea from what he considers to be the certainly real,
certainly all-human Polykrates of Samos, the first man of the
anthrōpēiē legomenē geneē ('the generation of humans as it is
called') whom he knows for sure to have been a thalassocrat.

Myth versus History

But how did Herodotus 'know' this, and why was he not
prepared to vouch for either the humanity or the thalassocracy
of Minos? Here we move to our final pairing—or polar
antithesis—of myth and history. For Herodotus knew this
(among much else) as a result of the *historiē* that he had
proudly proclaimed in the preface to his work, which begins
thus: 'This is the exposition (*apodexis*) of the *historiē* of
Herodotus of Halikarnassos'. In using this one word, *historiē*,
Herodotus was both pledging allegiance to a thoroughly modern
form of intellectual activity and at the same time announcing
his affiliation to an intellectual tradition that had originated
in the Miletos of Thales and his followers a century before
Herodotus' own birth and been mediated to him through
Hekataios (*fl. c.*500), who was also and not coincidentally a
Milesian.

Now, in early Greece, indeed down to the fourth century,
muthos and *logos* were not two different types of discourse,
the one as it were primitive and pre-logical, the other rational;
and mythology as a scholarly category is a surprisingly recent,

eighteenth-century invention. So it would be anachronistic to identify the achievement of Thales and his successors as a radical intellectual shift from *muthos* to *logos*, a conversion from mythical thinking to scientific rationality. Besides, myth may embody the most rational thinking imaginable when applied to subjects whose intrinsic obscurity or depth of cultural resonance render it most rational and appropriate to approach them through the symbolism or allegory of myth. On the other hand, intellectual attitudes to myth were indeed somehow transformed between the time of, say, Hesiod (*c.*700 BCE) and that of Herodotus, in such a way as to enable the 'Greek historical spirit' (Starr 1968) to awaken. J.-P. Vernant (1983*b*: 351) has captured this intellectual development particularly well, identifying

two major transformations of thought. The first is the emergence of positivist thought that excludes all forms of the supernatural and rejects the implicit assimilation, in myth, of physical phenomena with divine agents; the second is the development of abstract thought that strips reality of the power of change that myth ascribed to it.

Following Hekataios, ultimately, Herodotus was more interested in the human world than in the world of non-human nature (*phusis*). And although he did not, like Thucydides, exclude all forms of the supernatural from his intellectual armoury, neither did he allow his belief in supernatural agency to obstruct his secular *historiē* into human affairs through the critical scrutiny of traditional tales (another meaning of *logoi*, which he distinguished from *muthoi*; below). Above all, he did not see the hand of god or 'the divine' (*to theion*) as being incompatible with, let alone as ruling out in advance, the principal overriding aim of his *historiē* (see further Chapter 7). That aim, as he announced at the end of his preface, was to 'give the great and wondrous achievements (*erga*) of both the Greeks and the non-Greek barbarians their due renown, especially the explanation of (or responsibility for) (*aitiē*) why they had fought with one another'. The precise meaning of *aitiē* has been long and hotly debated, but the case has recently and persuasively been argued once again that Herodotus did have a cogent model for explaining why things happen. For this among other reasons, the seemingly tautologous dictum that 'there was no Herodotus before Herodotus' (Momigliano 1966*a*: 129) properly expresses Herodotus' pioneering historiographical achievement.

To illustrate Herodotus' deployment of history as opposed to myth, I give just three examples. In the first we find him beginning his work as he means to proceed, with characteristic emphasis on the personal pronoun: 'The learned ones (*logioi*) of the Persians say that the Phoenicians are *aitioi* of the clash between the Greeks and non-Greeks.' The myths are then rehearsed, for four chapters. 'But, as for me, whether that was how it was or not I shall not go into. I shall begin rather with the man whom I myself know to have been the first to inflict harm and injustice on the Greeks . . . Croesus' (1. 5. 3). So much, Herodotus implies (not without sardonic humour), for the stories of the 'learned' Persians. Although he does not actually use the term *muthos* in a derogatory sense here, that is precisely what he does do, twice, in book 2 (on Egypt: see further Chapter 3). These are his only two uses of *muthos* in the entire work (2. 23, 2. 45. 1), and it is highly significant that both are explicitly described as myths 'of the Greeks' (possibly an allusively plural reference to the singular Hekataios). Here, in other words, is Herodotus the 'scientific' historian, staking his claim to mastery of his new intellectual territory.

The second of these uses, moreover, offers a striking verbal parallel to my next illustration of Herodotus' critical attitude to myth. For the Greek *muthos* about Herakles that he records at 2. 45. 1 is dismissed as *euēthēs* ('simple-minded'), which is just what arouses his scorn in the story of a stratagem attributed to the sixth-century Athenian dictator Peisistratos at 1. 60. 3. This he lambasts as the *prēgma* ('transaction') the most *euēthēs* by far that he has discovered in his researches. The very idea of Peisistratos being allegedly escorted back to Athens by the goddess Athena herself—as if the Athenians of the mid-sixth century (shortly before Polykrates: see above) thought they were living in Homer's mythical Ithaca rather than at Athens in the time of men. The Athenians (including presumably

his contemporary Athenian informants) should be ashamed
of themselves for believing such a silly tale—indeed, they
especially, since all Greeks were supposed to be smarter
than all barbarians, and the Athenians prided themselves on
being the cleverest and most cunning of the Greeks. Not that
Herodotus himself was innocent of what we would consider
the grossest credulity on occasion (e.g. 1. 214. 5); the point is
rather the distinction and polar opposition that he draws in
principle between a *muthos* and a true or acceptable *logos*.
Indeed, elsewhere he even programmatically covers his back
and flanks as it were by saying that his job, as he conceives it,
is (merely) to 'tell what is told' (*legein ta legomena*), whether
or not he himself actually believes the *logoi* (7. 152. 3).

My third and final illustration of history as opposed to
myth nicely yokes as well as divides Herodotus and his major
successor Thucydides. The story of the Tyrannicides, Harmodios
and Aristogeiton, became the most important charter-myth of
the foundation of the Athenian democracy, since the Athenians
conceived and represented their system of popular self-rule,
both visually and verbally, as the antithesis of tyranny. Thus
the theft of the original statue-group of the Tyrannicides from
Athens by the Persian Great King Xerxes in 480 not only was
symbolically apt but was also especially keenly resented by
the democratic Athenians, who immediately commissioned a
replacement. In 477 this was duly erected in the Athenian
agora (civic centre), the only such images of mortal men then
permitted within that sacred civic space. However, the reason
for this exception was that Harmodios and Aristogeiton were
by then no longer considered mere mortals but had long since
been transmogrified into honorary heroes in the technical
religious sense (objects of worship of more than human, but
less than fully divine, status)—by the magic wand of myth.

Herodotus the historian, however, was not deceived by
Athenian popular oral tradition. As he drily observed (6. 123),
it was not in actual fact Harmodios and Aristogeiton, but the
Alkmaionids led by Kleisthenes, who—of the Athenians—were
most responsible for overthrowing the Peisistratid tyranny.
Thucydides, the even more 'scientific' historian, went one

better. In a lengthy retrospective digression from his narrative context of the events of 415 he stated (6. 53. 3) that ordinary Athenians 'knew' (*epistamenos*) from 'oral tradition' (*akoē*) that it was neither Harmodios and Aristogeiton nor the Athenian people, but the Spartans, who had in reality got rid of the Peisistratid tyranny. However, what they did not know—but Thucydides did—was that, strictly speaking, Harmodios and Aristogeiton were not even tyrant-slayers. For the man they had assassinated some four years before the overthrow of the tyranny itself, and in honour of whose assassination they had been heroized, was not the reigning tyrant, but only his younger brother. Then in a *tour de force* of more laborious and exact enquiry (*zētēsis*—Thucydides is careful never to use the Herodotus-tainted term *historiē*), eked out by critical use of documentary inscriptions from Lampsakos in the Hellespont as well as Athens, Thucydides proceeded to demonstrate how the true history of the end of the Peisistratids could and should be (to use his term) 'written up'.

That it was now possible to conduct such antiquarian research is revealing enough; here, at last, is unambiguous testimony to the historiographical impact of literacy. That it had to be conducted, in order to rectify the vagaries of popular misbelief, is in its way no less revealing. However, perhaps the most interesting and revealing thing of all about this brilliant piece of 'scientific' historical reconstruction is that for its author such *arkhaiologia* or 'ancient history' held no intrinsic importance whatsoever. For Thucydides was the contemporary historian *par excellence*, not a Herodotean purveyor of ancient *muthoi* or *logoi*, pleasant though those might certainly be for an audience's ephemeral entertainment. The age of historical scholarship had dawned, at the expense of a myth that was popular both in the technical and in our everyday senses.

An Archaeological Myth

This development helps to put into proper perspective my final text, the so-called 'Archaeology' of Thucydides (1. 1–19). The historian's ostensible purpose in including this excursus was to prove, by his own exacting standards of proof, that the

Peloponnesian War was the 'greatest *kinēsis* ('upheaval')' in all Greek (and some non-Greek) history. But in order to do so, Thucydides paradoxically found himself obliged to invent his own largely allegorical myth of the past. For his lightning *tour d'horizon* of Greek history, from the time of Hellen son of Deukalion 'up to this war', was not strictly speaking a historical tour at all, since his normal methods of testing and proving historical testimony could not be applied to a past that was not only non-eyewitnessed but also pre-documentary. The 'Archaeology' excursus, therefore, is really a theoretical exercise, based on a theory 'derived from prolonged meditation about the world in which Thucydides lived' (Finley 1986c: 18). This explains, in part, the inclusion of Minos and Theseus, not to mention Hellen (supposed eponym of the Hellenes), alongside and on all fours with Polykrates and Croesus—as if the evidence for all these characters were equally reliable, as if the time in which they and Thucydides lived were a continuum, and as if Herodotus had never written. It would be hard to find a more spectacular refutation of the linear evolutionary model of intellectual progress.

At the same time it would be hard to think of a more spectacular illustration of the power of myth in Classical Greece than the fact that even the rationalistic Thucydides, who affected to despise what he called the *muthōdes*, who warned against the deceitful seductiveness of agonistic public recitations, and who spoke slightingly of mere *logographoi*, meaning chiefly Herodotus (1. 20–2), should have found himself compelled either to reject in principle all traditional tales about the past precisely as 'myths' (in our popular sense, the polar opposite of facts) or to create his own myth of the distant past, as he did in the 'Archaeology'.

While Herodotus and Thucydides were embroiled in intellectual invention, the broad mass of Greek toilers, in whom the 'historical spirit' had yet to be awakened sufficiently, persisted in their old myth-loving ways. For that matter, the irreconcilable factual disagreements between, say, Ktesias and Xenophon over 'what was actually happening' at the Persian court in c.400, or between Xenophon and the 'Oxyrhynchus

Historian' over the course of the battle of Sardis in 395, suggest that not many would-be historians shared Thucydides' self-proclaimed passion for 'accuracy' (*akribeia*) above all else. History as entertainment generally prevailed over history as instruction throughout the course of ancient Greek historiography, barring conspicuously isolated exceptions like Polybius (second century BCE), the historian of Rome's emergence to Mediterranean suzerainty.

Indeed, such was the enduring power of myth that not only did Plato make a speciality of creating new, philosophical ones (like the Myth of Er in the *Republic*), but even stern old Aristotle, who had once derogatorily labelled Herodotus the 'myth-teller' (*muthologos*, *Generation of Animals* 756^{b}6), found himself confessing willy-nilly late in life that 'the more I am a selfer and a loner, the more fond have I become of *muthoi*' (fragment 668). Perhaps this was because they seemed to reveal to him, as they have more recently to the structural anthropologist Claude Lévi-Strauss, deep truths about the human condition. Or perhaps he was simply bowing to the inevitable, and conceding the attractive power of a kind of discourse that was deeply embedded in the received and reputable opinions, the *phainomena* and *endoxa*, of Greek culture. It is in the latter context that this book, at any rate, must attempt to come to terms with Classical Greek myth. For all that Herodotus and Thucydides did in a sense make a breakthrough from myth to history, their representation of the past was at the same time conditioned inevitably by the dominant paradigms of their culture's mentality, not least the paradigm of polarized thinking that we shall be exploring further under various rubrics.

Entr'acte

Others in Images and Images of Others

The Need for Images

The Greeks, as Alain Schnapp (1988) acutely observed, needed images, of many different kinds. Barbarians, or rather some barbarians in the eyes of some Greeks, did not need images at all (Schnapp 2000). Imagery, even more obviously than the proverbial beauty, was all in the eye of the beholder. In this new additional section I shall use a commentary on a selection of Greek images of various categories of 'others' as a counterpoint to the extended commentary on my four principal written sources, Herodotus, Thucydides, Xenophon, and Aristotle, that comprises the bulk of this small book. On occasions, the counterpoint shades into contradiction, a further complication of what is already a complex picture.

That the imagery of alterity or of Others is a subject in its own right, and a very lively one at that, is illustrated graphically not only by Brian Sparkes's most useful article (Sparkes 1997) but also by the appearance in 2000 of two major collections of articles devoted to the topic of ancient Greek (and Roman) visual representations or constructions of what one of them calls 'Counterworlds' (*Gegenwelten*: Hölscher ed. 2000; the other collection is Cohen ed. 2000). In that same year an aptly reflexive general study of Greek art self-consciously included a chapter entitled 'Greeks and Others' (Fullerton 2000: ch. 2). The most acute problem I have faced here therefore is, for once, an abundance, rather than a dearth, of potential sources. Although the preponderance of suitable images that survive derives as ever from the Athenian repertoire, as the title alone of the Cohen collection conveys, the visual evidence from the great 'pan-Hellenic' or 'interstate' sanctuaries of Olympia, Delphi, and so on suggests that images might be taken to 'mean' pretty much the same to Greeks whatever their civic origin. Exactly what they meant to any one Greek, however, at any one moment, is of course by no stretch of the imagination a straightforward matter to discern. To speak of a 'Greek' way of viewing must therefore be construed often, or perhaps usually, as in some sense just a manner of speaking.

Plate 1 *History v. Myth*

The Parthenon frieze

Perhaps the *locus classicus* of modern scholarly dispute over the meaning of a Classical Greek image is the Parthenon frieze. Does it depict the Panathenaia festival, or perhaps *a* Panathenaia festival? Does it look back to the Persian Wars, in which Athens stood shoulder to shoulder with Sparta to resist the barbarian invader, or forward to the (renewed) Peloponnesian War, in which Athens and Sparta went head to head in what Thucydides saw as a carnival of internecine Hellenic reaction? Was it intended to belong to the time of myth, set in the eternal past, or of utopia, projected into the eternal future? Or was it intended to be. as it certainly also is, a monument of as well as a memorial to its own time, the third quarter of the fifth century BCE? In any case, might not what was intended by its designer, putatively Pheidias, have been quite different from what was in the minds of the Athenian people or of its two chosen architects, who respectively voted for and designed the construction of the temple of Athena Parthenos as a whole ?

My own hunch is that the ordinary Athenians as they (he or she) viewed the Parthenon frieze would not have recognized the distinction between 'history' and 'myth' as adumbrated, for example, by Herodotus to be relevantly applicable. The scene depicted, whatever it was, belonged for them equally to both spheres. Or rather to neither: for that distinction, as Thucydides rather ruefully acknowledged (6. 59), had yet to be articulated in the popular Athenian consciousness and remained indeed a predominantly élite conception thereafter. When we speak of 'Greek historical images' (Hölscher 1973), in other words, history should probably be interpreted in this context more loosely as story rather than strictly as critical historiography.

Consider, in contrast, the following two images, the first of which was intended more for private viewing, the second for a less restricted public gaze. The impact of both depended on a shared, universally Greek understanding of the polar opposition between Greeks and the rest of mankind, the 'Barbarians'.

Plate 2 *Greeks v. Barbarians I*

Athens, Nat Mus Inv. 9683 [*World of Athens* (*WA*) 7: 6 p. 298] Herakles and King Busiris: *c*.470

On the face of it, the most 'civilized' of the barbarians or non-Greeks by whom the Greeks found themselves abutted or encircled were the Egyptians. So Greek-like were at least some of them thought to be that Herodotus (2. 2) could amusingly represent a Pharaoh of the late seventh century whom he calls Psammetichos (Psamtik in Egyptian) as behaving uncannily like a Greek intellectual of the second half of the fifth century, conducting a social-scientific experiment to discover which was the aboriginal, the absolute first, human language.

Of course, there was a sting in that tale, as Psammetichos finds his confident expectation that it would be Egyptian confounded by the 'discovery' that it was in 'fact' Phrygian; and later on in that same second Book devoted chiefly to Egyptian matters Herodotus (2. 147) comments slyly that the Egyptians are incapable of living without kings—unlike, he implies, the more politically developed, republican Greeks. Yet one suspects that Herodotus' long drawn out catalogue of polar cultural oppositions between the *nomoi* of the Greeks and those of the Egyptians (2. 35–6) owes much to the awkward recognition that the Egyptians' culture was at least a good deal older than that of the Greeks and that their civilization, though very different, was at least impressively cultured and not barbarous or barbaric in the way, for example, of the justice-less 'man-eating' Androphagoi Scythians.

Another Egyptian king in whom the Greeks showed great interest, a figure entirely of legend rather than of myth-history like Psammetichos, was one Busiris, the supposed eponym of the place of that name. This king had the unfortunate habit of treating all foreigners extremely badly, and more specifically of failing, like the above-mentioned Androphagoi, to realize that eating people is wrong. That is, he did the very opposite of treating visitors with the respect that Zeus Xenios, Zeus of strangers, would have required of his Greek devotees. Until, that is, a certain Greek stranger confronted him in his own backyard—none other than the universal Greek culture-hero, Herakles. True, Herakles' own eating habits were not entirely *comme il faut*—he ate too much, too often, and too indiscriminately, giving rise to a number of cautionary cultural stories (Bruit and Schmitt 1992: 171–2). But when it came to dealing with monsters who threatened civilized values, whether of the animal or the human variety, Herakles was your man. The Pan Painter has taken care here to emphasize visibly the negroid, non-Greek physical features of Busiris' cowardly minions, and above all the culturally decisive attribute of circumcision—a practice which the Greeks viewed (in more senses than one) with shock and horror.

Plate 3 *Greeks v. Barbarians II*
BM [Spivey 1997: fig. 141]
Bassai Amazonomachy

From an individual male barbarian we turn to a collectivity, indeed a society, of female ones, the Amazons. They are to be found, prominently, in tragedy, comedy, the funeral oration, historiography, and, not least, visual art. In the latter, they are popular both on privately owned and used vases and in publicly displayed sculpture. This is no mean feat for a people which was, in every sense, imaginary.

It is true that the Amazons had a special affinity for the Athenian sensibility and consciousness. The Athenians' local lore and tradition gloried in ancestors who repulsed an invasion of Amazons and, yet more interestingly, in a founder-hero, Theseus, who 'married' one and fathered on her Hippolytus, eponym of one of Euripides' most dramatically satisfying extant plays. All the same, the Amazons were by no means a peculiarly Athenian phenomenon, but rather a truly Greek invention. Their ubiquitousness in classical Greece is quite remarkable. They spoke to and spoke for a panhellenic mode of self-definition by polar opposition.

This local Athenian and panhellenic reception was given a spectacular boost by the Persian invasions of 490 and 480–479, since these too were incursions of exotic foreigners whose way of life threatened that of the Greeks both symbolically and physically, and incursions that were also spectacularly repulsed. Moreover, as was typically the case with Greek conceptual dualism, one set of oppositions, Greek v. Barbarian, was intercut with and reinforced by another, Men v. Women. For, as Lillian Doherty has recently put it (2001: 137), the versions of Amazon myths

that have survived are fully mythic in their neat reversals of Greek (especially Athenian) norms . . . they valued daughters above sons, to the point of killing or giving away male babies born to them (as unwanted daughters might be exposed in Greek society); they assumed all the roles reserved for males in Greece, administering their own affairs and engaging in warfare. Above all they rejected marriage outright, seeking sexual contact with men only sporadically and for their own purposes— that is, for their own pleasure or to reproduce their society of women . . . As might be expected, the Greeks consistently portrayed Amazons as losing their battles with Greek heroes, who represented the 'proper' patriarchal order.

Nowhere does the Greekness of the Amazon myth and representation obtrude more strikingly than in the interior frieze of a late fifth-century temple erected in the relatively isolated backwater of Bassai, in the territory of ancient Phigaleia in inland Arkadia. The architect of this magnificent limestone temple was reputedly the Athenian Iktinos, 'the Kite', joint architect with Kallikrates of the earlier Athenian Parthenon, where a battle of civilized Greeks and anti-civilized Amazons is also featured prominently. Yet the Phigaleians' honorand was not Athena the Virgin, a goddess with obviously relevant cultural and gender as well as military implications, but Apollo Epikourios, Apollo the Helper. For what help was the god of healing and song being specifically thanked?

The late writer Pausanias (8. 41. 8) had gleaned a connection with deliverance from a plague, analogously to a temple devoted to an Apollo who had 'turned away' a pestilence—presumably the Great Plague of 430 and following—at Athens. But, quite apart from the problem of the authenticity of that testimony at a distance of nearly six centuries, such an explanation seems a little too distant from Arkadian concerns and a little too Athens-influenced to carry complete conviction. Far more persuasive is the suggestion that the Apollo of Bassai was the Apollo of mercenaries (Greek *epikouroi*). From since well before the time of the Persian Wars (Herodotus 1. 66. 2) Arkadia had been famed as a hungry, unforgiving land, and from the Persian War period on (Herodotus 8. 26. 1; Hermippos 63. 18) as a source of hungry young men seeking a livelihood, at least temporarily, through mercenary service abroad. One thinks automatically of Xenophon's 'Ten Thousand' mercenaries, the largest ethnic contingent of whom was drawn from Arkadia. That expedition postdated the construction of the Temple of Apollo at Bassai by almost a generation, but the service of the Ten Thousand within the Persian empire provides just the oriental context within which the Greek imagination placed the race of the Amazons, the *ne plus ultra* (as the Greeks fervently hoped) of oriental barbarian female independence.

Plate 4 *Men v. Women*
BM, Inv. E 467 [*WA* 2: 5 p. 96]
Athene and Pandora

The myth of Pandora was foundational for the Greeks in the most basic way. As depicted in Hesiod's *Theogony*, she was the primordial woman, a sort of Greek Eve. But, as Lillian Doherty has pointed out (2001: 136), 'Hesiod does not call her the mother of all subsequent humans but only of the *genos gunaikôn*, the "race of women".' It would be hard to think of a sharper illustration of the extreme sexual dimorphism, the extreme polarization of gender, that the ancient Greeks fervently believed in and tried very hard to practise.

Pandora owed her name, 'All-Gifts', to the fact that all the gods and goddesses conspired to load her with suitable—and suitably positive—attributes. Athenians, however, who also worshipped their own local version of Pandora, might be forgiven for concentrating on the gift-giving of their own patron deity, Athena, such as is illustrated in this large red-figure kalyx krater (sympotic wine-mixing bowl) attributed to the Niobid Painter of the mid-fifth century, roughly contemporary with the Parthenon wherein a version of Pandora was also figured.

There remained, however, a certain irony as well as aptness in the juxtaposition of Athena and Pandora. For whereas Pandora was as female and feminine as it was possible to be, quintessentially so one might say, the feminine sexuality of Athena was, to say the least of it, somewhat challenged. Not only had she been born of a man, her father Zeus, not a woman, but she had not gone through the normal rituals of marriage and defloration that to Greek ways of thinking made an immature female human being into a woman in the full sense, a *gunê* as opposed to *parthenos*. 'Parthenos', virgin, was indeed precisely one of her cultic epithets, the one honoured and ritually celebrated in the shrine known as the Parthenon (actually only a part of the building we conventionally but inaccurately refer to as the Parthenon). Moreover, apart from her feminine craft skills of weaving and suchlike, Athena was surprisingly comfortably at home in the exclusively male preserve of the battlefield, and was indeed depicted as a warrior in, most conspicuously, her role as Athena Promachos or 'Frontline fighter'.

Thus Pandora and Athena, so far from standing shoulder to shoulder for femininity, might even be construed as standing for opposed gender ideals. This may explain why our painter is careful to show Athena as about to bedeck Pandora with a characteristically feminine adornment, a fancy necklace. In this case at least, the sexual proprieties were to be faithfully observed. Other elements in the other friezes of this exceptionally fine sympotic vase—actors dressed as satyrs, *aulos*-players (see further below, Plate 5)—indicate its strongly Dionysiac association.

Plate 5 *Citizens v. Aliens*

BM E 532 [Bérard 1989*a*: fig. 192]
Satyr as citizen, Pelike *c*.430

In Plato's *Symposium*, with its dramatic date of 416 BCE, Alkibiades starts his speech as follows:

> The way I am going to set out to praise Socrates, gentlemen, is through images. Now *he* will probably think it's meant to amuse everybody, but the purpose of the image will in fact be to tell the truth, not to be amusing. I declare that he is most like those silenuses that sit in statuary shops, the ones the craftsmen make, with *auloi*, and when you open them up by taking them apart, they turn out to have statues of gods inside them.

No such figures of Silenus happen to have survived from antiquity, though the idea of 'a god within' another statue or image is known from medieval Christian Europe and from Hindu India. But the likening of Socrates in his outward facial appearance to a Silenus is instructive enough for our purposes. A Silenus was an elderly form of satyr, and satyrs were part-man, part-beast, representing both the beast in man and the close association, sometimes even imagined kinship, of human and animal. Their association with Dionysus served, not incidentally, to help position mortal men on the moral scale somewhere between gods and beasts. Our chosen illustration of a demurely robed satyr, from an Athenian red-figure oenochoe (wine-jug) of *c*.430, stretches the humanity of the imaginary representation to its greatest possible—and therefore most satirical—degree by figuring him as a respectable citizen . . . on the outside. The effect, presumably intended by the artist, is to suggest that the bestial, the lawless, the wild lurk beneath, and not all that far beneath, the surface of the polished, humane civic identity of the idealized Greek male.

In controlled contexts such as the *orgia* or religious rituals of Dionysos, as celebrated by private companies (*thiasoi*) of initiates, such exotic licensed excess was considered not only tolerable but necessary; one of the civic lessons of Euripides' *Bacchae* of 406/5 was, presumably, that to deny the Dionysiac impulse could lead to appalling outrages, especially among women. Conversely, expression of Dionysiac bestiality in unlicensed, non-normative contexts, especially by males, was bound to be no less destructive. The mad havoc wreaked on all and sundry at Mykalessos in 413 by barbarian, and barbarous, mercenaries from Thrace, a land of noted Dionysiac associations, was a lesson for all Thucydides' readers. So too the fiendish destruction of the public and private Hermes figures in Athens two years earlier, on the ill-omened eve of sailing of the Athenian armada for Sicily.

The prime mover of that expedition, and implausibly alleged mastermind of that sacrilegious destruction, was Alcibiades. Plato's sympotic character Alkibiades, as quoted above, mentions that the statuaries' Silenuses were depicted with *auloi*, that is, a form of reed-pipe something like our oboe usually played in doubled form. The very instrument was itself also shot through with moral-psychological ambivalence. It was, on one hand, a necessary accompaniment of, for example, tragic drama, a properly civic Dionysiac ritual. Yet at the same time the *aulos* carried overtones of irrational and orgiastic excess, prompting Aristotle in Book 8 of the *Politics* (1341^a25) even to claim that it 'prevents the use of *logos*', that is the free and reasoned speech of the ideal Greek *polities* (Wilson 1999; 2001: 130–1).

Plate 6 *Free v. Slave*

Paris, Louvre 2587 [*WA* 4: 19 p. 185]
Thracian slave girl, Aigisthus Painter, *c.*475–50

A twisted, polemical Athenian writer of strongly oligarchic persuasion composed a paradoxical pamphlet somewhere in the second half of the fifth century, probably in the 420s or 410s. It is in fact the earliest extant substantial piece of Attic literary prose, and in the English-speaking world it goes by the familiar name of the Old Oligarch. At least the second half of that title is accurate. One of the many uncongenial features of life in contemporary, democratic Athens at which he (almost certainly the author is male) rails is the awkward circumstance that you could hardly tell apart a poor free citizen and a slave solely by their appearance. So difficult were they to distinguish indeed that you might get into serious trouble for doing physical violence to a free citizen, after mistaking him or her for a slave. That would have been to commit *hubris*, a categorical confusion of status with the most serious political and cultural implications.

A great deal of allowance has to be made for the author's sheer class prejudice, but implicit in his indignation is the thoroughly Greek notion that not only ought slaves to be different, in terms of their legal status and ideally their essentially servile 'nature', but they ought to look different also. Thus in Sparta, for example, one of the many indignities the Spartans heaped on their servile class of Helots was to force them to wear certain types of clothing, made of animal skin rather than woven fibres, in order both to reduce them symbolically to the status of beasts and to justify thereby as well as enforce their social degradation. But the Spartans had an added reason for taking this trouble, in that the unfree Helots were also Greeks like their masters. Most slaves in Greece, that is the imported chattel slaves, were not. Almost by definition they were barbarian outlanders, foreigners alienated from their natal condition by cultural difference as well as, usually, by physical force.

One of the prime areas from which the Greeks derived their slaves was the fringe northern territory of Thrace, which corresponds roughly to modern Bulgaria. So intimate was the linkage between Thrace and slavery that at Athens 'Thratta' and 'Thrax', the ethnics for 'Thracian female' and 'Thracian male', were standard slave names. On this pot we see represented just such a 'Thratta'. Though she is not named as such, her ethnic affiliation is made perfectly clear by the draughtsman for the benefit of his no doubt free Greek client or patron, both in her dress and hairstyle and in her tattoos on neck as well as arms.

One further thought must not be left unspoken, however. The draughtsman might well himself have been a slave, even possibly a Thracian by origin. At any rate, there was nothing incongruous or incompatible between servile status and outstanding craftsmanship. For instance, the elaborate architectural decoration of the Erekhtheion temple on the Athenian akropolis in the last decade of the fifth century was in part carved by slaves. Nor, of course, were slave status and literacy incompatible. A recently published lead letter from Athens, dated to the fourth century, is most easily interpreted as written by a slave. So far as fine pottery manufacture goes, one Athenian pot survives, of late sixth-century date, explicitly signed by 'Lydos the slave', or possibly 'the Lydian slave'. Now, one of the very best Attic early Classical potters, who was also perhaps a painter, went by the name of Brygos, and the Brygoi were a Thracian people. The accuracy and sensitivity of the portrayal of a Thracian slave woman on this pot might therefore have owed something to the shared ethnicity of the painter.

Plate 7 *Gods v. Mortals I*

Brauron Mus Inv. 1153 (32 + 32a)

Sacrifice relief scene, 4 c.

One modern definition of the ancient Greek gods, by A. D. Nock, labelled them as 'larger Greeks'. The definition aimed to capture three essential features of the Greek projection and representation of the divine. First, that the gods—and goddesses—were perceived according to human canons, in anthropomorphic forms; as Herodotus (2. 53. 2) put it, 'Homer and Hesiod were the first . . . to describe [the gods'] forms'. But not merely generically human, but specifically Greek, forms: Xenophanes of Kolophon (fr. 168) in the late sixth or early fifth century had memorably commented that the Thracians' gods had light blue eyes and red hair, the Ethiopians' snub noses and black skin. Third, the gods and goddesses were both physically and spiritually bigger than ordinary human beings—they were deathless, ageless, ate different food, could perform feats of aerial and terrestrial movement not available to humans, and so forth.

In many representations, especially on the pediments or metopes of temples, or in free-standing statuary, the divine pantheon received superhuman, larger than life bodies, none more so than the gargantuan figures used as column-substitutes on the fifth-century temple of Zeus at Akragas in Greek Sicily. In our more modest, indeed domestic image, the sculptor of this dedicatory relief from Brauron in east Attica has expressed the gulf between the gods and their mortal worshippers in terms of relative scale. Comparatively puny humans pay cult to their much larger divine protectress and patron, Artemis, chief divinity of

Brauron. And they do so in the characteristic manner of pre-Christian Greek religion, by way of animal blood-sacrifice. In addition to, and just in front of, the stag that symbolizes Artemis' function as goddess of hunting on the wild margins and is represented on a comparably supernatural scale, there is just detectable the head of a much smaller beast, presumably a real-world domesticated doe.

The human worshippers too are carefully graded in size according to their relative age and status. From the two tiniest figures, who like the woman bending over the doe may perhaps be slaves, through the young boy and the two adolescent males to the three fully adult bearded males and the adult female the sculptor has minutely observed, in an almost photographic way, the generational structure of this family at worship. The sacrificial ritual as depicted here emphasizes the necessary linkage of gods and men, but other representations in other media, for example the aboriginal myth in Hesiod of Prometheus' theft of fire against Zeus' will, at the same time underlined the unbridgeable distance between the divine and the human spheres.

Plate 8 *Gods v. Mortals II*
BM, Coins & Medals, Inv. 1871-11-7-1 [*WA* HI: 21 p. 50]
Gold Stater: Apollo (obv.) + Philip II (rev.)

In principle the human and the divine spheres were considered by the ancient Greeks to be separate, unequal, and untransgressible. Or rather, whereas gods and goddesses might freely penetrate the human world, mortal men and women could not become gods. One way indeed of cutting down to size an overweening mortal such as Pausanias, Regent of Sparta and commander-in-chief of the loyalist Greeks at Plataia in 479, was to remind him precisely that he was not a god, that he should 'think mortal' (*thnêta phronein*) as the tragic poets including Sophocles put it. Yet, late in the fifth century, or early in the fourth, a significant breach in that supposedly watertight barrier was effected—by the ruling group on the island of Samos in the immediate aftermath of the Peloponnesian War.

The man singled out for this unprecedentedly honorific attention was a Spartan Heraklid, that is, an aristocrat supposedly descended lineally on his father's side from Herakles; and Herakles, although he did admittedly start with the natural advantage of having Zeus for his father, had been accorded the singular honour of being received into the company of the immortal gods on the top of Mount Olympos—thanks to his Labours. Lysander, the Spartan honorand in question, could claim lineal descent from Zeus via Herakles, but, notwithstanding his own self-estimate, his practical achievements hardly stood comparison with those of the hero-god.

His claim to Samian fame was that he was a political saviour and restorer. He had ejected a fanatically pro-Athenian democratic regime and established in its place a very narrow form of oligarchic rule, an extreme *dunasteia*, placing power in the hands of just ten men, formerly exiles, who were equally devoted and fanatical followers of his. In gratitude to Lysander they repaid him, apparently in his lifetime, with the religious honours that were normally paid only to gods. They paid him, that is, superior honours even to those paid exceptionally to 'heroes'. The latter were wholly mortal men who were treated posthumously with especial reverence on account of their benefactions, men such as the Spartan Brasidas at Akanthos. There is good reason for believing that Lysander personally would have not have found this dangerously hybristic treatment unwelcome, and may perhaps have prompted it. But in 395 he was killed in central Greece, and the precedent set by the Samian oligarchs was not followed precisely anywhere in Greece that we know of.

In fact, the next Greek to whom we can say with confidence that divine honours were paid by Greeks in his lifetime was Alexander the Great of Macedon some eighty years or three generations later on, by when he was overlord of not only all Greece but also much of Asia. However, before Alexander, whose stupendous feats at least make the award understandable, his father Philip had already taken several steps along the road that might have led to a lifetime divinization—had he not been assassinated in 336. At the greatest panhellenic interstate sanctuary of Olympia, where he had won a victory early in his reign, a shrine known as the Philippeion appears to have been constructed before his death; the name suggests at least a hero-shrine. At the time of his assassination, a statue of him was being carried in procession at his daughter's wedding, in company with statues representing the Twelve Olympian gods. The gold coin illustrated here shows Philip in close association with one of the Twelve, Apollo. The historical allusion was unmistakable. But it is also rather specifically revealing.

Philip as a Macedonian had a problem establishing his Greekness, at any rate in the eyes of his enemies such as Demosthenes of Athens (below, p. 197). The officials responsible for organizing the Olympic Games in honour of Olympian Zeus did, to be fair, openly vouch for his Greekness by allowing him to compete, but that was a privilege accorded to him alone of all the Macedonians, not because he was Philip but because he was the Macedonians' king, on the (mythic) grounds that his ultimate lineal royal ancestor Temenos had been a pure Greek immigrant from Peloponnesian Argos. Thus the king was the one and only Macedonian deemed eligible to compete at Olympia, the oldest and the grandest of the pan-Hellenic festivals. One way in which Philip sought to establish more firmly his challenged Greek credentials— and thereby, probably, pave the way for the great Hellenic crusade of revenge that he proclaimed against the Persian infidel in the 330s—was to assume control of the religious Amphiktyony or league responsible for running the other major pan-Hellenic religious centre, Delphi, sacred to Zeus' son Apollo. The so-called Third Sacred War provided him with just the opportunity required.

The sanctuary had been taken over in 356 by the Phokians, allies of one of Philip's principal enemies, Athens. Three years later, Philip suffered two defeats while taking the side of the legitimate controllers of Delphi, chiefly the Thessalians. These proved to be the only two defeats in pitched battle that he was ever to suffer in an actively warlike reign of over twenty years. In 352 at the battle of the Krokos Field he avenged them with a neat touch of symbolic showmanship. His troops went into triumphantly successful battle against the Phokians sporting on their heads, not only regulation helmets, but also wreaths made from leaves of laurel, Apollo's sacred tree. Six years later, when final victory in the Sacred War was his, Philip assumed control of the Amphikty-ony and celebrated the quadrennial Pythian Games with especial magnificence. He had much to be grateful to Apollo for—and presumably the reverse was true too. At any rate that conjunction explains why a gold stater issued either by Philip in his lifetime or, after his death, in his name should carry on the obverse a laureate head of Apollo and on the reverse an illustration of a four-horse chariot with the name 'Philippos' in the exergue beneath.

3

Alien Wisdom

Greeks v. Barbarians

And now what will become of us without Barbarians?—
Those people were some sort of a solution

(C. P. Cavafy, 'Waiting for the Barbarians')

Constructing Ethnic Identities

One of the themes of Chapter 2 was the emergence of
'History' as an intellectual practice, in contradistinction to the
uncritical telling and retelling of stories for reasons other than
the desire to reconstruct and explicate a true human past.
Another was the impossibility, and undesirability, of drawing
too sharp a boundary between history and fiction in these
senses. Consider now the following two statements by leading
contemporary historians, which seem to me to capture this
tension perfectly with regard to this chapter's subject, 'ethnic'
self-definition through Greek history. According to the distinguished American historian of slavery and women, Carl
Degler (1983: 4): 'If history has any purpose as an intellectual
enterprise it is that through their conception of the past people
gain a sense of who they are through knowing where they
have been.' According to Gareth Stedman Jones, historian
of 'outcast' Victorian London: 'One of the uses of history
has always been (in Western society at least) the creation of
traditional mythologies attributing a historical sanctity to the
present self-images of groups, classes and societies' (Stedman
Jones 1972: 112).

The distinction between Degler's 'purpose' and Stedman
Jones's 'uses' is crucial: history has always been used ideologically for purposes other than those ideally professed by

historians. Such a slippage is particularly likely to occur, and arguably is even socially necessary, where ethnicity, the definition and self-definition of ethnic groups through such factors as language, blood, and religion, is at stake. Even Classical antiquity has been sucked into the current maelstrom of debate over ethnicity, by way of Martin Bernal's controversial *Black Athena* books. This learned but non-specialist author has the confessedly political aim of diminishing racial arrogance. This he seeks to achieve by rescuing what he regards as the authentic and decisive (Black) Egyptian and (Semitic) Phoenician inputs into Classical Greek civilization from what he sees as the racist-inspired oblivion imposed by the last two centuries of scholarship. The particular relevance of this project for us is that Bernal's star witness to his (genetic) view of the truth about the origins and nature of fully developed Classical Greek civilization is also one of our principal sources, namely Herodotus. However, laudable though Bernal's aim unquestionably is in our contemporary political terms, it is systematically frustrated by his inability to read the testimony of Herodotus in its original cultural context.

We shall be considering Herodotus' contribution in some detail below (and again, in a different context, in Chapter 7). But it is worth pointing out here that Herodotus himself was of mixed, not purely Hellenic, origins. He was born in Halikarnassos, modern Bodrum on the west coast of modern Turkey, perhaps somewhere in the 480s. Thus he was born a subject of the Persian Empire, which he was in turn to make the subject of his life's work, in the geographical region known as Caria within the Persian satrapy (province) of Lydia. But not only was the *polis* of Halikarnassos not politically independent; it was also not purely Greek. The names of Herodotus' father and uncle (or cousin) are both Carian or Carian-derived, the result of either intermarriage or some other close connection between Greek and 'native'. Or rather Greek and 'barbarian', in the technical sense that the Carians did not speak Greek. It was precisely they whom Homer in his unique use of the epithet had described as *barbarophōnoi* or '*bar-bar*-speakers'.

Moreover, the Greeks who had founded Halikarnassos among the Carians some five centuries before Herodotus' birth were themselves apparently not entirely ethnically homogeneous. The majority belonged to the Doric language group which predominated in southern Greece, the southern Aegean islands (including Crete), and southern Asia Minor. But while Herodotus was a young man the city began to publish official state documents in the Ionic alphabet, that used by Athens. By then, it is true, Halikarnassos was liberated from Persia and a member of the anti-Persian military alliance dominated by Athens that we call the 'Delian League'. But the use of the Ionic alphabet among non-Ionic-speaking east Greek states was generally avoided until much later, after the presumed date of Herodotus' death (*c*.425?). This argues the existence of an important Ionian strain in the Greek population of Halikarnassos, although dialect-affiliation was not a determinant of racial identity in the world of Classical Greece (any more than speaking a Semitic language is today). So too, perhaps, does Herodotus' apparent anti-Ionian prejudice, which contrasts so vividly with his tolerance of or even admiration for non-Greek barbarians.

The Invention of the Barbarian

Herodotus' attitude to non-Greeks, however, was hugely untypical, and before we consider his and other Classical Greek historical representations of them I want to set his attitude off against the stereotyped image prevalent in the consciousness of ordinary Greeks-in-the-*agora*-barbershop during the fifth and fourth centuries. The chronology is important here. Homer bears little or no trace of ethnocentric and derogatory stereotyping of barbarians, indeed does not actually use the word *barbaros* in any but a descriptive sense (of *barbarophōnoi* Carians). Nor is any such process of 'othering' apparent in the seventh and sixth centuries BCE. For example, Greeks like the brother of the aristocratic poet Alkaios (of Lesbos) who enlisted as mercenaries under Middle Eastern potentates seem to have incurred no social stigma thereby, and, as we saw in Chapter 2, the Athenian aristocrat Alkmaion actually increased his social kudos by allegedly founding his family's fortune on a windfall from just such an oriental source. Near-Eastern mythology and philosophy were absorbed into the mainstream of Greek religion and culture in the same period, just as Greek artists borrowed and domesticated such oriental ideas as the Egyptian colossal male nude statue of stone. A descendant of the said Alkmaion, who was presumably named Kroisos after the Lydian king, was commemorated by a statue of this type, prominently erected in the family burial plot during the third quarter of the sixth century. No doubt his father enjoyed a prestigious ancestral relationship of ritualized friendship (*xenia*) with the Lydian royal house.

However, by the time of Aeschylus' *Persians*, produced at the Athenian Great Dionysia festival of 472, the process of 'othering' and indeed inventing 'the barbarian' as a homogenized stereotype was well underway in Greece, in an early version of the specific form of derogatory stereotyping now known as 'orientalism'. The catalyst was the defeat of the Persian invasion of Greece in 480–479, upon the failure of which the Athenians grounded their anti-Persian empire. In cold historical fact the defeat had been effected by a shaky and improvised coalition of a mere thirty to forty Greek states—out of more than seven hundred in the Aegean world alone; and the Athenians' alliance was not as Hellenic as Athenian propaganda maintained. But that of course was all the more reason for celebrating the feat precisely as 'Greek', indeed pan-Hellenic or 'all-Greek', *pour encourager les autres*. However, any narrowly political dimension introduced into Greek self-awareness by the conflict with Persia remained intermittent and evanescent. Even if there was something that could be called Greek nationality, there was never any chance of there emerging from it a Greek nation-state. That fact was silently acknowledged by Herodotus in his famous definition of Hellenism (see the Prologue). But it was openly bemoaned by Aristotle in his *Politics*, and it is through Aristotle's text that we gain reliable access to 'popular' or at any rate 'dominant' Greek ideology.

'The Hellenic people,' Aristotle wrote (*Politics* 1327^{b}29–32), 'which is situated between them [Europe and Asia], is likewise intermediate in character. Hence it continues free and is the best-governed of any people and, if it could be formed into one state (*politeia*), would be able to rule the world.' Europe (meaning what he knew of it to north and west of the Greek world) was for Aristotle cold, spirited, but unintelligent, whereas Asia (meaning roughly the Persian Empire, minus the Greek pale of settlement at its western extremity) was hot, languid, but intelligent. Greece, in conformity with the classically Aristotelian notion of the golden mean, enjoyed a moderate warmth, and its people therefore managed to combine both spirit and intelligence in due measure and proportion. That combination, he asserted rather than argued, was the explanation of Greek freedom, which he represented as constituting a polar contrast to barbarian servility. Moreover, because the Greeks were 'naturally' free and the barbarians 'naturally' servile (a point that has special relevance to Aristotle's doctrine of 'natural' slavery: Chapter 6), it was right and proper for the Greeks to rule barbarians, if only for their own good. This was an open endorsement of and invitation to at any rate cultural imperialism by the Greeks.

This mishmash of ideology, illogicality, and wishful thinking from the stylus of the founder of Western philosophical logic betrays the emotional and cultural charge that the Greek–barbarian polarity aroused in him. But just how conventional such Greek pseudo-scientific 'ethnology' was emerges from an earlier exercise in the genre, by a fifth-century contributor to the corpus of medical writings ascribed to the great Hippokrates of Kos. In a tract entitled *Airs Waters Places* we read (ch. 16):

The small variations of climate to which the Asiatics are subject, extremes both of heat and of cold being avoided, account for their mental flabbiness and cowardice . . . They are less warlike than Europeans and tamer of spirit, for they are not subject to those physical changes and the mental stimulation which sharpen tempers and induce recklessness and hot-headedness. . . . Such things appear to me to be the cause of the feebleness of the Asiatic race, but a contributory cause lies in their customs; for the greater part is under monarchical rule. . . . [E]ven if a man be born brave and of stout heart, his character is ruined by this form of government.

Much as we might like to dismiss such reflections, which do not do much for the Greeks' reputation for genius, as aberrant and cranky, we are forbidden to do so by the basic feature of Aristotle's political-philosophical method mentioned in Chapter 1. Unlike his teacher Plato, Aristotle preferred to begin by 'positing the phenomena', starting off from propositions of good repute, which in the opinion of the majority or of the 'savvy' (the experts, the prudent) among the Greeks seemed valid or fruitful for the subject-matter in hand. In some cases Aristotle ended by modifying these received views in some significant way, but not here. In the case of barbarians, presumably, there was no need for special experience, expertise, or intelligence to understand them: being a barbarian boiled down to a combination (the wrong one) of temperament and intellect.

So through Aristotle we get access in not very rarefied form to the thinking or rather prejudice of 'ordinary' Greeks. Confirmation that this was indeed the standard view is easily found in a wide range of Athenian literature, for example the plays of Aeschylus and Euripides (though it is of course quite another matter whether the playwrights agreed with the sentiments they dramatized), and speeches delivered before mass juries in the Athenian popular jury-courts.

Dissentient Voices

A major—and arguably the major—incentive to unthinking acceptance of the standard stereotype was the fact that the majority of slaves in the Classical Greek world were by origin barbarian. Even Greeks who owned no slaves aspired to do so and identified themselves with their slave-owning compatriots in embracing wholeheartedly the ideology of freedom: Greeks (like the Britons of 'Rule Britannia') never, never shall be slaves, whereas barbarians were naturally slavish and so tailor-made for servitude. Fear of enslavement, even if only temporary or metaphorical (and, as we shall see in Chapter 6, Greeks considered a remarkably wide range of behaviours, attitudes, occupations, and lifestyles to be servile), was an ever-pressing motive for 'othering' the barbarian for the majority of ordinary free, citizen Greeks. But against the trend there were a few bold spirits who protested with various arguments and varying degrees of urgency, among them, happily, some of our principal literary sources.

I begin, however, not with a historian, but with a philosopher who may also have been a politically motivated man, namely Antiphon of Athens. He is usually called 'Antiphon the Sophist', partly because he is a characteristic product of the Sophistic movement, but also in order to distinguish him from Antiphon the legal speechwriter and politician. The latter was a man of extreme anti-democratic views who was executed for high treason in 411/10 after masterminding a successful but shortlived oligarchic coup. However, it is now widely believed that the two supposed Antiphons are really one. If so, the most exclusive and exclusionary brand of political ideology could coexist in one and the same brain (or *psukhē*, as the Greeks thought of it: see Chapter 4) with the most broadminded and humanistic radicalism. For Antiphon the Sophist, in accordance with the Sophists' typical intellectual move of questioning the intrinsic validity of all social norms, denied that there was such a category as barbarians by nature. Since all human beings shared the same nature, i.e. had an identical physical and intellectual makeup, barbarian difference, and *a fortiori* barbarian natural inferiority, had to be a matter of mere arbitrary social convention (*nomos*) and not a fact of essential and unalterable nature (*phusis*).

Pan-Hellenism

Few are known to have followed Antiphon down this intellectual path in Classical Greece, and none sought to convert his reflections on papyrus into concrete political reality. It was another century before the Stoic school of philosophy mooted the brotherhood of man as a serious moral tenet, and in practice even where Stoics acquired political influence, or the men with political power in the Hellenistic world were themselves Stoics, barbarians were still found good to think with in mundane political terms. Indeed, the coming of the Romans in the third and second centuries BCE merely aggravated the barbarians' categorical inferiority, since the new masters of the Greek world wanted to be regarded as cultured and thus not as barbarians (which, technically, in Greek eyes they inevitably were).

In the Classical period, as we might have inferred from the passage in Aristotle's *Politics* discussed above, the trend went in the opposite direction from Antiphon. Not only was it thought good to have barbarian slaves in the Greek world, but in the fourth century the more articulate and conservative Greeks began to formulate a theory of the relationship between Greeks and their barbarian neighbours that enshrined the negative, slavish stereotype. This theory (if that is not too grand a word) is known for short as 'pan-Hellenism'. It survives most extensively in the abundant political pamphleteering of the Athenian crypto-oligarch Isokrates (436–338). Terrified by what he saw (or affected to see) as the imminent threat of political revolution from below, involving confiscation and redistribution of the landed property owned by plutocrats like himself in favour of poor, rootless Greeks, he consistently advocated over a period of almost half a century a single panacea: the conquest of some part of the Persian Empire to act as a sump for the dregs of Greece under the slogan of all-Greek revenge and reparation for the sacrilege and material damage inflicted by Xerxes in 480–479. As it happened, the Persian Empire was in fact conquered from the west, and under just such a liberationist slogan, but the conqueror, Alexander the Great, was a Macedonian and only technically a Greek, in the sense that the king of Macedon alone of his people was permitted to compete in the pan-Hellenic Olympic Games (Herodotus 5. 22). To some Greeks, indeed, though not to Isokrates (or Aristotle, who tutored Alexander and whose father had ministered medically to Alexander's grandfather), all Macedonians were virtually or utterly barbarians, even though they probably spoke a Greek-based dialect.

Pan-Hellenism thus worked itself out somewhat paradoxically and ironically in practice, and Isokrates lived long enough (he died aged 98) to witness first the conquest of Greece by Alexander's father Philip and then the beginning of his assault on Persia, which had to be completed by Alexander following Philip's assassination in 336. Our other major source on pan-Hellenism, however, would have been considerably more astonished by this outcome, since he had died some twenty years earlier when Philip's rise to ascendancy was not very far advanced and the power of Persia still constituted a formidable factor in Greek thinking and politics. That source is Xenophon (c.427–354).

Two factors chiefly inspired Xenophon's pan-Hellenist outlook: first, his experience as a mercenary in Asia Minor and the Middle East from the Aegean to Mesopotamia between 402 and 400; second, his meeting, when still a mercenary, with King Agesilaos II of Sparta during his anti-Persian campaign of 396–394. The first convinced him that the western reaches of the Persian Empire were less formidable than was normally thought, the second that Persian-hating was a vital ingredient of Greek political correctness.

The story of Xenophon's 'March Up-Country' (*Anabasis*) to take part in a Persian royal succession struggle and of his triumphant return to the Black Sea (*thalassa, thalassa,* 'the sea! the sea!') and to (Greek) civilization is—or was—familiar to Macaulay's proverbial schoolboy. What may be less well known is that the *Anabasis* is also the earliest extant example of the genre of reflective autobiographical travelogue. I select just one passage to illustrate how travel narrows the mind, a classic piece of ethnocentric ethnography. The Mossynoeci tribe on the southern shore of the Black Sea (already mentioned by Herodotus, 3. 94, 7. 98) were, according to Xenophon, the most barbarous, that is, the most un-Greek, of all the many barbarian peoples that he and the 'Ten Thousand' mercenaries encountered. The main reason for this distinction was not a matter of their sexual usages (as it would have been for Herodotus: see below and next chapter), but of their food-habits. For the Mossynoeci did not normally eat bread. The force of that cultural lapse can be gauged by considering the importance to the Greeks of the earth-mother goddess of grain, Demeter, especially at Eleusis in Attica, where initiation into the Mysteries was pan-Hellenic in the precise sense that it was open to all who could speak Greek (regardless of ethnic origin and social status).

The *Anabasis* contains much historical material but was not itself a work of history. The so-called *Hellenica* or 'Greek History' (not Xenophon's own title) purported to be just that; indeed, it masqueraded as a continuation of Thucydides' truncated history of the Peloponnesian War. I say 'masqueraded' because what Xenophon considered 'worthy of record' (*axiologon*) in history was very different from what Thucydides had decided to treat, and his moralizing manner was almost the exact opposite of his predecessor's austerely self-denying stance of amoral objectivity. Pan-Hellenism therefore receives an overt seal of approval in the *Hellenica*, whether it is the Spartan Kallikratidas' pontificating that Greeks should not fawn on the barbarian for silver (1. 6. 7), or Agesilaos' pose as a new Agamemnon (3. 4. 3, 7. 1. 34), or an Arkadian ambassador's returning from the Persian court to quip about the fabulously rich Great King's minuscule golden plane-tree ('not big enough to shade a cicada'!) (7. 1. 38).

Some Barbarians More Equal than Others

Xenophon, however, did not speak with one voice on the barbarian question, even within the *Anabasis* and *Hellenica*. Moreover, as we shall see, he wrote an entire work, admittedly one of fiction or theory, with a barbarian as its hero. Not that this is all that surprising either in biographical or in cross-cultural terms. For is it not of the essence of 'othering' that the 'other' group be treated categorically and normatively as an undifferentiated homogeneous mass, while individual members with whom ego has a personal relationship that contradicts the stereotyped image are treated as being by definition exceptions who prove the rule? The 'some of my best friends are Persians, Jews, . . .' syndrome, at any rate, flourished both in Xenophon's life and in his writings.

Another linguistic upshot of the Graeco-Persian Wars of 480–479 besides the negative connotation of 'barbarian' was the coinage of *mēdismos* to mean passive sympathy or active collaboration with 'the Mede'. By that term the Greeks included or really meant the Persians. For it was part and parcel of their ethnocentric homogenization of the Iranian enemy that in their vocabulary they refused to distinguish between the related but distinct Medes and Persians; what we call the 'Persian Wars' were for Herodotus *ta Mēdika*, literally 'Median things'. To an extent, of course, the very coinage of the term was designed to be prophylactic or judgemental rather than descriptive, and it could easily degenerate into a mere party-political slogan. But Themistokles, for example, after masterminding the Persians' defeat at Salamis in 480, really did 'medize' by ending his days as a valued pensioner of the Persian Great King. So indeed might Xenophon have done, had his mercenary employer, the Persian pretender Cyrus the Younger, defeated his older brother King Artaxerxes II at Cunaxa near Nineveh in 401. Xenophon saw nothing ideologically demeaning, that is, in serving a barbarian prince for pay (that was not what he would have called 'fawning on the barbarian for silver'), or in painting a portrait of his former employer in the *Anabasis* that in no way relied on the standard Greek negative stereotype.

On the opposing side at the battle of Cunaxa, by a neat stroke of complementary opposition, there served, though in a medical not a military capacity, another Greek exile with literary pretensions. Ktesias of Knidos had been trained within Greece's second most distinguished medical centre (after Hippokrates' Kos) at a time when Greek medicine was judged by the Persian court to be superior to the age-old traditions of Egypt, which happened also to be one of the Persian Empire's most troublesome provinces and from 405 to 343 actually in open revolt. Artaxerxes was therefore as glad of Ktesias' services as Ktesias was happy to exploit his keyhole view of Persian royalty. Ktesias' *Persika* unfortunately survives mainly in the abridgement made by the ninth-century Constantinopolitan patriarch Photius, but there is enough left to show that, whatever Ktesias thought privately of his barbarian employer, he did not present him in terms of the standard Greek stereotype. Not that his memoir often rises much above the level of boudoir gossip, either, but through his association with the king-making queen

mother Parysatis he gives us an invaluable, non-judgemental
insight into an alien harem-based system of dynastic power.
There is no suggestion, at any rate, that he would have agreed
with a Euripidean character that the (deplorable) behaviour of
the Persian court could be generalized to all barbarians. Indeed,
his no doubt pseudo-historical representation depended for its
credibility on the assumption (a Herodotean one, as we shall
see) that these particular barbarians anyway were just different
from, and maybe in a soap-opera sort of way rather more
fascinating than, but certainly not necessarily inferior in nature
to, Greeks.

A similar equality of respect, though no doubt manipulated
to cross-cultural moralizing effect, shines through Xenophon's
brilliantly dramatic account in the *Hellenica* (4. 1. 29–39)
of the interview between Agesilaos and the Persian satrap
Pharnabazus conducted on the latter's home territory in the
winter of 395/4. Xenophon perhaps was in attendance and
certainly received a first-hand report from his friend Agesilaos,
but his fictionalized version was deliberately spoken in his
'other' voice. The interview was arranged by a Greek go-
between called Apollophanes of Kyzikos, who Xenophon goes
out of his way to state had long been a *xenos* of the satrap and
had recently become one of Agesilaos too.

Now, *xenos* is the most general Greek word for a stranger or
outsider, someone who is not a full member of your community,
whether Greek or non-Greek; typically, though, a linguistic
distinction was drawn according to context between *xenoi* who
were Greek and those who were *barbaroi*—only the Spartans
refused this, being so xenophobic that they called all non-
Spartans *xenoi* regardless of their origins (Herodotus 9. 11,
55). But, as the passage under discussion illustrates, there
were *xenoi* and *xenoi*, because *xenos* here does not mean
'foreigner' or (as some translations have it) merely 'friend',
but something like 'ritualized guest-friend' or 'spiritual kins-
man'. The solemnly binding relationship of *xenia* in this technical
sense involved specified rituals of contract and reciprocal
obligations, and—more to our point—implied equality of
usually aristocratic status. Above all, it by definition crossed

not only *polis* lines, so that one could not be the *xenos* of a fellow-citizen, but also national or ethnic lines, so that one could be the *xenos* of a *barbaros*. Some barbarians, that is to say, were more equal—or less unequal—than others, and they were not all indifferently slavish, effeminate, disorderly, and so on in the opinion of those élite Greeks who dealt with them on an individual and sometimes intimately familiar basis.

The details of the interview between Agesilaos and Pharnabazus have their own interest too in terms of our Greek–barbarian discourse. Agesilaos and his Spartan advisers sit directly on the grass—no throne or dais or other regalia for a Spartan king, not even soft rugs, which 'of course' the vice-regal Pharnabazus in accordance with effeminate, soft, luxurious, oriental custom has had brought along. But now Xenophon springs his first cultural surprise: Pharnabazus dispenses with the soft furnishings and joins Agesilaos on the grass, ashamed (it is said) of his fine clothing by the side of Agesilaos' homespun. Once the interview is underway Pharnabazus shows himself as in no way on the defensive, but rather counterattacks the crusading Agesilaos in thoroughly Greek moral terms (honour, justice, helping friends), terms that were nicely calculated to exploit *xenia* obligations. Agesilaos is forced back first on an appeal to the supposedly higher claims of patriotism—even *xenoi*, he points out, must fight each other, if their states are at war. But to that he adds the crushing political argument from liberty. If Pharnabazus revolts from Artaxerxes, he will not be merely changing masters, but exchanging Persian servitude for Greek liberty. Pharnabazus, however, was prepared for that one too. He both is personally obligated to Artaxerxes and considers retention of his satrapy to be a matter of honour. Agesilaos can only recognize the force of these considerations, and the two potentates part amicably, so amicably indeed that Agesilaos becomes on the spot the *xenos*, not of Pharnabazus (that would have been too awkward politically), but of a son of his.

If anything, it is Pharnabazus who in Xenophon's version emerges from the interview with the greater credit, greater even than the Greek whom Xenophon revered sufficiently to publish a glowing obituary of him in *c*.359. Some barbarians, in other words, could on occasion be represented as honorary Greeks, without seriously tarnishing or denting the normal and normative Greek image of the barbarian other. But if that is surprising enough, Xenophon has a bigger surprise still in store.

A Righteous Barbarian

Xenophon turned his hand to all the recognized genres of Greek prose literature, and he pioneered at least one more—the *Tendenzroman* or historical novel with one or several messages. Edward Gibbon dismissed the *Cyropaedia* ('Education of Cyrus') as 'vague and languid' by comparison with what he found to be the 'circumstantial and animated' *Anabasis*, and he put the latter's superiority down to 'the eternal difference between fiction and truth'. Like Pontius Pilate, I do not propose to stay for an answer to the question, what is (historical) truth? But it may be useful to restate firmly that the *Cyropaedia* was a work of fiction, since it has recently been taken seriously as giving authentic facts about the life and times of the eponymous Cyrus the Great, founder of the Achaemenid Persian Empire (*c*.559–530). In so far as Xenophon did get his facts right, these were facts of his own day, the fourth century, gained from personal observation or gleaned from his Greek or Hellenophone non-Greek *xenoi*. What matters to us, therefore, as it did to Xenophon, is the message or messages he was seeking to convey to his readers by his choice of a barbarian, largely Persian, milieu for his ostensibly realistic prose narrative.

One of those messages, surely, was precisely the same as that conveyed by the Pharnabazus–Agesilaos interview. Although all barbarians as a category are by definition inferior to all Greeks, some individual barbarians might be not only as good as but actually, on occasion, superior even to model Greeks like Agesilaos. That should not, however, be taken to imply that Xenophon was consciously seeking (as I shall suggest Herodotus had been) to weaken somewhat the symbolic and cultural impact of the Greek–barbarian polarity. Rather, in the *Cyropaedia* he was much more interested in the moral-political lessons to be derived from his representation of Cyrus' career (see further Chapter 5) than he was in Cyrus' ethnicity, which he minimized to vanishing point. However, Xenophon was surely not unaware of the emollient effect that his version of Cyrus was likely to have. If even one barbarian could achieve Hellenic standards of moral and political conduct, then merely belonging categorically to the *genos* of barbarians was not by itself a sufficient reason for a person's being denigrated as inferior by nature. On the other hand, his liberalism of outlook extended only a very short way down the barbarian social scale, no further indeed than his liberalism towards Greek womankind (Chapter 4).

Inasmuch as Xenophon's Cyrus was a fictional prototype of what W. W. Tarn called 'culture-Greeks' (Tarn and Griffith 1952: 160), he, like his phil-Hellenic real-world contemporary Maussollos satrap of Caria (377–353), pointed forward to the post-Classical Hellenistic epoch of Greek history opened up by Alexander the Great's conquest of the Persian Empire that the historical Cyrus had founded. In this era (conventionally dated 323–330 BCE) many members of the upper classes among the non-Greeks who had been forcibly incorporated in the new Graeco-Macedonian territorial monarchies, including even some Jews, found the force of Hellenic culture compellingly attractive. Without ceasing for a moment to be barbarians by *genos* and blood, yet they engaged in a Greek style of life and so realized practically what a few untypical Classical Greeks (Euripides, Isokrates, the Sophist Alkidamas, the Cynics) had mooted as a theoretical ideal. However, for what the ordinary Greek of the fifth and fourth centuries thought about the 'intelligence' (*dianoia*) of the barbarians, and the impossibility of barbarians 'becoming' Greeks, we have only to recall the triumphally ethnocentric passage of Aristotle's *Politics* from which we began—or consider some telling passages in the work of Xenophon's major historian predecessor, to whom we now turn.

Savagery and Civilization

For Isokrates and Xenophon pan-Hellenism was not just a cultural ideal but a political programme. The 'Greeks of Asia'

whom the Hellenic and Delian Leagues had successively liberated and kept independent from Persian domination between
479 and 404 had been returned to formal Persian control in
386 under the terms of the protocol known alternatively as the
'King's Peace' or the 'Peace of Antalkidas' (after the Spartan
who acted as the chief Greek negotiator). Thucydides, however,
grew up in that happy interval of freedom, when the Persians
posed no real threat to the Asiatic Greeks and none whatsoever
to the Greeks of the mainland. Indeed, it is more than probable
that in about 450, shortly after Thucydides' birth, the Athenians
and their allies concluded a formal peace treaty with the Persian
Great King, symbolized by the massive building programme
on the Athenian Akropolis that has bequeathed us among
much else the Parthenon and its long shadow. At any rate
between then and 412 the Persian Empire was a sufficiently
negligible factor in Greek political history to account for or
excuse Thucydides' more or less ignoring it in his *History* of
the war between the Athenians and the Spartans and their
respective allies (431–404).

However, the outcome of that war was in fact decided by
Persian intervention, financial rather than military, on the
Spartan side, as Thucydides (2. 65. 12) was well aware. And
had he lived to complete his work (which breaks off in mid-
sentence in a context of 411) he might perhaps have given
greater weight, retrospectively, to the Persian factor. As it is,
the contrast in this regard between his sparing treatment and
Xenophon's far fuller one is glaring enough, but it is as nothing
compared to the disparity between his and Herodotus'. Indeed,
it was quite likely the very concentration of his main predecessor
on Persian imperial power that determined his own emulous
silence.

However that may be, it cannot be said that Thucydides has
singled out the Persians for special neglect. With only a few
exceptions, he is in general barely interested in barbarians of
any stripe or hue in his determinedly Hellenic history. However,
the exceptions are all the more striking, especially when they
include explicit authorial judgements, which are as rare for him
as they are commonplace (almost 1100 examples, according to
one count) for Herodotus. I select just three such exceptions.

First, the 'Archaeology' at the beginning of book 1, which was introduced in Chapter 2 as an example of the lasting power of myth in Classical Greek mentality. In seeking to prove that 'his' war was the greatest ever fought by Greeks, greater specifically than Herodotus' Persian Wars, Thucydides sketched an evolutionary schema of progressive development, chiefly economic, from deepest prehistory (as he, the contemporary historian *par excellence*, was most acutely aware) down to the outbreak of the Peloponnesian War in 431. Unlike the remainder of his work, this passage is shot through with the Greek–barbarian polarity. For example, some culturally backward Greeks (as they seemed to a sophisticated Athenian) living to the north of the Corinthian Gulf in West Lokris, Aitolia, and Akarnania are said to follow still the 'old' Greek custom of regularly carrying weapons in their everyday life. Such behaviour was to Thucydides literally barbarian, since he cites this as one among several instances 'where the manners of the ancient Hellenic world are very similar to the manners of barbarians today' (1. 6). A major purpose of the 'Archaeology', therefore, apart from its ostensible one, was to set the scene of his history firmly in Greece, indicate the level of cultural advance some parts of Greece at least had achieved by 431, and thereby the more dramatically bring out the moral depths to which the war eventually reduced the Greek world. 'Greece as a whole, *to Hellenikon*, or the Greeks themselves, *hoi Hellenes*, become the standard of greatness and significance in the work' (Connor 1991: 65).

In view of Thucydides' pose of magisterial objectivity those rare occasions when he does intervene to 'read a lecture, moral and political, upon his own text' (Hobbes's words) deserve particular attention. One such occurs towards the end of the work as preserved, in book 7 (29. 4–5, 30. 3), where Thucydides for once turns his gaze away from the major theatres of the war to follow the 'progress' of a band of mercenaries (another meaning of the word *xenoi*, because by definition a Greek city never hired its own citizens to fight for it). As the Peloponnesian War dragged on, mercenaries were used ever more heavily by both sides, and a disproportionate number of the Greeks who fought in this way were from poverty-stricken, upland Arkadia (no idyll, whatever the early modern poets and painters might suggest). But the mercenaries Thucydides is discussing were barbarians, from Thrace (roughly modern Bulgaria), who had been hired by the Athenians in 413. The original idea was to send them to Sicily to aid Athens's doomed attempt at conquest, but they arrived too late to join the final batch of reinforcements. So an Athenian commander was deputed to lead them back home, with instructions to do what damage they could *en route* to Sparta's allies in Boiotia. But when they got to Mykalessos, the Thracians reportedly went berserk and ran amuck. They not only killed all the human beings they could lay their hands on, including women and children, but they also slaughtered the farm animals and indeed 'every living creature in sight'.

This carnage so affected Thucydides that it prompted not one but two personal reflections. He noted, first, that like the most barbaric of the barbarian 'breed' (*genos*) the Thracian 'breed' is most bloodthirstily murderous when it has its 'boldness' (*tharsos*) up. If we are to translate that observation in cultural terms, Thucydides is implying that in a fair fight with adult male Greek citizen soldiers, barbarians do not even have *tharsos*, let alone truly Greek 'courage' (*andreia*, literally 'manliness'); but when taking on women, children, old men, farm animals, household pets, and so forth, they do get their inferior form of boldness up, but instead of directing their appetite to strictly military ends, they slake it on senselessly indiscriminate slaughter. Thucydides' second personal reflection was aroused by the slaughter of children in a school. This he describes hyperbolically as a disaster for the whole city, second to none in magnitude, and more deserving of lamentation than any other of its kind in the war as a whole.

There can be no doubt that it was the barbarian-ness of this slaughter that particularly exercised Thucydides. Not that he elsewhere mitigates inter- or intra-Greek savagery (see Chapter 5); that was grist to his thesis about the 'barbarization' of Greek behaviour induced by the Peloponnesian War. But the fact that the barbarians in question here were Thracians might also have something to do with this outburst of passion. For

Thrace and Thracians had come to be associated peculiarly
with slavery in Classical Greece (Chapter 6). Still more to the
point, Thucydides himself had Thracian connections, indeed a
Thracian patronymic (Oloros), as a result of either intermarriage
or a *xenia* relationship between one of Thucydides' paternal
ancestors and some noble, even royal, Thracian house. For
some Thracians, no doubt, Thucydides had a lot of respect,
but precisely because of his Thracian connections (which
extended to hereditary mining-rights) he could equally have
been anxious to emphasize his own purely Hellenic, not-
barbarian credentials.

Thracians feature centrally, too, in one of Thucydides' very
rare ventures into 'Herodotean' ethnography, his excursus on
two barbarian kingdoms (Macedon and Odrysian Thrace) in
book 2 (95–101). Two authorial interventions, both in 2. 97,
leap to the eye, though it is in terms of Thucydidean rather
than Greek mentality that they are eye-catching. A discussion
of Thracian gift-giving, first, prompts a snide, inter-barbarian
comparison: throughout Odrysian Thrace receiving (even asking
for) gifts was the accepted norm, whereas in Persia it was the
custom (*nomos*) of royalty to give rather than receive them.
Not that Thucydides thought the Persian custom intrinsically
good; rather, he was using it, as being rather more Hellenic
and less barbaric, as a stick with which to beat the more
barbarous Thracians. Herodotus, likewise, could make the
Persians appear surprisingly Hellenic by the side of the, for
him, most barbarous of barbarians, the Scythians.

In fact, it is precisely to the Scythians that Thucydides'
second authorial comment applies in the excursus on Greece's
northern barbarian neighbours. In respect of their military
strength, Thucydides reports, the Scythians are said to be
without doubt unequalled in all Europe; nay more, in all Asia,
too, no other people (*ethnos*) would be able to resist them—if
only they were *homognōmones*, 'capable of achieving reasoned
unanimity'. However, of that they are congenitally, by nature,
incapable, since they lack the requisite *euboulia* ('wisdom in
counsel') and *xunesis* ('intelligence'); in those respects, indeed,
they are inferior 'to all others'! Thucydides had almost certainly

conducted no *historiē* among the Scythians, although his low opinion of them in their homelands could have been reinforced by his personal experience of the Scythian archers at Athens, a small force of publicly owned slaves used for certain law-and-order functions. Certainly, too, the representation of these pseudo-policemen on the Athenian comic stage, for instance in the *Thesmophoriazousài* of Aristophanes, was by no means a flattering one. On the other hand, no amount of historical research could have supported Thucydides' emphatic cross-cultural judgement of Scythian inferiority. So it is hard to resist the conclusions, first, and more disappointingly, that despite his own towering intellectual achievement in other respects his attitude to barbarians was no less prejudicially ethnocentric than the average Greek's, and second, and more interestingly, that this remarkably unflattering view of the Scythians was essentially lifted, silently as ever, from Herodotus.

Holding Up the Mirror

Herodotus' account of Scythia, his 'Scythian *logos*', occupies the first three-quarters of book 4 (1–144) and is one of the two major ethnographic digressions in his work, the other being the whole of book 2 on Egypt. Since the Scythian *logos* has been the subject of one of the most illuminating books to have been written recently on any Greek author (Hartog 1988), I shall concentrate rather on book 2. But it may be helpful if I summarize first what it is about Hartog's book that I have found so inspiring. The work is an exercise in translation, not merely the rendering of Herodotus' Greek vernacular into its rough French or English equivalent, but translation as interpretation—that is, the exploration, exegesis, and explication of what Hartog calls Herodotus' 'rhetoric of otherness'. Hence his subtitle: 'Essai sur la représentation de l'Autre' or 'the representation of the Other in the writing of history'.

In order to capture the essence of what reading Herodotus could and should be like Hartog resorts to the metaphor of the mirror, in three main applications. First, there is Herodotus' text itself, not just the words transmitted palaeographically and in print, but all the interpretations of it too: into this enlarged text we peer as into a glass darkly to descry who we are, seeking our own identities and activities. Typically, Hartog observes, the question generated by this concern has been, is the image reflected by Herodotus' mirror true? But Hartog finds this constricting, preferring to resist a move outside the text to Herodotus' cultural and political environment or the *ex hypothesi* factual basis of his narrative long enough (some would say too long) to conduct a more subtle metahistorical reading of his polysemous subtexts.

Secondly, Hartog's mirror is the one held up by Herodotus to his 'addressee', which is Hartog's shorthand collective term for all those Greek groups and individuals who heard and/or read some or all of Herodotus' work in the fifth century BCE, and for whom Herodotus was consciously or unconsciously composing. Mirrors, of course, reflect back in reverse, so that in Herodotus' composite mirror of history Greeks were presented with a series of overlapping but not identical images of the barbarian Other. The Scythians—or at any rate most of them, characteristically—represented that Other in its purest, polarized form, being the ideal type of the anti-Greek: non-agricultural, non-urban, uncivilized, nomadic.

The third chief use of the mirror metaphor by Hartog is for Herodotus' own conceptualization of his field of vision, his canvas as it were. On this Herodotus depicts both the physical *oecumenē*, inhabited space, and the recent Graeco-barbarian past, employing a variety of rhetorical figures and tropes such as analogy, concern for number and quantity, preoccupation with the miraculous, and—not the least significant for us—opposed tables of customs linked by inversion.

Herodotus' Egyptian Grid

Book 2 on Egypt is a conspicuous anomaly in Herodotus' work, raising in a particularly acute way all the most awkward questions about the author's literary project as a whole. Father of History—or lies? Critical student of scrupulously collated oral traditions—or credulous tourist retailing mere travellers' tales? Historical geographer belatedly converted to history proper—or geographical historian with a special interest in Egypt? Father of comparative ethnography and cross-cultural history—or mere narrative artist in prose? I begin with a consideration of the book as such, which in its present form and location constitutes a kind of giant excursus from his main project of 'the Median things'.

Not that Herodotus would have seen anything contradictory in that: for him, as he put it in the middle of his Scythian *logos* (4. 30), digressions or excursuses (*prosthēkai*, literally 'additions') were an integral part of his plan of exposition. However, what makes the Egyptian *logos* seem more than just a digression, or a digression of a special kind, are its exceptional length and the exceptional care with which Herodotus parades his learning and methodology. This has led some to suppose that it was originally written as a self-sufficient composition, before Herodotus had settled on his main theme of Graeco-barbarian military conflict and when he was still working in the tradition of Ionian rationalizing ethnography pioneered by Hekataios. My own inclination goes the other way, since I believe that Herodotus partly for reasons of his personal biography embraced his theme early in his career, and I prefer to see book 2 as the outcome of purposively directed and critically informed travel. But whatever the truth, there is no doubt that it is uniquely informative in defining Herodotus' viewpoint, first on historical method and secondly on ethnographic interpretation.

In chapter 99 Herodotus looks back at the Egyptian space, mental as well as physical, that he has 'surveyed' (Hartog's word) and comments: 'Thus far it is my own *opsis* and *gnōmē* and *historiē* that have been relating these things; but from this point on I proceed to relate the Egyptian *logoi* as I have heard them.' When he gets to chapter 147, he adds: 'In what follows I have the authority, not of the Egyptians only, but of others also who agree with them. I shall speak likewise in part from my own *opsis*.' It is generally granted that Herodotus did exercise judgement (*gnōmē*) and practise enquiry (*historiē*), but for well over a century a debate has raged over whether he really did conduct autopsy (*opsis*) of Egypt. Did he in fact talk (through interpreters, since he was monoglot) to the *logioi* ('those versed in *logoi*') among the Egyptians, such as the priests of 'Hephaistos' (Ptah) at Memphis? Or did he merely talk to people who had been to Egypt and read the available published accounts, almost aggressively advertising the authenticity of his personal research because this was now the necessary language of advanced Greek 'scientific' discourse? That debate, it seems to me, is largely futile and infertile. Better, rather, to follow Hartog's advice and consider the matter within the terms of Herodotus' own text.

For, as he says in his preface, the preservation in memory of 'the great and wondrous *erga* of the . . . non-Greeks' was one of the explicit aims of his *historiē*, and Egypt contained more 'wonders' than anywhere else (2. 35. 1). For Herodotus, that is, wonder 'is the beginning of wisdom when it leads to further thought' (Redfield 1985), and there is no doubt as to the principal kind of thought to which *theōria* (contemplation and probably also visual inspection) of Egyptian marvels led Herodotus: binary opposition or polar classification. Or perhaps we should say that Herodotus had inherited this kind of thinking from his general Greek intellectual legacy and found in Egypt the ideal cultural space to apply his polarizing grid. At any rate, polar opposition is what shapes Herodotus' Egyptian *logos* throughout and yields the *locus classicus* of 'reversed world' othering. 'Not only is the climate different from that of the rest of the world, and the rivers unlike any other rivers, but the people also, in most of their *ēthea* ('manners') and *nomoi*, exactly reverse the common practice of mankind'—by which he means his Greek 'addressee' (2. 35–6).

Two of the no fewer than eighteen oppositions he proceeds to enumerate will have to serve as proxy for the list as a whole. 'The women urinate standing, the men sitting down.' As we shall see in the next chapter, the practices or usages of a society's womenfolk are for Herodotus among the most significant cultural markers. But this Egyptian polarity is also a good example of how polar classification is less than straightforward. For in the matter of urination Greek men thus find themselves in the same cultural pigeonhole as Egyptian, that is barbarian, women, which puts into question the general validity of not only the Greeks' polarization of themselves and barbarians but also what we shall discover to be their polarization of men and women. Second example: 'When they write or calculate, instead of going, like the Greeks, from left to right, they move their hand from right to left—and yet the Egyptians insist that it is they who go to the right, and the Greeks who go to the left.' At first sight, this looks like a classic case of mutual misperception, but on reflection it tells us more about Herodotus' aims and outlook than it does about the true direction of Egyptian writing and calculation. Not only does it show us Herodotus reversing and thus relativizing the Egyptians' reversal, but it also exemplifies a supposedly universal rule of human society which Herodotus enunciates and illustrates by a famous anecdote in book 3 (ch. 38).

'Custom is King'

Once upon a time Great King Darius I of Persia (reigned 522–486) summoned to his presence at the royal capital of Susa some Greeks and asked them what he would have to pay them to eat the corpses of their kindred dead. They replied with horror that no amount of money would induce them to eat rather than cremate their dead. So Darius summoned in turn some Indians, who did customarily eat their dead, and asked them what it would cost him to induce them to cremate. To which suggestion they responded with if anything even greater horror and no less flat a refusal than the Greeks. Herodotus, rather than registering his own horror at the Indians' cannibalism, as Greek ideas would surely have entitled him to do, preferred to quote (out of context) a phrase of the lyric poet Pindar: 'custom (*nomos*) is king (*basileus*) of all'. All mankind, that is, Greeks and barbarians alike, are ruled by custom, and all equally are of the unshakeable opinion that their own customary usages are not just the best for them but absolutely morally superior to those of all other peoples.

Herodotus, however, as the very telling of this story indicates, was not a typical Greek in this respect. On the contrary, he was both an ethnographic comparativist and—in principle at least—a radical ethical relativist. Whether the report is true or not, it is at least not incredible that Herodotus should have been on friendly terms with the Sophist Protagoras of Abdera, who formulated the famous *homo mensura* ('Man is the measure . . .') doctrine—although he is unlikely to have had much sympathy for Protagoras' equally unconventional theological agnosticism (see Chapter 7). Like all the Sophists, Protagoras spent much time at Athens, and perhaps because of his democratic views he was reputedly asked to draft the constitution for the new Athenian-inspired foundation of Thouria in south Italy (on the former site of Sybaris) in 444/3. Herodotus, in exile from his home city of Halikarnassos, seized this rare opportunity to re-establish his civic status and became a citizen of the new city, where one source indeed says he was buried, honorifically, in the Agora.

'Herodotus' Law' (of Oriental Despotism)

It was among other things for his toleration of barbarian custom, extending even to cannibalism in the acutely sensitive cultural area of the disposal of dead kin, that the conservatively patriotic Plutarch (*Moralia* 857a) misguidedly derided Herodotus as a *philobarbaros* or 'wog-lover'. As a matter of fact, Herodotus did not love either all barbarians or all things barbarian. The cultural habits of the Scythian tribe of the Androphagoi (literally, 'Man-eaters'), for example, earned from him the label *agriōtata* ('most savage') of all mankind'; indeed, Herodotus asserted, they 'believe in no justice (*dikē*) and use no law (*nomos*)' (4. 106). However, it should not be thought that Herodotus regarded each and every *nomos* as equally good, even for the people in question. On the contrary, what I have called 'Herodotus' Law', as he applied it to the Persian monarchy and Persian imperialism, was arguably the leitmotif of the entire work, and it was this interpretative construct, partly moral, partly analytical, which provided him with the answer to the problem of explanation he set himself in the preface—'the reason why the Greeks and the non-Greeks fought with one another'.

In book 1 Herodotus introduces the Persians in his usual manner: 'these are the customs (*nomoi*) which I know the Persians to observe' (1. 131). There follows a catalogue reminiscent of the Egyptian list (above) which reveals (these) Persian *nomoi* to be the exact opposite of the Greek. But that by itself is insufficient for Herodotus to cast the Persians—or at any rate all of them—any more than the Egyptians in the role of stereotypical barbarians. In fact, some of them turn out to behave, indeed to philosophize, strangely like the most advanced Greek thinkers of Herodotus' day. For example, the so-called 'Persian Debate' (3. 80–2), which is the earliest surviving developed example of Western political theory (and perhaps another of Herodotus' debts to Protagoras), is placed in the mouths of noble Persian speakers (but see Chapter 5). Xenophon's Cyrus, therefore, had perfectly respectable literary antecedents.

On the other hand, when it came to monarchy—not the sort of constitutional monarchy advocated by 'Darius' in the 'Persian Debate', but despotic tyranny—then Herodotus was quite clear that that was without qualification a bad thing, for its immediate subjects no less than for those against whom the despot might seek to extend his power through imperialistic conquest. That judgement, moreover, was applied to Greeks as well as barbarians. Peisistratos of Athens, for instance, earned mild credit from Herodotus for not disturbing the existing political institutions during his first tyranny (*c*.560) but strong discredit for subsequently having sex with his noble Athenian wife 'not after the customary manner' (Herodotus 1. 59, 61).

As just such a tyranny—barbaric, royal, despotic—did Herodotus present the Persian *basileia*, from its relatively benign origins under Cyrus, through the sacrilegious madness of Cambyses, and the vengeful but calculated ruthlessness of Darius I, to its climactic incarnation of *hubris* in the person of Xerxes. Time and again, implicitly and explicitly, Herodotus draws a polar contrast between what we might call Greek republican freedom and self-government and Persian oriental despotism. Again, it is through an emblematic story or parable that Herodotus most forcefully drives his point home.

Among Xerxes' retinue of advisers during his attempted conquest of Greece in 480 was a Spartan exile, not just any Spartan but ex-king Damaratos, who after his (unjust) dethronement had 'medized'. Herodotus cannot possibly have known what Damaratos and Xerxes ever said to each other, let alone the details of any formal interview. Yet such, nothing daunted, is what he professes to reproduce more than once in book 7. In one of these (7. 104), somewhat implausibly, Damaratos is made to speak as it were for Hellenism, though he gives it a Spartan spin. To the Persians, he says, you, Xerxes, are a *despotēs*, an absolute ruler over subjects who are no freer than slaves. The Spartans, however (standing proxy for 'the Greeks'), recognize no *despotēs* except *nomos*, Law (meaning both customary law and positive enactments by the citizenry). It was the Persian monarchy's despotic *nomos*, Herodotus implies, that inevitably stimulated Xerxes' imperialist aggression and in that sense caused the Persian Wars. But, no less unavoidably, it and he met their match in the freely chosen *nomos* which 'ruled' the Greeks. To that, considerable, extent did Herodotus endorse, as almost all Greeks unthinkingly did, a negative stereotype of the barbarian Other.

4

Engendering History

Men v. Women

> The goal of a feminist struggle must precisely be to
> deconstruct the death-dealing binary oppositions of
> masculinity and femininity
>
> (Moi 1985: 13)

Genesis as Myth

It has long been clear that the story of Adam and Eve is a
myth in the technical senses discussed in Chapter 2, but it was
not before 1959 that genetic research proved it to be a myth in
the popular sense too. We now know that the basic body-plan
of the human species is female and that males, genetically,
are a secondary development of the mammalian embryo (the
discovery of the determining gene, SRY for 'Sex-determining
Region of the Y chromosome', being finally announced in May
1991). However, even in our supposedly science-worshipping
culture such mere biological and anatomical facts of life as
these are unlikely to shake let alone shatter the dominant
cultural paradigm of phallocentric patriarchalism. *A fortiori* it
comes as no surprise to be told that

> how sexual difference was imagined in the past [from the Greeks to
> Freud] was largely unconstrained by what was known about this or
> that bit of anatomy, this or that physiological process. It derived
> instead from particular rhetorical, cultural and political exigencies of
> the moment. (Thomas Laqueur in the *London Review of Books*,
> 6 December 1990; cf. Laqueur 1989)

'No surprise', but is it true of 'the Greeks', all of them all
the time? The purpose of this chapter is precisely to test the
validity and explore the ideological ramifications of those

alleged exigencies in the context of Classical Greece, with special reference to explicit or implicit manipulations of the polar opposition between 'nature' and 'culture' in our privileged historical texts. Where do our main sources stand, in other words, on what is still perhaps the major issue of feminist politics both inside and outside the academy, namely whether there is a natural essence of 'woman' as a sex, or rather only a social construct of 'woman' as a gender? I put it thus in polarized terms, since in this area at any rate the Greek legacy appears remarkably potent: either male power or female power, but never shall the twain co-operate in mutuality.

The 'Second' Sex

Just over forty years ago a publication event occurred, the relevance of which to this book has already been stressed (see Prologue): the appearance of Simone de Beauvoir's *Le Deuxième Sexe* (1949). Perhaps the title was also meant to convey a message to her longstanding lover Jean-Paul Sartre, but what is certain is that from the book of Genesis on, in the Judaeo-Christian religious tradition, and from Hesiod and Semonides on, in the Greek-inspired 'Western' cultural tradition, women have indeed been marked down as number two—categorically defined as secondary.

One major difference, however, separates the Classical Greek discourse on women radically and unbridgeably from that of the Judaeo-Christian tradition: the latter is inscribed within a dogmatic religious frame foreign to the religion of Classical Greece (Chapter 7). Consider, for instance, the following quotation: 'The superiority of the male is an ideological fact of the Middle Ages; it is socially and theologically orthodox; therefore it is an absolute and unquestioned truth, like God' (Helen Cooper in the *Times Literary Supplement*, 19 July 1991). As Jewish and Christian feminists today can readily testify, such a religious sanction for negative discrimination (woman is 'not in God's image' and so forth) makes the argument for equality of status and treatment for women very much harder to ground internally. By contrast, Classical Greek religion lacked even the concept of religious dogma and hence of orthodoxy. The 'nature of woman' question could not therefore simply be settled by appeal to theological overdetermination, even if Classical Greek men did their level best with the principal equivalent weapon at their disposal, mythology. Nevertheless, in Classical Greece the question did still have to be contested, formally at least, *es meson* or 'in the middle of the public arena'—up front, as we might say. Thus Classical Greek literature, which like the culture as a whole was quintessentially agonal or competitive, provides an especially fruitful body of evidence for the debate over the true nature and proper place of women.

Male Ordering

Two methodological provisos must be registered *ab initio*. First, all the sources upon whom I shall draw here were themselves male. Even where a female character in an Athenian tragedy speaks with almost violently feminine authenticity, it must be remembered that the words were written by a male playwright and the character impersonated by a male actor before a largely or wholly male audience. In a predominantly sex-segregated society, as the world of Classical Greece was, it remains a question whether and how far a man can experience or sympathetically represent the reality of women's lives, particularly when his 'addressee' is also male. *A fortiori*, there is a question-mark over the Greeks' (especially Herodotus') ethnography of barbarian women.

This doubt has recently become acute as a result of one of the major theoretical contributions of modern anthropological participant observation of Greek rural societies: an awareness of the gap between social and symbolic appearance and reality. For example, the apparent spatial, social, and political subordination of women as a category may fool even the most sensitive ethnographer into overlooking the scope for women to negotiate, largely in the private domain, within the externally imposed constraints.

The other methodological caveat, which is intimately connected to the fact that the sources are male, applies with equal force to historians of all societies down to the nineteenth century. It is that what has conventionally been taken to be the appropriate subject-matter of history is precisely his-story, the story of what men have done or had done to them. Herodotus, as we shall see, is an exception to this rule, but only a partial exception. Although he has dozens of references (375, to be exact) to women collectively or individually, women very rarely feature in the main storyline, so to speak. That is to say, they appear under the 'wonders' rubric of his preface rather than the 'why the Greeks and non-Greeks fought with one another'.

It should at once be added that these methodological problems are far less serious for us, who are primarily concerned with our sources' constructions of reality and images of women, than they are for historians concerned to reconstruct and explain the ostensible truth about the social, political, or economic status of women in Classical Greece. Not that they are not serious at all, however, because ideology—in this case, male ideology—is an important part of what constituted reality for ancient Greek women. Nor are the historical sources by any means uniquely informative on Greek normative gendering. Other genres of fifth- and fourth-century literature provide perhaps more strikingly obvious *points d'appui*, above all Athenian tragedy and comedy and the philosophy of Plato and Aristotle. As with the Greek–barbarian polarity (Chapter 3), it is not only convenient but almost obligatory to begin with and from the latter.

Aristotle's Woman

In terms both of his output and of his outlook Aristotle was primarily a scientist, an enquirer into nature, rather than a philosopher in our sense. The archaic term 'natural philosopher' captures his position rather nicely. In particular, he was a zoologist and biologist, so that his concept of nature (*phusis*, literally 'process of growth'), like that of many Greeks, was derived ultimately from his understanding of the animal and plant worlds, as opposed to the human. Thus in his 'Enquiry into Living Creatures' (*historia zōōn*) he speaks of a continuum between the animal and human worlds. However, to this scientific view he added a quasi-metaphysical gloss, his own peculiar brand of teleology.

Every living thing, he held, has its *telos*, or 'end', that of the acorn for instance being the oak-tree. But *teleios*, the Greek adjective from *telos*, did not only mean 'eventual' or 'completed' but 'complete' in the sense of 'perfect' in an evaluative or normative as well as a scientifically descriptive sense. So on Aristotle's animal-to-human spectrum humans occupy the 'most complete' or perfected end of it. 'Speciesism', as Richard Ryder has dubbed it, begins here in the Western tradition of natural science. So far, so predictable, perhaps. But then comes a surprise. The completion or perfection, for Aristotle, is not just of form, but of essence. Most relevantly for us, completeness in Aristotelian teleology also embraces gender. Thus male humans are the most perfectly masculine of all living things, female humans the most feminine.

But are 'masculine' and 'feminine' equipollent for Aristotle? Emphatically not: Aristotle's teleology is as sexist as it is normative. For women, according to his 'Generation of Animals', are both 'opposite' (*enantion*) and inferior to men, indeed are a sort of freak of nature. As a eunuch is to a complete male, so a woman is (inferior) to a male child, which is also—but in a different sense from the eunuch—an incomplete male. How could that come to be? With a characteristically Greek combination of polarized thinking and inadequate attention to empirical evidence Aristotle simply asserts the received dogmas that female offspring are generated from the left testicle, male offspring from the right, and that, once implanted in the uterus, female foetuses grow on the left of the womb, male on the right—the old right–left hierarchical polarity again, almost wearisomely familiar from a wide range of otherwise utterly disparate societies. Now, Aristotle and his pupils did carry out anatomical dissection, but no amount of scientific instrumentation or exploration could have demonstrated these 'laws of nature'. They are pure sexist ideology.

However, before we leap to condemn Aristotle outright, we should take cognizance that his views on women's biological nature were in no way out of line with the most 'progressive' medical thought and research of his day, as represented in the Hippokratic Corpus. For instance, although the Hippokratic author of *On Seed* was convinced that 'both the man and the woman have male and female sperm', he was equally sure that 'the male being stronger than the female must of course originate from the male sperm' (ch. 6). In fact, it was not until the early modern era that women's equal and active part in human reproduction through ovulation was scientifically established, let alone the identification of SRY. The Hippokratic doctors were apparently no less anxious than their modern successors to raise the standard of the treatment of women's diseases, but in their diagnosis of and recommended cures for the by definition feminine malady of hysteria (literally 'wombiness') they 'were not concerned so much with physical healing as with upholding the established values of society' (Lefkowitz 1981: 13)— masculine values, it hardly needs to be added.

The status of science in relation to gender remains problematic. Very recently it has been established that, although women's brains are on average smaller than men's, the isthmus of the *corpus callosum* linking the two hemispheres of the human brain is on average larger and therefore more conductive in the female than the male. However, what that scientific fact implies for sexual difference or gender differentiation is rather less perspicuous. Does a better connection between the centres of reason and emotion enable a better handling of the emotions—or make it more difficult to separate emotion from reason? Indeed, are we not in danger here of slipping back into Aristotelian pseudo-scientific natural determinism?

That danger, however, is inherent in Aristotle's project, since it was by way of his understanding of female psychology, his construction of women's *psukhē* ('soul', 'mind', 'spirit'), that he moved from the postulated 'natural' to the inferred 'cultural' inferiority of women as a gender. A crucial bridge between them was formed by the cardinal virtue of courage, for which the Greek word was literally 'manliness' (*andreia*). By identifying manliness with bravery, courage, and pugnaciousness, the Greeks virtually excluded women etymologically from the possibility of experiencing those good emotions or displaying that kind of virtuous behaviour. Brecht's 'Mother Courage' character would have struck Classical Greeks like Aristotle as oxymoronic. (The fact that the Greek noun *andreia* is feminine in grammatical gender is, of course, immaterial.)

Consider, first, Aristotle's delvings into the animal kingdom. Female Indian elephants, he admits, show bravery of a sort, but it is an inferior, feminine sort, and among molluscs too the males are braver than the female ones. The spider, however, posed a ticklish problem for his socio-biological system, since in some species the female had the preposterous temerity to eat her mate after or even during copulation. All Aristotle could do was record this precisely as a contradiction of his assumed norm, an inversion that by its exceptionalism confirmed and reinforced the norm of essentially and exclusively masculine bravery. At the very most, Aristotle was prepared to concede to female animals their maternal instinct, which as he saw it not only enabled them to rear offspring but also generated a kind of courage and intelligence.

But with intelligence (*dianoia*) we have reached the most elevated of Aristotle's six divisions of the human *psukhē*, the part which does the reasoning (*logismos*, *to logistikon*). It is here, too, that we find the properly political expression of Aristotle's idea of gender polarity. The *polis* on Aristotle's analysis is an amalgam of individual households (*oikoi*), and each household, to be a household, must contain both a male and a female component, for reproductive purposes if no other. Specifically, it must contain a husband (*posis*) and a wife (*alokhos*—Aristotle prefers this more literary term to the standard *gunē*). But which of the two is to rule? The male–husband, according to Aristotle, because ruling requires the exercise of reason, and in that department women are congenitally inferior to men. How so? Because the ratiocinative capacity (*logistikon*, *bouleutikon*) of their *psukhē* is *akuron*, 'inauthoritative', 'without authority'.

But what on earth can this sign mean, exactly? How, for example, would Aristotle have defended this view to his mentor Plato who, although by no stretch of the imagination a 'feminist' in our sense, was apparently prepared to regard some few, highly exceptional women as in some intellectual respects the equals of men? Aristotle unfortunately does not trouble to spell out the import of *akuron*. Possible explications include the following: women are unable to follow an argument or process of reasoning through to its logical conclusion; alternatively, although they can reason intellectually, they are unable to translate their reasoning into effective action because of their congenital lack of self-control (so that they are unreliable, irresponsible, fickle, light-minded); or, thirdly, thanks to their inferior social status, their reasoning lacks authority over their menfolk.

The Silent Women of Thucydides

Whatever Aristotle himself may have had in mind, the third of these was undoubtedly the case, both socio-politically and ideologically, in Classical Greece. So what Aristotle may well have been intending to do in regard to women, as we know he was trying to do for slaves (Chapter 6), was provide a philosophical rationalization or gloss on their *de iure* situation in all Greek states, that is their formal exclusion from public decision-making, and on the normative male Greek citizen view that within the *oikos* too the chain of command should ideally run from man to woman. Small wonder, therefore, that he should have found the alleged 'rule of women' (*gunaikokratia*) at Sparta so profoundly distasteful, indeed the world turned upside down (see further below).

Presumably, though, despite his general downgrading of history as 'what Alkibiades did and what happened to him' (*Poetics* 1451[b]10–11), Aristotle nevertheless found the history of Thucydides (the prime source on Alkibiades) utterly satisfactory in its treatment of women at any rate. Or rather its non-treatment of them, which is especially striking by comparison with Herodotus' relative—almost eight times as many references—garrulity on their account. Several explanations for this silence could be offered. War, like its peculiar emotion and virtue, *andreia*, was an exclusively male prerogative, and Thucydides much more fixedly than Herodotus was a war-historian. Secondly, as with barbarians, Thucydides was consciously staking his claim to difference from Herodotus by excluding women from his frame. But although there is force in both of these, they cannot be a complete explanation. The nearest to that, I believe, may be inferred from one of the most famous pieces of Classical Greek prose, the 'Funeral Speech of Perikles'—that is, Thucydides' version of the *epitaphios* which Perikles delivered over the Athenian war-dead during their state funeral early in 430 BCE, at the end of the first year of the Peloponnesian War:

If it is necessary to make some mention of the virtue of the women who will now be widows, I shall define it all in a brief admonition; for great is the glory for you [widows] not to be worse than your existing nature, and ⟨great is the glory⟩ of her whose celebrity, whether for virtue or reproach, exists least among males (2. 45)

Through his own historiography, in other words, Thucydides by his silence would have been obeying the advice of 'Perikles', which was in fact the normative view of all Greek citizen males, not to speak about their womenfolk in public among unrelated men.

However, Thucydides' silence was not total, and in one respect it speaks louder than words. Let me consider first just one passage where he does decide to mention women playing an active role in the masculine sphere of war (3. 74. 2): 'Their womenfolk too joined in the fighting audaciously (*tolmērōs*), hurling tiles from the roof-tops and withstanding the uproar with a courage beyond their sex.' The last six words (taken from Rex Warner's translation) translate, or rather interpret, just two words in Thucydides, *para phusin* or literally 'contrary to their nature'. True bravery, that is, the sort that was required in pitched battle, was in Thucydides' conventional formula beyond women's natural capacity. The best they could show was a combination of audaciousness and fortitude, elements of true bravery perhaps but not the whole of it, and only in the sort of situation Thucydides is here describing—civil war in the streets of Kerkyra (modern Corfu), rather than pitched battle on the open plains between armies from different communities. As if to underline the topsy-turvy abnormality of the

Kerkyra civil war, Thucydides points out that not only the women but also slaves fought on the democrats' side. The very conjunction of women and slaves, openly active in a public, civic context, was antinomian.

The respect in which Thucydides' silence is peculiarly telling concerns the woman most talked about of all in Athens in 430, Perikles' 'common-law wife' Aspasia. In that very year, perhaps, the comic playwright Kratinos had his *Dionysalexandros* performed, in which Paris and Helen were surrogates for Perikles and Aspasia. Five years later, when Perikles was safely dead, Aristophanes' Dikaiopolis (hero of his *Akharnians*) claimed Perikles had been so intoxicated with Aspasia that he had had war declared on Sparta in 432/1 just to retrieve two prostitutes stolen from Aspasia's whorehouse! Thucydides was of course right to have no truck with such *cherchez la femme* mudslinging. But it is worth our while briefly to ask what it was about Aspasia that excited such male gossip. The answer, in short, is that, though free and of citizen status by origin, she was a foreigner from Miletos and so not entitled to claim Athenian citizen prerogatives at Athens, above all legal marriage to an Athenian citizen like Perikles. Ironically, it was a law proposed by Perikles himself, the citizenship law of 451/0, that had thus disqualified Aspasia. The irony was further compounded in 430, just after Perikles delivered his Funeral Speech, by the deaths from the plague of his two legitimate sons by his divorced Athenian wife, which left him heirless. To prevent his *oikos* from dying out, the Athenian people passed an extraordinary decree legitimating his son with Aspasia.

Down to 451/0 Athenian citizens—i.e. freeborn adult males duly registered with the deme and thus inscribed in the *politeuma* (see further Chapter 5)—required only single descent on their father's side to qualify as such: 'naturally' enough, according to one theory of procreation, articulated (in)famously by Apollo in Aeschylus' *Eumenides* (458). This held that it was the male alone who was the true, active genitor, the mother being merely the seedbed, as it were, wherein the male sperm (Greek *sperma* means 'seed') germinated. Apollo's view was explicitly endorsed by Athena, patron deity of Athens, who as a virginal warrior-goddess of craft and wisdom was far from typically feminine, and the Athenians' autochthony myth (Chapter 2) could also be pressed into useful service in denying the procreative equivalence of women. However, from 451/0 onwards, being a citizen at Athens required double descent, having an Athenian mother as well as an Athenian father.

The motives behind Perikles' proposal and the reasons why the Assembly voted for it (not necessarily the same thing) have been endlessly canvassed. Prejudice against aristocrats like Kimon who had non-Athenian mothers thanks to personal connections abroad; a politically motivated desire to restrict the burgeoning privileges of Athenian citizenship to a manageable group; an ethnocentric wish to etch more sharply the line dividing Athenian from non-Athenian (both Greek and non-Greek)—these are probably the three best candidates. But one consequence, whether intended or not, was to put a premium on Athenian daughters, since henceforth only they could confer legitimacy and thereby title to property and citizenship on an Athenian male. That seeming privilege, however, could cut more ways than one. If marriage was perhaps now more or less guaranteed to an Athenian girl, provided she could offer some sort of dowry, the burdens of surveillance imposed on her by her father or other male guardian (*kurios*, meaning literally 'sovereign' or 'lord and master') before, and by her new *kurios*, her husband, after her marriage, also increased in proportion, with a view to preventing unwanted pregnancy or simply sexual access of any sort.

Moreover, 'Athenian' did not mean the same as applied to adult males and adult females. Females of whatever age were always technically in tutelage, under the 'sovereignty' (*kurieia*) of some man. Ideologically, as we have seen, that sorted well with the Aristotelian analysis of the feminine *psukhē*. Politically, it meant that women were not citizens (*politis*, the feminine form of *politēs*, did exist but was hardly ever used; the standard formulas for 'women of citizen status' were *hai Attikai*, 'women of Athens', and *hai astai*, 'women of the urban centre'). Or rather, they were not citizens on all fours with the men, except in the one—far from unimportant—area of public and private religion. To cite the most conspicuous instance of this exception, the chief, strictly religious, official of the Athenian state was the priestess of Athena Polias, a hereditary position restricted to members of an ancient aristocratic family. The holder of that post might occasionally be called upon to undertake some narrowly political action, as was the incumbent of 508, who debarred King Kleomenes I of Sparta from the Akropolis. Her name, too, would be generally known, unlike the names of most Athenian men's immediate female relatives, since it was a point of honour among men not to divulge them to unrelated males—carried to the extreme (in ideology, anyway) of its being open to doubt whether they actually had such female relatives or not.

Dramatic Women

What's in a name? Apparently a very great deal. Lysimakhe ('she who dissolves the battle'), chief priestess of Athena Polias in 411, would have smelled just as sweet by any other name, but she would not have been immortalized in the title of a play—as she was in Aristophanes' punning *Lysistrata* ('she who dissolves armies'). Perhaps he felt he could not use Lysimakhe's real name for the make-believe heroine of an irreverent sex-war comedy, but on the other hand he did feel the need to write such a comedy about the identities of and relations between men and women; indeed, more than one, since this was a theme to which he returned in the late 390s with his *Ekklesiazousai* or 'Women attending the Assembly' (as in real life they could not).

This raises a point often but contradictorily commented upon since antiquity. In everyday life actual Athenian women were supposed to be neither seen nor heard of in public, but twice a year, at the Lenaia and Great Dionysia play festivals in honour of Dionysos, fictitious women took conspicuous roles on the Athenian civic stage (though impersonated by men). One of the functions of Aristophanic comedy, as indeed of all comedy at all times and in all places, was to laugh at and thereby somewhat diminish (male) anxiety or fear. Tragedy, however, as interpreted by the great Athenian dramatists, would appear to have had the opposite function (see further Epilogue): to bring into question out in the open, and thereby set at risk, all the society's most deeply held traditional norms (*nomoi*), including those affecting the role and status of women. Indeed, the Athenian tragedy we know about is in some sense a more female than male theatre. The dynamics of male–female relationships at Athens, not to mention Athenian misogyny, are in play in numerous surviving tragedies, notably the *Oresteia* trilogy of Aeschylus (458 BCE) and the *Medea* of Euripides. But perhaps no other extant tragedy more centrally or acutely points up the 'problem of women' within the context of the *polis* than Sophokles' *Antigone*, staged in 441 and so written within a decade of Perikles' citizenship law.

Interpretations, readings, and reworkings of this play have been legion—hence George Steiner's book-title *Antigones*. One that both corroborates the view of tragedy's function expressed above and slots neatly into the discourse of woman as polarized 'other' may be worth summarizing here. Sophokles, it is argued (Sourvinou-Inwood 1989), pits an individual woman (and a 'bad' one, labouring under inherited pollution as a product of her father Oedipus' incest with his own mother, who is thus both Antigone's mother and grandmother) against a man, Kreon, who stands for the male citizenry of the city of Thebes (a kind of anti-Athens, used symbolically as an English playwright might use France). A woman, moreover, who violates the norm (*nomos*) that women should be invisible, confined within the domestic household, and have nothing to do with the public, male space of politics; and who does so in flagrant contravention of *nomos* in another sense, the law decreed by Kreon that traitors shall not be given the proper burial rites that allow a corpse's shade to descend in peace to the underworld of Hades. A woman, therefore (according to the cultural 'logic' of the Greek city), who must herself die a 'bad' death—suicide by hanging.

Or is her death really 'bad'? On Sourvinou-Inwood's reading, it is not. For it is Antigone (or rather the principle for which she stands, and in the name of which she buries her formally traitorous brother Polyneikes) who wins the *agōn* with Kreon, and she with whom Sophokles is inviting the audience to side. Although she has indeed flouted Kreon's temporal and secular decree, yet she has obeyed the traditional 'unwritten', divine law that kinsmen must give due burial to dead relatives, whatever the circumstances of their death. To rephrase that reading in terms of polar oppositions, we could say that Sophokles has privileged the 'gods v. mortals' rubric above both the 'men v. women' and the 'citizen v. non-citizen' polarities, not to mention such cultural sub-polarities as 'public v. private' and 'outside v. inside'.

Whether or not that reading is the (or a) right one, or true to Sophokles' intentions, can never be known. But, if it is, it has to be said that Sophokles was taking an unconventional line on both treason and political power. In the conservative view of a Thucydides, at least, Antigone would surely have been guilty of gross *atasthaliē* or *hubris*, the violent transgression of society's recognized status-barriers. Indeed, her very name Antigone might, on this reading, be construed to mean 'anti-procreation', that is, stiff-necked resistance to what were normatively deemed to be the female roles in Greek society, lawful marriage and legitimate motherhood.

An Ethnography of Alterity: Between Myth and Utopia

Staying for the moment with male Greek notions of proper feminine behaviour I turn from the rich and complex discourse of tragedy to the no less complex and if anything richer discourse of Herodotus, which can itself carry strong tragic echoes. In particular, I shall begin by examining his 'ethnographic' treatment of the 'usages' of women—how women behaved or were treated collectively in a range of barbarian and in one Greek societies.

Of all such Herodotean ethnography it can be asked, first, is it true and, secondly, even (and especially) if it is not, what might it mean for his addressee? I start with an instance where the truth test yields a certain answer. The Lykians (of southwest Anatolia) are alleged to have 'one singular custom in which they differ from every other people in the world, namely they take the mother's not the father's name' (1. 173. 4)—calling

themselves, as it were, Perikles son of Agariste, not son of
Xanthippos. Moreover, Herodotus adds, the child of a slave
man and a free woman may become a full Lykian citizen,
whereas if the mother is a slave and the father a Lykian he
does not. The first allegation is demonstrably false: Lykians
did not use matronymics. The second is unprovable either
way, but likely also to be false, since its meaning for the
addressee was that the barbarians do things upside down, the
exact opposite of Greek ways. (Strictly, though, that too would
have been false as a generalization, since at Gortyn on Crete
the son of a slave father and citizen mother counted as free,
though not a citizen; but elsewhere in Greece having one slave
parent legally consigned the child to servitude.)

The Greek way, it is implied, is the right way, the norm,
and that message is made abundantly clear in a spate of passages
dealing with sexual and especially marital (or the absence of
marital) relationships among barbarian peoples. Consciously
or unconsciously Herodotus constructs for his addressee a
spectrum of civilization and savagery in terms of these relationships, extending from the pole of Greek normality at one end,
monogamous matrimony, to the extreme of savagery at the
other, free love without benefit of marriage. I begin with the
latter.

The Scythian Androphagoi, as we noted in Chapter 3, counted
for Herodotus as the most savage of all mankind, since they
were entirely innocent of *dikē* and *nomos*. We may safely
infer, what Herodotus explicitly states of the Libyan Ausoi (4.
180), that 'they copulate promiscuously with their women', not
only not setting up a regular *oikos* together in lawful wedlock
but actually having intercourse (*meixis*) 'in the manner of
flocks and herds' (*ktēnēdon*). That does not mean that they
practised 'bestiality', as we legally define anal intercourse (giving
it the archaic but revealing gloss of 'unnatural vice'), but that
they copulated openly, thereby transgressing the boundaries
drawn by Greeks between inside and outside and public and
private, as Herodotus relates of the tribes of the Caucasus (1.
203): 'sexual intercourse among these fellows [*anthrōpoi*, as
often, bore a derogatory overtone here] takes place in the full

sight of all, as among the beasts'. Thus the Ausoi and Caucasian tribes not only violated the Greek norm of monogamous marriage but they also transgressed the sharp boundaries drawn by Greeks between men and beasts, public and private, and outside and inside.

Just slightly more civilized, that is, nearer the Greek norm, were the Libyan Gindanes (4. 176). In their society the way to public esteem for a woman was to maximize the number of her lovers, the conquest of whom she advertised by the number of leather rings she wore round her ankles, each supplied by a male lover. It is difficult not to recall Aeschylus' epithet for Helen of Troy, *poluanōr* or 'much-manned' (*Agamemnon* 62), a memory that may well have struck Herodotus' audience too and reminds us that Helen was no less ambiguous a role model than her sister Klytemnestra.

Yet more 'Hellenic' were two peoples, one northern, one southern, who did practise legal marriage but did not recognize exclusive monogamy with its corollary of adultery. Herodotus (4. 172. 2, 1. 216. 1) explicitly compares the mode of *meixis* practised by the southern Nasamones and the northern Massagetai. When a man wants to sleep with a woman, he displays prominently outside the door of her wagon or hut an appropriate masculine symbol (quiver or staff) and then copulates 'without fear'—that is, without fear of what an enraged Athenian husband might do if he found another man in bed with his wife (as in the famous lawcourt speech of Lysias written *c*.400 for a client accused of murder, who pleaded lawful killing of an adulterer *in flagrante*).

However, Herodotus the ethnographer was careful to draw distinctions even as he made comparisons. Besides having women 'in common', the Nasamones differed from the Massagetai in practising a kind of group marriage ceremony, in which the *droit de seigneur* was extended to all male wedding guests; they were thus relatively the less 'Hellenic' of the two. Nevertheless, there was no question about the barbarianness of the Massagetai. They were a Scythian tribe once ruled by a warrior queen called Tomyris, who had a baroque taste for gruesomely dramatic spectacle; the story of Cyrus the Great's death that Herodotus found most plausible had the queen dunking his decapitated head in a bucket of blood (a scene captured memorably by Rubens).

Tomyris, as we shall see, served as a barbarian forerunner and counterpart of Greek Artemisia, but for Herodotus' addressee she also had a more formidable resonance. To the Greeks any barbarian warrior-female (a formal contradiction in Greek terms) conjured up a vision of the race of such women they called Amazons. These functioned mythically as the ideal anti-type of the not-Greek/citizen/warrior/male, above all thanks to their alarming repudiation of Greek marriage. 'The imaginary polity of the Amazons is the inverse, set in a precise location, of the Greek city' (Vidal-Naquet 1986a: 208). Herodotus, however, not only sets the Amazons in direct, unmediated opposition to Greeks, but also complicates their difference by opposing them to the Scythians, the most outlandish and un-Hellenic of barbarians *grosso modo*. 'We', he has the Amazons say to the latter, 'could not live with your women: our customs (*nomaia*) are not the same as theirs. We draw the bow, we hurl the javelin, we ride horses—but womanly employments (*erga gunaikēïa*) we have not learned. Your women . . . never go out from their waggons to hunt or for any other purpose.' In this discourse, in other words, the Scythians have been transmogrified into honorary Greeks, the more sharply to bring out the barbarian character of the Amazons. But another effect of this move, surely not unnoticed nor unintended, is to assimilate Greek women to Scythian women by exploiting a kind of nostalgic primitivism. For Herodotus, that is, not everything barbarian was *ipso facto* barbaric, and some of his male Greek audience will have been left somewhat dazed by the Halikarnassian's fancy footwork.

To illustrate that point, literally, we may consider the scene of armed Amazons depicted by a fifth-century Attic painter on a fancy clay *epinētron*, a woman's utensil employed in the working of wool (Lissarrague 1992: 227, fig. 61). The transgressiveness of the barbarian warrior-women without a city is here highlighted by being reproduced on a quintessentially domestic and civilized Greek implement. There was nothing threatening or abnormal in that image. On the contrary: the masculine Amazons corroborated the domestic normality of an Athenian citizen-woman's wifely role as provider of the household's clothing. Herodotus' picture of Amazon history, by contrast, was not univocal nor merely comforting.

Herodotus, in short, has employed the 'usages' of barbarian women to construct a historian's discourse of a spatiotemporally grounded and more or less inverted non- and un-Greek world, located between the worlds of myth (in the distant and timeless past, the space of tragedy) and utopia (projected into the distant and vague future, the space of comedy). However, it remains to ask whether the Greek world that serves as foil and counterpart to the barbarian Other world is itself as stable and uniform as the normative discourse of polarity would seem to demand.

Sparta through the Looking-Glass

It is a little noticed or appreciated fact that Sparta is the only Greek state that Herodotus treats in his ethnographic manner, describing some of the Spartans' customs as if they might be as unfamiliar and outlandish to his audience as those of the Nasamones. The Spartans, that is, function as Herodotus' Greek Other, a kind of control on the Greek side of the Greek–barbarian polarity. This, I think, is why he was so careful to stress the uniqueness of the Spartans' own linguistic code for describing non-Spartans (see Chapter 3).

Not surprisingly, therefore, it is women of Sparta who both individually and collectively feature most prominently among the women of all the Greek communities he mentions. Unlike Xenophon (in his mistitled *Constitution of the Spartans* 1.9; cf. Plutarch's *Life of Lykourgos* 15), Herodotus does not treat us to the range of un-Greek, extra-marital pairing arrangements allegedly legally sanctioned in Sparta, where adultery (on the Athenian model) was said to be unknown. But he does tell the story of the bigamy practised by one Spartan king, adding quickly—too quickly—that Anaxandridas had behaved in an 'utterly un-Spartan way' (5. 39–40). And although, unlike Aristotle, he does not go so far as to speak of Sparta as a gynecocracy, he does more than hint at the possibility of female power.

In a long passage (6. 51–60) devoted to the two Spartan royal houses (hereditary kingship in itself being pretty odd for a Greek *polis* by the fifth century) he mentions among their hereditary prerogatives (*gerea*, good Homeric word) their power of adjudication in inheritance cases: 'When a maiden has been left heiress (*patroukhos*, literally 'holder of the patrimony') of her father's estate, and has not been affianced by him to anyone, [the kings] decide who is to marry her.' Women in Sparta (unlike their Athenian sisters) inherited in their own right, a contributory cause of the concentration of privately owned land in their hands—allegedly they possessed around two fifths in Aristotle's day, greatly to his chagrin. Heiresses were therefore not only a desirable economic proposition but capable of wielding what Aristotle took to be misplaced power: during the period of the Spartans' ascendancy over the Aegean Greek world between 404 and 371 'many things were managed by the women' (*Politics* 1269^{b}32–3).

In such a context it seems almost natural that Herodotus should write of dynastic machinations involving women that one would otherwise have assigned to the Arabian Nights' world of Ktesias. Succession disputes involving accusations of illegitimacy 'belong to the courts of tyrants and barbarian monarchs, not to a Greek *polis*' (Finley 1981*g*: 32)—precisely as Herodotus himself might have put it, since he explicitly compared Spartan royal practices with both Scythian and Persian equivalents (6. 58, 59), and there is a clear intratextual relationship between his accounts of the careers of Cambyses and Kleomenes I of Sparta. Indeed, one of the many stories he tells—with a little help from folklore, epic, and tragedy—immediately after the excursus on royal prerogatives contains an exact parallel with stories involving Darius and Xerxes.

The story (Herodotus 6. 63–9) concerns the birth, or rather procreation, of Damaratos, and is related as a flashback in the context of his deposition from the throne. Formally, the ground for his deposition (fraudulently and impiously manœuvred by the aforementioned Kleomenes, according to Herodotus) was his illegitimacy, which had been vouched for by Delphic Apollo. Shades of Oedipus' children! But Damaratos' mother, unlike Jocasta, knew the truth of Damaratos' conception, though she at least slightly embroidered it with folktale. As she told the story to her son, his natural father was either his legal father Ariston or the semi-divine Spartan hero Astrabakos in the guise of Ariston, and the conception had taken place on precisely the third night after their nuptials. It was behind their marriage that there lay the tale with a central motif in common with tales involving Darius and Xerxes, the motif of a wholly unexpected but equally wholly irresistible request for a gift. For Ariston had compelled his best friend under oath to surrender to him his beautiful—and, more importantly, fertile—wife.

The story as a whole is a tissue of fabrication from start to finish, but it perfectly illustrates the significance of women at the highest level in a society where the institution of monogamous marriage was vital but unstable, and women might have great social cachet and economic pull combined with formal political impotence and ritualized subordination to their husbands.

A Greek Wonderwoman

From Herodotean ethnography to a trio of individual Herodotean portraits or vignettes, one Greek, two barbarian. Herodotus had pledged prefatorily to record for posterity the great and marvellous *erga*—deeds, achievements, works—of both Greeks and non-Greeks. With Artemisia, 'queen' of his own Halikarnassos, he was dealing with a human marvel, someone he found simply 'wondrous' (7. 99. 1), though one suspects a certain *campanilismo* here. Like Tomyris (above) and Xenophon's Mania (below), and indeed 'our' Boudicca/ Boadicea, she was a widow who took the reins of government in her own very strong and capable hands after the decease of her husband. Like Mania and Boudicca, again, she was technically a client-queen, ruling Halikarnassos as a female tyrant in the Persian interest. By her very situation—of Greek birth (half-Halikarnassian, half-Kydonian), ruling a Greek *polis*, sub-

ject to the barbarian Persian Empire, a woman in charge—she
was a marginal and ambiguous figure; and marginality can
either challenge or reinforce the normative status boundaries
or do both simultaneously. Artemisia—or rather Herodotus'
Artemisia—was far more of a challenge than a reinforcement.

For a start she was reportedly admitted to the charmed
circle of Xerxes' advisers during his 480 campaign of invasion.
That royal device would inescapably have recalled Homer's
Agamemnon and his councils of war at Troy, but his advisers
in the *Iliad* were all men. Artemisia, however, gave Xerxes the
'best judgements' (7. 99. 3), and surely deserves the epithet of
androboulos ('manly-counselling') no less than Aeschylus'
Klytemnestra (*Agamemnon* 14).

Nor was it only her words that were as good as any man's:
uniquely, Herodotus applies to her conduct the standard
Greek word for bravery, *andreia*, despite the formal gender-
contradiction that involved. Indeed, Herodotus makes Xerxes
exclaim as he watches the battle of Salamis that his men have
become women (a thoroughly Greek insult), whereas Artemisia
fights as a man (8. 88. 3). For Herodotus' addressee, though,
that exclamation would not have cut much ice, since 'womanish'
was precisely how Greek men imaginatively represented Persian
men, most dramatically in Aeschylus' *Persians* of 472. But the
deed of Artemisia which occasioned Xerxes' exclamation—she
rammed a ship on the Persian side to avoid being rammed by
an Athenian ship—may have given them pause, since it was an
act of deception, of cunning intelligence (*mētis*), characteristic
of the thoroughly masculine eponymous hero of the *Odyssey*.
Gender-bending again, though at least Artemisia's feminine
wile deceived Xerxes as well as her Greek opponents.

Moreover, Artemisia's *sauve qui peut* attitude was at odds
with the Greek civic military-political ethic of remaining at
one's post and dying for the *polis* rather than saving one's own
skin. So possibly here Herodotus may have been protesting
too much. In an attempt to exculpate his native *polis* from the
opprobrious charge of medism, he has presented its leader
in too favourably masculine a guise. The man-in-the-street's
view of Artemisia, at any rate, was very different—and

utterly predictable: she was a latterday Amazon (Aristophanes, *Lysistrata* 671 ff.). But that view, too, carried its ideological hazards, since Artemisia was undeniably Greek and not barbarian. It seems appropriate to end this section as we began it, on a note of ambivalence.

Two Oriental Cautionary Tales

Similar suspicions of androgyny linger over my last but one Herodotean case-study, a love-story concerning an oriental royal wife taken from the very beginning of the *Histories* (1. 8–12). Such are its mythic qualities and dramatic intensity that it has inspired paintings, such as William Etty's 1830 *Candaules, King of Lydia, Shews his Wife by Stealth to Gyges*, and more recently a modern revision in the form of a novel, Frederic Raphael's *The Hidden I*.

King Kandaules of Lydia (real date: early seventh century) 'was fated to come to a bad end' (1. 8. 2). Does this mean that his end was decreed by Providence, God, or Fate? Or did he just end badly? Herodotus does not say. But he certainly did come to a sticky end, for although he died in his bed, it was not of natural causes. Kandaules' tragic flaw was to be passionately in love with his beautiful wife. So enamoured of her physical charms was he that he could not wait to expose them, all of them, to another male's gaze. That 'lucky' man was the captain of his bodyguard, Gyges, chosen both for his loyalty and because he was not a native Lydian. But the plan misfired horribly, and Kandaules' wife—unnamed, as was a respectable woman's due—caught sight of Gyges spying on her nakedness behind the bedroom door. Utterly shamed (even for a barbarian man, in polar opposition to a male Greek citizen, it was shaming to be seen naked; *a fortiori* for a barbarian woman), she made Gyges an offer he could not refuse: to kill Kandaules and become king—or himself be killed. He sensibly chose the first option and with poetic justice stabbed Kandaules to death in bed.

The motif of a woman as the foil for a man's weakness neatly subverts the dominant ideological paradigm of strong man:weak woman. Kandaules' wife, too, like Artemisia, had brains as well as beauty. Her revenge, though extreme and therefore perhaps vaguely barbarian, was also symmetrically apt, a clear case of *tisis* (compensatory retribution); and the manner of its execution was Greek in its *mētis*. The wife of Kandaules' story, in short, subverts both the Greek–barbarian and the man–woman polarities, all the more effectively for containing genuine oriental colour and detail.

My final Herodotean tale (9. 108–13) comes from the other end of the *Histories* and nicely complements it. If the lesson of the Kandaules–Gyges tale is ambiguous, even unsettling, this one is intended to leave his audience with an indelible impression of oriental despotism, of the 'otherness' of barbarian Persian harem politics. Xerxes had many wives and even more mistresses, as Persians were supposed to have (1. 135). But like Kandaules Xerxes made the mistake of falling in love, conceiving an erotic desire, for a wife—not one of his own, but of his brother Masistes. When direct entreaty failed to woo his sister-in-law, Xerxes resorted to indirect means, arranging a marriage between her daughter and one of his sons. But that merely compounded the felony, since he now fell for his daughter-in-law Artaÿnte (named by Herodotus, unlike the respectably anonymous wife of Masistes) who did respond to his advances. But at a price—she demanded as a gift the 'coat of many colours' woven for Xerxes by his principal wife Amestris. The tangled tale unravelled to its messy conclusion, as Amestris discovered that Xerxes had given away the robe to Artaÿnte and exacted a truly savage and 'oriental' revenge, rather unfairly, on her innocent mother.

Xerxes, in short, had failed to control his desire as a Greek citizen-man ideally should; and as a result not only was he a failure at playing the macho Great King role abroad but at home he was not even the master of his own house. His usage of women was a salient index of his moral and political deficiencies. The womanly violence of Persian Queen Amestris will have confirmed Herodotus' addressees in their stereotyped view both of female barbarians and of oriental despotism. Even Herodotus' Sophist-inspired enlightenment and sympathy for barbarians had its limits where women and power were concerned. But for the view of the Greek *homme moyen sensuel*, somewhere between those of Herodotus and Aristotle perhaps, we should turn finally to Xenophon.

A Modest Proposal

Poor Xenophon—fated not necessarily to come to a bad end, but to be judged customarily by posterity as a poor man's Thucydides, rather than for what he was: a historical writer of a very different stamp, far more akin to Herodotus than to his immediate predecessor, not least in the limpidity and ready comprehensibility of his Greek prose (as many a grateful novice learner of the language will know). Xenophon, however, had all the ambition of a Greek, and he combined that with a penchant for originality and innovation belied by his simple-seeming prose style. Yet for the most part we find nothing but reassuring 'normality' in Xenophon's representations of the man–woman polarity—his men are masculine men, his women feminine women, and they each know their place within a division of labour and hierarchy of command sanctioned by god.

For the most part . . . Although I am out of sympathy with the revisionist picture of Xenophon that figures him as subtle, allusive, and ironic, I do agree that there is more to his writing than meets the casual eye. If he was much less of a Socratic philosopher than he wanted to be taken for, he was also somewhat more of one than he has traditionally been taken to be.

Compare and contrast, to begin with, his Woman with that of Aristotle, as exposed in his *Oeconomicus* or treatise on the proper management of an *oikos*. Aristotle, too, starts from the *oikos* in the *Politics*, seeing the *polis* as an aggregate of *oikoi*. But for Aristotle a change in quantity meant a change in quality; the aggregate *polis* is different in kind from any one individual household, and one cannot live the good life for man, cannot realize the human *telos*, within the latter's confines. That would be to live like the Cyclops Polyphemos. Xenophon, however, in the *Oeconomicus* treats the *oikos* as a self-sufficient context for the display of human moral-political virtue, *aretē*.

And when he turns away from the micro- to the macro-level of properly political theorizing he does not construct his argument in the Greek present or future, as Aristotle does in the *Politics*, but retrojects it into the non-Greek past.

On the other hand, in his ideological construction of the man–woman polarity within the confines of the *oikos*, Xenophon saw pretty much eye-to-eye with Aristotle. For both men, the division between the sexes of nature, function, and power was of divine origin, and it was god too who (or which) had implanted in women their maternal instinct. The purpose of marriage was chiefly legitimate procreation, not companionship, let alone intellectual stimulation: Socrates' principal interlocutor in the *Oeconomicus*, Iskhomakhos, is very firm on the desirability of marrying a girl-woman aged no more than 14, so that the husband (probably twice her age) can teach her what he deems necessary to make her the model household supervisor and conjugal adjunct. The only hint of a serious difference between Xenophon and Aristotle comes in a coyly complimentary remark of Socrates that Iskhomakhos' wife would seem to have a masculine intellect (*dianoia*), but the remark was only meant half-seriously and of course anyway presupposed the standard Greek polarized and hierarchical view of gender difference. At most, therefore, one might say that Xenophon was relatively broadminded towards a certain very few women (women like the wife of Iskhomakhos are clearly represented as belonging to the Athenian élite).

Xenophon's historiography of women confirms this general impression of a certain repressive tolerance that the author considers to be rather daring. Two Greek widows, both from Asiatic Greece under Persian control, earn his approval. In the *Anabasis* (7. 8) he recounts how during his period as a mercenary commander he met and was well received by Hellas (a speaking name, if ever there was one), who gave him and her son good advice. In the *Hellenica* (3. 1. 10–14) he gives a more extended treatment to Mania, who had succeeded her late husband as under-satrap of a Greek enclave within the Persian satrapy of Hellespontine Phrygia. Like Tomyris the Massagetan and, more particularly, Artemisia of Halikarnassos,

Mania showed herself no whit less able as a leader than her spouse. Indeed, so successfully did she perform, in male Greek terms, that men at her court started a whispering campaign against her, saying that it 'was a disgrace for the country to be ruled by a woman'. Mania's son-in-law took the hint and murdered her—not a very good mother-in-law joke. At first sight, then, Xenophon's Mania is a reprise of Herodotus' Artemisia. On closer inspection she is revealed to be far less threatening a figure, being not only respectful towards her Persian overlord in a way that Artemisia was not towards Xerxes, but also overfond and too trusting of her son-in-law—'as a woman would be', in Xenophon's revealing editorializing phrase.

The Perfect Wife

Mania and Hellas lived on the margins, between the worlds of men and women and of Greeks and Persians. Xenophon's most extended female characterization, however, was located very firmly within the barbarian world of Persia, though she is an entirely fictional character. The main plot of the *Cyropaedia* is the education of Cyrus the Great, specifically the education of a paradigmatically good ruler. Among the sub-plots none is more memorable than the love-story of Abradatas of Susa and his devoted wife Pantheia.

Her Greek name, meaning 'thoroughly divine', was carefully chosen. The equivalent of Eve in Greek myth was Pandora, 'All-Gift', so called because she had been endowed with gifts by all the Olympians. But she had proved a bane, a curse, to Greek men, whereas Xenophon's Pantheia was intended as his very model of conjugal womanhood, the precise inverse of mythical Pandora. She was of course physically beautiful, but it was the beauty of her soul rather than of her body upon which Xenophon chose to dwell, emphasizing above all else her absolute and unwavering fidelity to her husband up to and indeed beyond his grave. For after he had been killed and horribly mangled in battle, she gathered up his remains and gave them due burial before killing herself.

'Look to the end', so wise Solon is supposed to have advised Croesus (Herodotus I. 32), and Pantheia's end was certainly tragic and heroic. The only, mild surprise is that Xenophon does not have her die in the usual manner of female suicides on (or rather off) the Athenian tragic stage, by hanging; instead, Pantheia ends all with a sword, a masculine implement. Perhaps here Xenophon is meaning to hint that in death as in life Pantheia was, in her separate and subordinate feminine way, the peer of her husband, and that her *dianoia*, like that of Iskhomakhos' unnamed wife, was just a touch masculine. But perhaps, too, that is why Xenophon felt obliged to retroject Pantheia, not only into the distant and fictional past, but also safely into the alien world of the barbarian Other.

5

In the Club

Citizens v. Aliens

> The *polis* teaches a man
>
> (Simonides)

> Whatever the principles for allocating specific political
> rights and functions within a citizen body, the global
> demarcation between citizens—all citizens—and others—
> all others—was conceptually paramount
>
> (Whitehead 1991: 144)

The Primacy of Politics?

Karl Marx, once a promising postgraduate student of ancient
Greek philosophy, never lost touch with the ancient world in
his groundbreaking explorations of the modern. In one of his
more aphoristic moods he opined that the ancient world did
not live on politics, any more than the medieval world lived on
religion. What came through forcefully, in other words, from
the ancient Greek sources, not least the historians and Marx's
revered Aristotle, was the idea that the *polis* and the privilege
of being a *politēs* were the be-all and end-all of human existence,
the fount and origin of the good life for man. That idea
or ideal, Marx noted with regret, was typically presented in
sublime isolation from the more sordid realities of production,
distribution, and exchange—of economics, in a word—without
which there could have been no rarefied politics, let alone
properly political thought.

Marx's materialism, his stress on the primacy of the production and reproduction of material life, has been variously
interpreted and developed over the century and a half since
The German Ideology of 1845. Perhaps its most enduring

legacy has been in the historiography of the so-called '*Annales* School' founded by Marc Bloch and Lucien Febvre and associated most recently with Fernand Braudel. Though not in any strict or dogmatic sense Marxist themselves, and the more widely influential for that very reason, the *Annalistes* agreed with Marx in not privileging the realm of the political in their writing of history. At the stroke of a pen, Thucydidean political history, and especially the history of political events (war, diplomacy, politics), were thus conscientiously abjured, and the tradition of post-Renaissance admiration and emulation of Thucydides that ran from Guicciardini through Hobbes and Macaulay to von Ranke was replaced by what we might call a Herodotean concern for the history of custom, mores, and mentality.

Not without protest and reaction from within the ranks of contemporary ancient historians. According to some of the protesters (e.g. Rahe 1984), politics—in the sense of the sorts of things that went on in the public spaces of a Greek city (assembly, lawcourts, *agora*, theatre, and so on), or on the battlefield—quite simply was more important than any other aspect of life in Classical Greece, and so Thucydides and his epigones were right to concentrate on it. The Greeks may not have lived on politics, in Marx's materialist sense, but it was politics that gave their lived experience its distinctive meaning and value. This view can fairly be accused of being unduly blinkered, in that it leaves out of account all those Greeks— the majority—who could never or only rarely operate actively within those public spaces: women, children, and aliens; not to mention the typically barbarian slaves, whom Marx occasionally (and questionably: see Chapter 6) envisaged as the pedestal upon which Greek politics rested. On the other hand, it cannot fairly be accused of sheer blindness. From Tyrtaios (mid-seventh century) to Aristotle, all genres of Greek public discourse, whether lyric and elegiac poetry, epinician odes, tragedy, comedy, history, oratory, or political theory, did indeed privilege the public, communal, political sphere above the private and the personal. Two examples from either end of those three centuries clearly illustrate the point.

Alkaios (*fl. c.*600) has a certain posthumous reputation among poets for his technical accomplishment; both Horace and Thomas Hardy, for example, wrote in his alcaic metre. But in his own day Alkaios composed his verses as a continuation of politics by other means, articulating the views of a conservative aristocrat from Mytilene on Lesbos who was struggling to maintain his and his peers' place amid a series of upheavals that led to a succession of dictatorships and, for him, disgruntled banishment. As an exile what he missed above all was Mytilene's *agora* or civic centre. The word means literally 'a place of gathering', and so for example it became the usual Greek term for a market. But for Alkaios it had a specifically political connotation, meaning the space where political assemblies were held and decisions and struggles affecting the governance of Mytilene were enacted.

Two and a half centuries later, the Athenian Isokrates in a couple of his crypto-oligarchic pamphlets (12. 138; 15. 14) employed a remarkable (to us, anyway) metaphor, describing the *politeia* of a Greek city as its *psukhē*, its 'life and soul' or 'beating heart'. In Classical Greek, *politeia* had two main senses (Bordes 1982 is exhaustive). First, it could mean something like what we understand by 'citizenship' (from the Latin *civitas*), the peculiar attribute of a *politēs* or '*polis*-person'. Secondly, it denoted the framework of rules and conventions within which the *politēs* exercised his (in the gender sense) *politeia*. In this second sense it is conventionally translated 'constitution', but a moment's reflection on the Isokratean usage suggests that may be highly misleading. If asked today what most gave our collective or social existence its meaning and purpose few of us, I suspect, would reply unhesitatingly 'the British (or whatever) constitution'.

Thus the Alkaios and Isokrates passages serve two useful purposes. They indicate a broad gulf between ancient and modern perceptions or constructions of politics and they lend initial credibility to the anti-Marxist, anti-*Annaliste* view that in Classical Greece politics was primary and should not be treated as a mere epiphenomenon. But what we must ask next is whether and, if so, how far and in what way the majority of their fellow citizens, the fellow-sharers in the *politeia* of Mytilene and Athens who collectively constituted their respective *politeuma* ('citizen body'), would have endorsed Alkaios' view of the *agora* and Isokrates' of the *politeia*. Our principal authors offer a variety of approaches and insights.

Herodotus and the Tyranny of Nomos

Herodotus was by no means uninterested in political life broadly defined, but he was conspicuously, almost notoriously, uninterested in the niceties of constitutional structure and practice. If, for instance, one were seeking enlightenment on the mode of government of Sparta and Athens, or on how their very different political institutions affected their behaviour in the run-up to and during the Persian Wars, one would not derive much from Herodotus. Indeed, he has but one use of the word *politeia*, in its citizenship sense, in the entire work— though this instance is interesting enough, since it records the only example known to Herodotus of Sparta's conferring its citizenship on a *xenos*, or rather on two of them, brothers from Elis who specialized in divination (9. 34–5).

Yet it is still perfectly possible to argue without self-contradiction that Herodotus was a thoroughly political and politicized historian, indeed no less so than Thucydides or Aristotle (and considerably more so than Xenophon). For running through his work is a discourse on power, above all despotic rule, and Herodotus enquires into its implications both in theory and in practice with as much vigour as he conducts his ethnography of gender and sexuality (see Chapter 4). In particular, he is obsessed with the relationship between *nomos* in the sense of custom or convention and *nomos* meaning law, whether a particular enactment or the rule of law (as opposed to arbitrary, individual despotism); and with the further relationship between *nomos* in either sense and *phusis* in the sense of what human beings deem natural or do because they can achieve their ends by sheer physical might.

It is not therefore quite so surprising that the least 'constitutional' of historians should have wished to include in his *History* what is by some way the earliest surviving piece of developed political theory in all western literature, the 'Persian Debate' (3. 80–2). The intellectual breakthrough involved is in retrospect stunningly simple, like all the most fruitful inventions. Some Greek somewhere discovered that all forms of political rule must be species of just three genera—rule by one, rule by some, rule by all (a relatively rare instance of Greek tripartition). That classification is logically and pragmatically exhaustive. But in order for that breakthrough of thought to be possible, some Greeks somewhere had first to have invented practical politics, in the strong sense of the taking of decisions of major, communal significance in public (*es meson*, 'into the middle', as they put it) after open debate between relevantly specified peers. But for that to occur required in its turn the prior invention of the necessary 'civic space' of the *polis*, whence sprang the idea of citizen equality. This is not of course to deny the invention of polities and political activity much earlier, in Sumer, say, nor the (possibly prior) creation of a state-form akin to the *polis* by the Phoenicians and Etruscans. But political theory in the precise sense under discussion here was a Greek breakthrough, the culmination of a largely endogenous political development.

We shall return to the genesis and nature of the *polis* in our discussion of Aristotle's political theory below. Now Herodotus' 'Persian Debate' demands our attention, for two main reasons. First, the fact that it is ostensibly Persian may not say much for Herodotus' understanding of cultural or intellectual possibility. The authenticity of the debate was challenged, quite rightly, on the ground that the idea of any Persian's ever seriously propounding a version of democracy was preposterous, and Herodotus' defence (6. 43)—that in 493, some thirty years after the dramatic date of the 'Debate', Darius had allegedly authorized the establishment of democracies in Greek Ionia—is singularly lame. For in 522 there had been no democracy anywhere in the world; it was one thing to set up or tolerate democracy at the western extremity of the empire among Greeks and quite another to establish it as the norm for the governance of the empire as a whole, beginning with the Persian court; and, thirdly, these

Ionian democracies were in any case not terribly democratic. In fact, the 'Debate' is a pioneering exercise in Greek political philosophy, originating no earlier than 500. In the form in which it is presented by Herodotus, each speaker countering the arguments of his opponents as well as advocating the positive merits of his own preferred political system, it may well owe something to Protagoras of Abdera (*fl.* *c.*450–430), who was apparently a democrat and the author of works entitled 'Knockdown Arguments' and 'Adversarial Debates' among others.

However, the 'Debate' does speak worlds for Herodotus' relatively enlarged vision of the barbarian Other—or at least of some barbarian others. Like Xenophon's Cyrus (Chapter 3) Herodotus' three noble Persian debaters Megabyzus, Otanes, and Darius embody wisdom that was by no means alien to Greek thought. On the other hand, the gap between Persian theory and practice, as it were, was also entirely grist to Herodotus' Hellenist mill. In the 'Debate' his Darius had of course advocated monarchy, in its 'good' form of constitutional monarchy, which he had opposed to the 'bad' forms of rule-by-some (factional oligarchy) and rule-by-all (mob-rule, ochlocracy). But in practice the Persian monarchy re-established by Darius in the late 520s and inherited by his son Xerxes in 486 proved to be the bad form of rule-by-one to which Megabyzus and Otanes had taken exception. It had become, that is to say, a classic exemplar of oriental despotism. So although rule-by-one won the 'Persian Debate', in Herodotus' own discourse rule-by-some and rule-by-all, the republican forms of government that predominated in the world of the Classical Greek city, won by a long way. Two passages, concerning the most famous Greek instances of respectively rule-by-all (Athens) and rule-by-some (Sparta), put beyond all question Herodotus' own confidence in the superiority and desirability of the *polis* as the site of the good life for political man.

First, in a context of 506 BCE, shortly after the establishment of democracy at Athens by Kleisthenes the Alkmaionid (6. 131; Chapter 2), Herodotus describes how the Athenians repulsed a pincer attack on Athens launched from the south-west by Sparta and her Peloponnesian League allies, from the north by the Boiotians, and from the east by the Khalkidians of Euboia. He then editorializes—or rather hymns the peculiar quality that in his view accounted for this unprecedented Athenian military prowess (5. 78):

So Athens had increased in greatness. It is not only in respect of one thing but of everything that equality and free speech are clearly a good; take the case of Athens, which under the rule of princes proved no better in war than any of her neighbours but, once rid of those princes, was far the first of all. What this makes clear is that when held in subjection they would not do their best, for they were working for a taskmaster, but, when freed, they sought to win, because each was trying to achieve for his very self.

David Grene's recent translation reproduced here is consciously archaizing, but in other respects its verbal fidelity to the original does nicely capture the flavour of Herodotus' oral style of delivery. So too it does full justice to the implications of the key words in the text, with one exception: 'princes' (as in Machiavelli's *Il principe*) hides the fact that Herodotus' Greek uses the original of our own word 'tyrants' meaning illegitimate, autocratic rulers.

The tyrants in question were the Peisistratidai, Peisistratos (545–528/7) and his son Hippias (528/7–510), who had ruled Athens for a generation and provided an essential bridge of stability between the civil disorder of the late seventh and early sixth centuries and the inauguration of democracy at the end of the sixth. But towards the end of his reign, following the murder of his brother by the heroic 'Tyrannicides', Hippias had allegedly become despotic or as we say tyrannical, and his foreign connections with Persia were grounds for reasonable suspicion of his patriotism. In 510 he was at last overthrown, though by Spartan intervention rather than internal uprising (despite the Tyrannicide myth: see Chapter 2). A further period of domestic instability supervened, resolved temporarily by Kleisthenes' securing the passage of his democatic reform bill through Council and Assembly in 508/7. Sparta's political sympathies and King Kleomenes' personal connections, however, ran in favour of Kleisthenes' principal opponent, Isagoras: hence the multipronged invasion of Attica in 506 spearheaded by Sparta that the democratic Athenians successfully resisted.

The emphasis, in Herodotus' explanation above, rests firmly on the 'democratic'. What Grene translates as 'equality and free speech' is in Greek the one word *isēgoriē*, literally equality of public speech in Athenian political assemblies, and that by Herodotus' day was construed as a peculiarly democratic feature of Athens's civic life. Whether *isēgoriē* had in fact been institutionalized as an integral feature of Athenian public decision-making as early as 506 is far more doubtful; Herodotus is probably as guilty of anachronism here as he was in the 'Persian Debate'. But what matters is the unbridgeable gap and polar opposition, for him, between democracy and equality of free speech, on the one hand, and tyranny on the other. Indeed, Herodotus spells it out for his addressee. Under a tyranny the Athenian citizenry, though technically free, were like slaves working for a 'taskmaster' (*despotēs*, the usual Greek for master of slaves). A final exegesis is perhaps necessary of the last sentence of 5.78: *isēgoriē*, Herodotus says, is a morally admirable thing (*spoudaion khrēma*), because it allows each to achieve for his very self—as a part of the community, he means, an equal member of the civic community, and not, as might too easily be supposed today, for his own self as opposed to the community.

The discourse of power is developed further and with more subtle refinement in book 7, where Herodotus employs the familiar folktale storyteller's device of the wise adviser. But his chosen mouthpiece is not an Athenian this time. He is a Spartan, and no ordinary Spartan but a deposed ex-king, Damaratos the 'medizer' (cf. Chapter 3). Given the circumstances of his exile, illegally even sacrilegiously rigged by his co-king Kleomenes I, one might have expected Damaratos to be an embittered and implacable enemy of Sparta, vowing death, destruction, and revenge on his ungrateful native *polis*. Not a bit of it. Not only does he serve the tragic function of the adviser whose good advice is rejected but, had it been followed, would have assured success. He also serves as spokesman of and for Spartan and by extension Greek freedom. What is at stake is once more the relationship between political system and martial valour, and 'Damaratos', like Herodotus himself, derives military prowess from political, civic condition (7. 104):

Fighting singly [says 'Damaratos' to 'Xerxes'] they [the Spartans] are no worse than any other people; together, they are the most gallant men on earth. For they are free—but not altogether so. They have as the despot over them Nomos and they fear *nomos* much more than your men fear you.

There is a truly sophistical paradox at work here. *Nomos*, meaning either a particular custom or law or, as here, the rule of law, by definition cannot rule in the same sense as the master rules slaves. For it is citizens—guided, according to a widespread form of myth, by an all-wise lawgiver (*nomothetēs*) such as the Spartan Lykourgos—who have made the laws and established the rule of law, by their own free volition. By mutual consent they agree to abide by the laws they have so made, and other things being equal they prefer to observe the existing laws rather than change them. Since they are not above the laws, and the laws rule, they must necessarily be under them. So by a paradoxical twist and semantic slippage 'Damaratos the Sophist' is able to present this Greek contractual, egalitarian, and civic idea of the rule of law as the polar opposite and inverse of the Persian *nomos* (custom) of rule by a despot. For Herodotus' Greek addressee, moreover, that was a particularly easy shift to comprehend, since in the Greeks' opinion all Xerxes' subjects were indeed political slaves, and they were slaves because, being barbarians, they were naturally slavish (Chapter 6). Persian political custom, in other words, was in accordance with Persian nature. Herodotus himself, however, would surely not have gone so far. One of the implications of the 'Persian Debate', at all events, is that not all Persians were *ipso facto* incapable of perceiving the merits of civic self-government.

Thucydides and the Utility of History

Thucydides, too, was distinctly reticent on constitutional history in the narrow sense. What exactly, for instance, was the 'Constitution of the 5,000' at Athens in 411–410? We shall never know, since Thucydides chose not to say, although he did approve mightily of it, at least in its first phase (8. 97. 2). Nor was he much more interested in politics in our conventional contemporary sense of interpersonal or interfactional infighting—until, that is, it erupted into outright civil war. To select just one of his plangent silences, he says virtually nothing in detail about the vital internal struggle at Athens in about 417, which ought to have resulted in the ostracism of either Alkibiades or Nikias but was somehow fixed so that a third party, Hyperbolos, received the grand order of the People's boot. (For the ostracism procedure to be valid at least 6,000 Athenian citizens had to cast their vote, in the form of an inscribed potsherd (*ostrakon*), against the politician whom they wished to have exiled from Athens for ten years. The candidate with the most such votes 'won' this reverse election, and the roll-call of 'winners' was a distinguished one.) This miscarriage had the unhappy consequence of divided counsels that played no small role in Athens's disaster in Sicily in 415–413, but all Thucydides (8. 73) says, with untypically undisguised moral prejudice, is that Hyperbolos 'had been ostracized, not for fear of his power or prestige, but because he was a wretched character and a disgrace to the city'.

Yet in other senses Thucydides' historiography was as political and civic as could be, indeed more obviously so than Herodotus' in that he deliberately excluded the mythic or romantic element of storytelling (1. 21, 22). For Thucydides devoted his enquiry to war, the most visible and tangible and fraught expression of relations between Greeks organized in political communities, and, secondly, to civil war within and for the control of a state's *politeia*. But to justify Hobbes's characterization of Thucydides as 'the most politick historiographer that ever writ' a further ingredient is necessary. This is provided by Thucydides' explicit concern with the permanent utility of his history above and beyond its immediate focus on a 'world' war between Greeks. As he expressed it in the famous conclusion to his exordium (1. 22. 4): 'My work is not a prize composition designed to meet the taste of an immediate public, but was done to be a possession for ever.'

Despite the rhetorical *suggestio falsi*, Thucydides' *History* was indeed written competitively, and probably to defeat above all Herodotus in the struggle for readers' immediate attention. Paradoxically, though, the burden of his claim to superiority rests on the last two words, 'for ever'. Thucydides, that is, supposed that his work would have permanent value because he assumed that there was something unalterable at work in human history. That constant he labelled variously 'human nature' or 'the human thing', and he located its most crucial sphere of operation in the arena of interstate relations. Although Thucydides did not recite his work in public like Herodotus, he too composed to be read aloud; and situated as he was within a tradition that extended back ultimately to Homer, he found it quite natural to include speeches as well as narrative, as had Herodotus. But such was Thucydides' passion for accuracy that he felt obliged to warn readers in advance of the licence he had necessarily given himself to invent the content of his speeches, to put words into his speakers' mouths: 'I have found it necessary to make the speakers say what in my opinion was called for by the situation at hand' (1. 22. 2). Nowhere was this licence more liberally exploited than in two passages in which Thucydides put words into the mouths of anonymously collective Athenian speakers in contexts where the historian himself had not been present at the time and where there was no chance of his receiving even an accurate précis of what had actually been said. Not coincidentally, it is in these two passages that Thucydides departs most completely from the immediate situation in order to generalize stratospherically about the constant features of human nature as they seemed to him to operate in interstate relations.

First, in his so-called 'Melian Dialogue' of book 5 (84–112). The context is a pause, a phoney peace, in the fighting between Athens and Sparta and their allies. Neutral but pro-Spartan Melos, an island-city in the southern Cyclades, is resisting Athens's attempt to coerce her into alliance in 416/15. To the Melian oligarchs' confident appeals to human and divine justice Thucydides' Athenians reply with brutal frankness (5. 105):

So far as the favour of the gods is concerned, we think we have as much right to it as you have ... Our opinion of the gods and our knowledge of men lead us to conclude that it is a general and necessary law of nature to rule wherever one can. This is not a law we made ourselves, nor were we the first to act upon it when it was made. We found it already in existence, and we shall leave it to exist for ever among those who come after us. We are merely acting in accordance with it, and we know that you or anybody else with the same power as ours would be acting in precisely the same way. (trans. Rex Warner)

The key words here are 'law', 'nature', 'for ever', and 'power'. (We shall return to Thucydides' attitude to the gods in Chapter 7.) Against the backdrop of the Sophistic *nomos–phusis* polarity, the Athenian speakers stress the rule of the strong as a fact of human nature in interstate relations. But this is not simply the law of the jungle. Reason, rationality, and prudent calculation are not excluded by the logic of power—far from it. It is precisely those statesmen (like Perikles) who possess these civic capacities, and those communities which find the arguments of such statesmen persuasive and act upon them prudently, who survive and win through in Thucydides' pitilessly amoral universe.

To discover the motives which should in his view weigh most in the prudent calculation of collective civic self-interest we may look to his other anonymously attributed Athenian policy speech. The original was ostensibly delivered before the Spartan assembly in 432 with a view to dissuading the Spartans from declaring that Athens had broken the Peace of 445. But if its main purpose was really to assuage Spartan fears and mollify Spartan resentment, in Thucydides' version it hardly set about accomplishing that in the most obvious way. Instead, Thucydides' 'Athenians' reiterate the three motives which, they insist, determine interstate policymaking: fear, honour, and profit (1. 75. 3, 76. 2). Fear, in the sense not of sheer terror, but prudential calculation, concern for collective security. Honour in the sense of *amour propre*, self-esteem, prestige—again, a characteristic preoccupation of the free Greek citizen and civic community. Thirdly, and finally, material advantage. And the greatest of the three, Thucydides said unto his readers, was fear. 'What made war inevitable was the growth of Athenian power and the fear this instilled in the Spartans' (1. 23. 6). With this glaring exception to his normal rule of avoiding first-person authorial judgement Thucydides closes the circle and makes watertight the connection between the views of his anonymous Athenians and the view he himself held.

Such was the stuff of his political history, whereby he sought to teach lessons of utility 'for ever', and many historians after him—from his anonymous continuator known to us only as the 'Oxyrhynchus Historian' down to Leopold von Ranke in the nineteenth century and beyond—have taken his brand of political history as a kind of supra-historical model. But although Thucydides' historiography is in an important sense universal and universalizable, it was also the product of his Greek civic milieu, and in particular of the Athenian democracy within which he was formed. That facet will be treated more fully below in connection with the Periklean Funeral Speech. Immediately, the quality of Thucydides' engagement with the political may be brought out further by contrasting his historiography with that of another of his continuators, Xenophon.

Xenophon and the Privatization of the Political

Thucydides' *History*, in short, confirms our reading of Herodotus' *Histories*: *historia* as a genre, new-minted in its critical application to the great and wondrous (or horrific) deeds of Greeks and/or non-Greeks, was itself a form of civic and political discourse. It was not, however, in any sense official. Indeed, when compared with the annals of the Assyrian kings or the biblical book of Kings, for example, it represents the very denial of official history, whether dynastic or religious.

But it does nevertheless present itself as a contribution to political debate *es meson*, 'into the central space' of the *polis*. Here their Greek citizen addressees were invited to reflect upon its messages and redeploy them in the ceaseless round of competitive public debate that constituted Classical Greek politics.

Judged against this lofty intellectual and social achievement Xenophon's historiography has often seemed to be a declension, a descent from good to bad historiography, both technically and civically. That, however, is a misreading. Xenophon, too, aimed to write history in his *Hellenica*, in the then accepted sense of a record of public, political events (above all, wars). But conditioned as he was by the outcome of the Peloponnesian War and the ensuing impotent stalemate between the great powers of fourth-century Greece, he preferred a different, quietist approach. Thucydides had wanted to be 'useful' primarily to practical politicians who might have a direct influence on public affairs. Xenophon, by contrast, wrote a privatized sort of history, deeming to be *axiologon* ('worthy of account', so 'important') moral instruction of a frankly conventional kind.

At two points he sets out his credo explicitly. First, in connection with an in itself trivial incident in the Corinthian War (395–386) (*Hellenica* 5. 1. 4):

I know that in this description I am recounting no expenditure, danger, or stratagem worthy of report (*axiologon*)—but, by Zeus, it seems to me that this is worthy of a man's consideration, what it was that Teleutias did to produce such a disposition in his men. That is an achievement (*ergon*) of a man most worthy of report (*axiologōtaton*), more than great wealth or many dangers.

The repetition of 'man' (in the gender sense) and *axiologon* and the interjection of 'by Zeus' indicate the passion with which Xenophon wrote this; the use of *ergon* implies that the passion was directed specifically against Herodotus and Thucydides, the historians of great wealth and great dangers respectively. The fact that Teleutias was half-brother of his own patron Agesilaos merely added fuel to the flames.

Two books later, Xenophon had occasion to laud collective rather than individual 'achievement' (7. 2. 1):

If any of the large cities has a single fine deed to its credit, all the historians (*sungrapheis*) record it. But it seems to me that if a small city has many fine achievements (*erga*) to its credit, that is even more worthy of exposition.

The small city that prompted this outburst was Phleious in the north-east Peloponnese, a city which—unlike most of Sparta's Peloponnesian League allies—remained consistently loyal after Sparta's crushing defeat at Leuktra in 371. Again, the fact that Phleious was pro-Spartan, indeed was governed by an oligarchic regime that Agesilaos had imposed on a largely unwilling democratic citizenry in 379, simply increased the warmth with which Xenophon expressed a view that he anyway held. For him the function of the historian was essentially to praise moral virtue and, by implication, to castigate vice, public and private, individual and collective. Not that Herodotus or Thucydides was innocent of moral purpose, but their emphasis was not primarily on moral improvement. Xenophon's emphasis, however, throughout the *Hellenica* is on individual or collective moral achievement, not civic and political analysis or explanation.

Oriental Despotism Revalued

It is in this light that the *Cyropaedia* is properly to be read. *Paideia*, usually translated as 'education', was for some Greeks, as we shall see, an integral part of the definition and formation of a Greek citizen; without the appropriate *paideia* active membership of a state's *politeuma* would be put at risk, if not rendered impossible. Xenophon, however, devoted his longest exercise in the study of *paideia* to that of a barbarian, Cyrus II 'the Great'. Moreover, Xenophon gives to *paideia* an extended meaning that was not habitual when applied to an individual. Etymologically, *paideia* was a matter for *paides*, 'children', but Xenophon applies the term to all of Cyrus' career that he chooses to represent, including his early maturity as king and emperor. This Xenophontic *paideia*, in other words, is a school for monarchs, not citizens.

The originality of this conceit stems from its conflicting with the dominant Greek paradigm of the monarch, especially the oriental monarch, as a despot or tyrant, an autocrat above the laws. The Egyptians, Herodotus (2. 147) had rather snidely observed, appeared incapable of living without kings, whereas the Athenians defined themselves democratically in terms of the overthrow and permanent rejection of tyranny (5. 78). The *Cyropaedia* thus not only introduces a new genre of literature, the pseudo-historical novel or romance, but also reflects a new model of political theory, pro-monarchist and not so much anti- as non-civic. For the inhabitants of Cyrus' world are all subjects, the ruled, people subjected to a unidirectional flow of monarchical power from the top down, whereas it was the essence of being a Greek citizen to 'rule and be ruled in turn'. Early on in the *Cyropaedia* (1. 6. 20) Xenophon does use this standard expression—but he applies it, paradoxically, to Cyrus personally. One of the basic lessons of the *Cyropaedia* is, no doubt, that 'human beings resist no one so quickly as the person they see trying to rule over them' (Tatum 1989: p. xviii). But the most basic lesson, the message, of the work as a whole is that such resistance not only can but should be overcome—by an enlightened prince such as Cyrus is depicted to be.

It is easy to see, then, how the *Cyropaedia* should have been lined up with other Xenophontic works, the *Hiero* (how to be a good Greek tyrant) and *Agesilaos* (how to be a good Greek hereditary king), and with other contemporary works of monarchist propaganda (Isokrates' *Evagoras* and *To Nikokles*, both Cypriot Greek tyrants), and with Plato's *Republic* (with its philosopher-kings) as exemplifying a new, fourth-century willingness to allow virtue and wisdom to a sole ruler, who is somehow elevated above the common herd of his subjects. But it is important not to freight this intellectual trend with too heavy a burden of causal significance in the real world, for example by seeing it as somehow necessarily explaining the political and military triumph of the kingdom of Macedon over the Greek city during the third quarter of the fourth century. That is surely a case of confusing *post hoc* with *propter hoc*. The reasons why the Greeks were defeated by Philip of Macedon at Khaironeia in 338, whereas the Greeks had defeated Xerxes of Persia in 480–479, cannot be simply reduced to a question of monarchist propaganda and alleged loss of confidence in Greek civic republicanism. Aristotle's *Politics*, for instance, a living testament to the vitality of the latter, was written after rather than before Khaironeia. More to the point, even Xenophon's *œuvre* is by no means entirely predicated on the desirability of the triumph of enlightened despotism.

Reluctant Mercenaries

Consider the *Poroi* ('Revenues'), *Hipparkhikos* ('Cavalry Commander'), *Oeconomicus* ('Household-Management'): all presuppose the continued existence of the *polis* of Athens as a going concern, despite the buffetings and setbacks of the 350s, especially the all too successful revolt by important allies in Athens's Second Sea League (founded 378, against Sparta this time, not Persia). But perhaps Xenophon's most striking because least expected testimony to the values of *politeia* is to be found in his *Anabasis*. Here surely, one would have thought, is to be found the very embodiment of the new alternative model of Greek lifestyle outside the framework of the *polis*, as lived by a footloose band of several thousand 'free lance' mercenaries, *xenoi* (in a double sense) who sell their military services to the highest bidder in direct contravention of the 'political' norm of the citizen militia?

Well, yes, but only up to a point, Lord Copper. If there was a 'general crisis of the fourth century', then the proliferating bands of would-be mercenaries are certainly the best evidence for it. Not only were there ever more Greeks willing to exercise their strong right hands outside the framework of their native *politeia*, but ever more Greek states were willing to employ them, non-citizens, to fight on their behalf and in their stead. It was one thing for individuals like the brother of Alkaios in *c*.600 to sign up with an oriental potentate to help him fight other barbarians, quite another for Greek *poleis* fighting other Greek *poleis* to rely heavily on such mercenaries as their principal fighting-force, as the Greek states increasingly did in the fourth century. Aristotle (*Nicomachean Ethics* 1116^{b}15–24) was moved to protest against this trend. However, Xenophon's *Anabasis* is, surprisingly, not the place to look for a theoretical justification of it. On the contrary: not only do the Ten Thousand (the survivors of the 13,000 or more who had fought the Battle of Cunaxa in 401 on behalf of Cyrus, the young pretender to the Persian throne) turn themselves into a '*polis* on the move' (Austin and Vidal-Naquet 1977: 380, quoting Hippolyte Taine), but Xenophon actually considered—or so he claims—turning them into the *politeuma* of a new *polis*, a Greek colony to be planted on the southern shore of the Black Sea. For he 'thought that it would be a glorious achievement to increase the territory and power of Hellas through the foundation of a city'. Unfortunately, the majority of the Ten Thousand decided, democratically (be it noted), against Xenophon's plan (*Anabasis* 5. 6. 15–19).

Aristotle and the Teleological *Polis*

Xenophon, in short, for all his monarchist yearnings, was no more convinced that the Greek *polis* had had its day than was his coeval Plato, whose last work, the *Laws*, was a detailed blueprint for such a colony as Xenophon had projected, only in Crete rather than Asia Minor. We may therefore be more than usually confident that in the *Politics* Aristotle was indeed basing his view of the *polis* on the *phainomena* and the *endoxa* and representing the outlook of the *phronimoi*. Not for Aristotle the world-state possibly dreamt of by his one-time pupil, Alexander the Great of Macedon (reigned 336–323), nor yet the 'United States of Europe' dreamt of by modern federalists looking through rose-tinted spectacles at the League of Corinth founded in 338/7 by his father Philip. For Aristotle, like E. F. Schumacher, small was beautiful, and the *polis* was just the right size and type of political community (*koinōnia*) to realize the good life for mankind.

That, indeed, was the meaning of Aristotle's famous—and usually mistranslated and misunderstood—dictum that man (as a species, mankind) was a *zōön politikon*: not tritely 'a political animal', but a living creature designed by its nature to realize its full, human potential, its 'end' (*telos*) in Aristotle's sociobiological sense, within and only within the political framework constituted by the Greek *polis*. Man was by nature a 'community-animal' (*zōön koinōnikon*: *Eudemian Ethics* 1242^a23–5), but, although other forms of community could provide the means of bare subsistence or existence, only the *polis* could enable mankind to live the true morally good life, the life of 'well-faring' (*eudaimonia*) analysed and argued for in the *Nicomachean Ethics* (a sort of part 1 of a bipartite work of which the *Politics* formed part 2).

There is no reason to believe that all or even most of Aristotle's readers, let alone most Greeks of the third quarter of the fourth century, went all the way with him in their own specifications of the good life for mankind. But they will assuredly have agreed with him, first, on the uniqueness and indispensability of the *polis*-framework, and, secondly, that the *polis* was a 'natural' organism in that it represented an agglomeration of the basic, minimal, human associational units called *oikoi*—households consisting of man, wife, children, and property. So when Aristotle echoes Isokrates (see beginning of this chapter) in claiming that the *politeia* of a *polis*, its rules and regulations governing public civic decision-making, was its 'life as it were' (*Politics* 1295^a40 ff.), there can be no doubt left in our minds that politics, 'the political', really did matter fundamentally both in theory and in practice to the average Greek citizen.

Who Was the Greek Citizen?

And yet, and yet . . . Although Aristotle was himself of citizen status by birth, in his native Stageira in Khalkidikē, he chose to spend most of his adult life in Athens—where his Stagirite citizenship was inoperative. It is time, then, to ask what were the formal, legal qualifications for *politeia* (citizenship) in a given Greek city, and why those criteria were adopted: what ideological or theoretical considerations underlay the granting of citizen-rights, and what civic activities most encapsulated or expressed *politeia* in action? Aristotle the non-citizen still, remarkably, provides more than enough material for adequate answers.

Aristotle's civic man, as we saw, is intrinsically sociable by nature. He must therefore live a life sufficient not only unto itself but also for his nearest and dearest, the *oikeioi* (those who are 'like' oneself, or members of one's *oikos*) and *philoi* ('one's own', 'friends'). Books 8 and 9 of the *Nicomachean Ethics* attempt to answer the question who one's friends are and gives a firmly instrumental response: they are those whom you need and who need you. For this relationship of friendship to work, even if lopsidedly, there must be a certain amount of reciprocity and mutuality, and that in turn presupposes a certain minimum of equality, an equality of nature. It is because women are not (deemed to be) by nature equal to men, for the reasons given in the first book of the *Politics* (see Chapter 4), that they cannot be citizens, because they are incapable of ruling in a truly civic way and must therefore be ruled by the men, for their own good.

The *Politics*, from one point of view, is precisely a treatise on different kinds of rule. The type appropriate for citizens is the 'political' or 'statesmanlike' kind, not the 'kingly', since citizens rule and are ruled in turn reciprocally (1259^b4); indeed, this principle of reciprocity is nothing less than 'the salvation of [*polis*-type] states' (1261^a30-^b5). But such generalizations fail to capture the specific qualities of the citizen, to the definition of which he eventually addresses himself in book 3 ($1274^b31-1278^b5$, esp. 1275^b18-20): 'He [not she] who has the power to take part in the deliberative and judicial administration of a state is said by us [the *phronimoi*] to be a citizen of that state.'

Yet even this definition does not entirely satisfy Aristotle. Theoretically, it would do for all citizens of all states, but pragmatically speaking 'it is best adapted to the citizen of a democracy' (1275^b4-5). Only under a democratic constitution, that is to say, are citizens in fact treated more or less equally, and only there do they genuinely rule each other in turn both judicially and deliberatively. For Aristotle, however, that was not in itself a commendation, since his own oligarchic or aristocratic preference was for a more restrictive definition, one that would have excluded from the citizenship of his ideal state not only manual craftsmen but also working farmers, the very people who constituted the majority of the citizen body of a real-life fourth-century Greek democracy. Why, then, did he wish to exclude the *banausoi* and the *geōrgoi*? Because the nature of their work allegedly rendered their souls servile and slavish, whereas 'political' ruling was by definition something practised by, over, and for entirely free men (1277^b3-7, 1325^a28-30). There was thus for Aristotle a mutually reinforcing implication between the citizen–alien and the free–slave polarities, a view which we shall re-examine in the context of his doctrine of natural slavery (Chapter 6).

Put differently, on Aristotle's largely representative view citizenship was a matter primarily of birth (*genos*), in two senses: first, it depended on a 'natural' condition of *psukhē*, which should be male, free, and Greek; and, secondly, it was a status transmissible by—and usually solely by—heredity. A state like democratic Athens that required double descent (citizen parentage on both sides) took this standard Greek view to its logical limits, adding for good measure the ideological glue of aboriginal autochthony (Chapter 2). Extraordinarily powerful and helpful foreigners, non-Greek as well as Greek, might exceptionally be granted Athenian citizenship, but the status normally accorded to free foreigners like Aristotle who chose to reside permanently at Athens was the status of metic (*metoikos*). That, however, was not in itself a privilege, but rather a strictly limited concession: for it excluded the possessor from landownership as well as political rights, it made him or her dependent on a citizen patron, and, not least, it required the payment of a poll tax. Since the latter necessitated registration of residence and so restriction on one's freedom of movement, it not only was a financial burden but was apparently found no less degrading than the versions imposed in fourteenth-century or twentieth-century England.

Secondarily, citizenship was a matter of occupation—or freedom from certain productive occupations such as mining (reserved for slaves) or working in a mill (a punishment for disobedient slaves). But neither birth nor occupation precluded a role for education. If it had, there would have been no call for political theory of the Aristotelian type, whose principal objective was to devise institutions and practices conducive to civic virtue (*Nicomachean Ethics* 1099^{b}31). Political theory, however, on its own was inadequate. The *polis* itself, too, by means of its laws had the function of educating its prospective and actual citizens in the appropriate virtuous behaviour. As the fifth-century epigrammatist Simonides of Keos put it, *polis andra didaskei*—'the *polis* teaches a man [how to be a true citizen]'. The question therefore was what laws, what form of *politeia* (constitution), what education, should a *polis* have in order to produce good citizens.

Stasis, not Stasis

One answer, a negative one, was those laws, that constitution, and that education which pre-empted the occurrence of *stasis*, a word which in Classical Greek did not have its primary modern sense of 'steady state' but meant a divisive 'standing apart' of hostile political factions that at its most extreme took the form of outright civil war. Greek politics being what they were, an agonistic and zero-sum competition, such an extreme situation was all too often realized. Even in Athens, which was abnormally free from this scourge, the political assassination of Ephialtes in about 460 prompted a profoundly contemporary rejoinder from Aeschylus in his *Eumenides* of 458, and the oligarchic counter-revolutions of 411 and 404 had a lasting impact on Athenian civic practice and ideology. The different reactions to *stasis* of Aristotle, Thucydides, and Xenophon are singularly instructive.

Aristotle's classification of the citizenry of the (any) Greek city was, in the final analysis, both binary and polar. Stated thus baldly, such a dichotomous classification should occasion no surprise to readers of this book. But it deserves particular emphasis in light of Aristotle's desperate wish for there to have been a third term, a middling stratum of moderately disposed citizens who would hold the balance between the other two. However, attention to the empirical facts and intellectual honesty compelled him to admit that, even in those cities where the 'in-between' (*mesoi*) citizens were numerically significant, they did not in fact carry the necessary political weight to make a difference (below).

Thus each and every *politeuma* was composed entirely or overwhelmingly of two mutually exclusive, opposed, and exhaustive groups, namely 'the rich' (*plousioi*) and 'the poor' (*penētes*). This was a quintessentially Aristotelian analysis: it was based on *ta phainomena* and *endoxa*, according to which one's economic status determined one's political outlook and behaviour for the most part, other things being equal, but was given 'scientific' precision and explanatory force. Thus the rich, who were few (*oligoi*), tended to strive to establish or maintain some form of oligarchic (literally, 'the rule of the few') constitution, whereas the poor, who were many, countered by struggling for democracy (literally, 'the sovereign power of the *dēmos*' or 'people'). Aristotle, however, was not satisfied with a merely numerical distinction. The difference in number between the (few) rich and the (many) poor was for him contingent and accidental. What distinguished oligarchy and democracy essentially was real and perceived economic interest. Even if the rich happened (*per impossibile*) to be in the majority, their preferred constitution would still be an oligarchy, since oligarchy was essentially the rule of, by, and for the rich—and vice versa for the poor and democracy (1290^{a}40–^{b}3, 17–20).

At one point, however, Aristotle did concede that the rich–poor dichotomy might be too simplistic, for between the (super) rich and the (very) poor there were citizens of 'middling' (*mesoi*) economic status and correspondingly 'moderate' (*metrioi*) views. Indeed, his own advocacy of a 'mixed' form of constitution, which he rather confusingly labelled *politeia* ('polity'), was actually based on the notion that these *mesoi* would hold the balance of power (1294^{a}30 ff.). But, however desirable they might be in theory, in practice they were never a sufficiently large or homogeneous component to act as a balancing force between the two great classes of citizens. Hence book 5 of the *Politics*, in which Aristotle prescribed various other ways of pre-empting *stasis*. But the practicability of these schemes too was severely limited, as he himself silently admitted by devoting the last two Books to constructing a rather halfhearted paper utopia.

By 338, in fact, *stasis* had become so endemic and destabilizing in Greece that Philip of Macedon sought to outlaw it under the terms of his League of Corinth. Herodotus would surely have been surprised at this, although *stasis* was in itself nothing new to him (e.g. 5. 30; cf. 8. 3. 3). Thucydides, on the other hand, would not have been surprised at all. Indeed, he had both described and unforgettably analysed the phenomenon as a defining feature of his Peloponnesian War. The civil war of 427 between oligarchs and democrats in Kerkyra (modern Corfu) was, he wrote, the first major outbreak, but later on *stasis* 'convulsed practically the whole of the Greek world' (3. 82. 1). For 'convulsed' here he used the verb from which was derived the noun *kinēsis*, 'movement' or 'upheaval', and in his preface he had characterized the Peloponnesian War as precisely 'the greatest *kinēsis* hitherto known both for the Greeks and for a portion of the non-Greeks, and one might almost say for the whole of mankind' (1. 1. 2).

Thucydides' account of the Kerkyra civil war is a classic in the full sense, giving further substance to his boast that his work was written as 'a possession for ever'. What sticks in the memory, above all, is his pungent analysis of the relationship of words and deeds. To correspond to the unprecedented enormity of the horrendous acts of deceit and violence, words too had to be transvalued, sometimes being applied in the exactly opposite sense to their normal usage. For example, an action that normally would have been ranked as the depth of cowardice (*deilia*) was now called the height of bravery (*andreia*). Words, that is to say, did not change their meanings so much as their reference, and in such a world there was no place for reason (*logos* means 'reason' as well as 'word' or 'speech') as conventionally understood. That too is presumably

Plate 1 Myth v. History: Detail of the Parthenon Frieze

Plate 2 Greeks v. Barbarians I: Herakles and
King Busiris on vase, c.470

Plate 3 Greeks v. Barbarians II: Frieze from the Temple of Apollo at Bassae showing Greeks battling Amazons, c.420–410

Plate 4 Men v. Women: Athene decks out Pandora for the
temptation of Epimetheus, vase painting, c.460–450

Plate 5 Citizens v. Aliens: Clothed satyr in conversation
with a young man, vase painting, *c*.430

Plate 6 Free v. Slave: Athenian vase with Thracian slave-girl fetching water, by Aigisthus painter, c.475–450

why Thucydides found no place for *logoi* in the sense of 'speeches' in either his narrative or his analysis of the Kerkyra *stasis*, or in his other extended treatment of this theme in book 8 (45–98, describing the oligarchic counter-revolution of 411 at Athens). For to Thucydides speech connoted a degree of (Thucydidean) rationality, and he simply could not bear to compose speeches consisting of nothing but passionate emotion.

Compare and contrast the practice and theory of Xenophon in the *Hellenica*. For him the second bout of *stasis* at Athens, in 404–403, offered a golden opportunity not to be passed up to indulge his passion for moralizing judgements. His debate (between the oligarchs Kritias and Theramenes: 2. 3. 24–34, 35–49) and his speeches (two by the moderate democrat Thrasyboulos: 2. 4. 13–17, 40–2; one by the herald of the Eleusinian Mysteries, Kleokritos: 2. 4. 20–2) are not about the pragmatics of politics, what Thucydides would have called *ta deonta*, but rather the ethics of loyalty and treachery, the private relationship of friendship and betrayal. What Xenophon approves are the forgetting of past injuries and the forgoing of vengeance or, if revenge be inescapable, the exaction of a limited vengeance compatible with the imperatives of religious piety. Piety, however, although in 'normal' circumstances it may have been 'one of the great unifying forces in any Greek community' (Gray 1989: 101), had done nothing to prevent or moderate *stasis* at Athens in 411 and 404–403. Xenophon's linkage of citizenship and piety was therefore ideological rather than analytical or explanatory, a nice measure of the difference and gulf between his historiography and that of Thucydides (see further Chapter 7).

A Discourse of Civic Harmony

The flipside of *stasis*, its polar opposite, was civic solidarity and harmony. If Aristotle's *Politics* was importantly a response to the kinds of civil war described by Xenophon and Thucydides, the peculiarly Athenian genre of the *epitaphios* (sc. *logos*) or funeral speech was, by contrast, both a celebration of and an encouragement towards maintaining the unusual civic harmony that characterized the Classical Athenian democracy. Unfortunately, we have only six surviving examples of the genre, one a pastiche (Plato's *Menexenos*, attributed to 'Aspasia'), one a literary reworking (by Thucydides of Perikles' original of 430), one a mere fragment (by Gorgias, who, along with Lysias, was not an Athenian citizen), and only two both composed and delivered by the same person (Demosthenes and Hypereides). But despite their diverse origins and present conditions, they constitute a remarkably homogeneous 'corpus'. The Thucydidean *epitaphios* (2. 35–46) may thus serve as a surrogate for them all, making due allowance for Thucydides' personal contribution.

Two features deserve special emphasis from the point of view of the political. First, this is the Athenian civic discourse *par excellence*, even more so than tragedy, since it is directly and exclusively about Athenian citizens, past, present, and future, and their *oikeioi*. 'Men are the *polis*', said Thucydides' Nikias in 413 following the major disaster at Syracuse, when many thousands of Athenian citizens were about to die (7. 77. 7). It was precisely to celebrate and commemorate eternally such dead Athenians, citizens who had died on campaign for the *polis*, that the institution of the *epitaphios* had been originally devised (perhaps in about 460). For not only was it *dulce et decorum pro patria mori*, but death in battle or on campaign was the sweetest and most fitting, the best, sort of death for an Athenian citizen. According to Herodotus' Solon (1. 30), notionally addressing Croesus of Lydia and citing the example of the otherwise unknown Athenian Tellos, human happiness consisted in just such a death.

Thus the major civic lesson of Perikles' *epitaphios* was, *in nuce*, that a man who had died bravely had done everything expected of him; and it was indeed expected of him, since etymologically manliness (the literal meaning of *andreia*) was equated with bravery, and bravery in battle on behalf of the *polis* was an essential component in the hierarchy of citizen values. Yet 'Perikles' was at pains to stress also that these were values that the Athenian citizen had freely chosen—no oriental slavery for Athenian citizens. 'The fine death is the model of a civic choice that is both free and determined' (Loraux 1986*a*: 104).

But Perikles' *epitaphios* was political in a second, narrower sense as well. It was a specifically democratic discourse, and thus both implicitly and explicitly contrasted Athens's 'rule of all by all, freely and openly' with the governance of heteronomous and authoritarian Sparta. The passion and conviction with which Thucydides makes his Perikles laud Athens's democratic institutions and culture ('an education for all Hellas') has sometimes been misinterpreted as an expression of Thucydides' own feelings towards the radical Athenian democracy under which he grew up. Closer attention to the surprisingly aristocratic features of the *epitaphios*, coupled with Thucydides' own explicitly hostile judgements on democracy in both theory and practice (2. 65. 7, 9; 8. 97. 2), rule such a reading out of court. Thucydides was no ideological democrat, nor can his historiography in general be called in any useful sense democratic (*pace* Farrar 1988).

Rather, the context in which the speech was delivered—a collective state funeral for Athens's war dead in the Kerameikos cemetery located at the very heart of the city—demanded an ideological construction that was fully in harmony with the city's democratic *politeia*. But, as is often—perhaps necessarily—the case with ideologies, what it left out, what it did not say, was as important as what it included. Two major exclusions were *de rigueur*. First, metics. Although by definition not citizens, those resident aliens who were male, of military age, and could afford to equip themselves as heavy-armed infantrymen were required to fight for Athens as hoplites. Such metic hoplites were, we know from Thucydides' narrative, recruited to the standards in large numbers at the beginning of the Peloponnesian War and suffered casualties; and since Xenophon in a pamphlet on revenues (*Poroi* 2. 3) refers to 'Lydians, Phrygians, Syrians, and barbarians of all sorts' among the metic hoplites, some of them at least in the mid-fourth century were freed slaves. Yet of their very existence Thucydides' Perikles breathes not a word. They, along with the men and women kept in slavery, constituted the Other within.

Secondly, the democratic *politeia* of Athens, notoriously (as it may now seem to us), excluded women formally and publicly from all but a religious role and function; and their exclusion constituted a problem. The one massively jarring note in the Periklean *epitaphios* was struck near its end, by the seemingly reluctant and grudging reference to 'the virtue of the women who will now be widows' (2. 45. 2). Institutionally, as we have seen (Chapter 4), the problem arose from the male Athenian citizens' preoccupation with legitimacy of descent and inheritance, a legitimacy that had to be conferred by Athenian women no less than by themselves. Ideologically, however, it stemmed above all from the universal Greek construction of male–female difference by analogy with the free–slave polarity—or so I shall argue in the next chapter.

6

Of Inhuman Bondage

Free v. Slave

> This is all contrary to reason, in conflict both with itself
> and with common sense, like Simonides' 'long story', the
> sort that slaves tell when they have no sound excuse to
> offer.
>
> (Aristotle, *Metaphysics* 1091^{a}5)

> How can I love Mount Vernon
> with its green alleys and its river perspective
> and its slave quarters?
>
> (from Marge Piercy, 'Contribution to
> Our Museum')

Slavery Begins at Home

Periodically, the position and condition of female domestic
'staff' of Filipino origin working in London surface in the
British national press, usually in connection with some particularly lurid court case. Properly classified as 'slaves', these
women have also been referred to as 'second-class citizens',
wrongly, since they are not citizens of the United Kingdom in
any sense. The Classical Greeks would not have made that
mistake. For them, 'slave' was by extension the antithesis of
'citizen', since a Greek citizen was by definition free (if sometimes, very exceptionally, of servile origin). On the other hand,
given that the Filipino slaves are foreign women, the Greeks
would not have found their status entirely odd. For most of
the non-Greek women who were domiciled in Classical Greek
lands were slaves. Indeed, as we shall see, Greek women too
might be literally enslaved in Greece; and even if they escaped
that fate, they typically suffered the next greatest indignity of

being categorically lumped together with or assimilated to slaves in the male supremacist thinking of free Greek citizens.

We shall return in due course to the ways in which slaves were used, and what their rights were, in Classical Greece. But the Filipino women of London also raise an important issue of moral principle and historical method. For they provide a tart reminder that, despite the undoubted successes of William Wilberforce and the Anti-Slavery Society he helped to found a century and a half ago, slavery still 'flourishes' today. In fact, there are estimated to be some 3,000 slaves in Britain (mostly belonging to the economically and sexually exploited type of the Filipino domestic staff); and in the world as a whole there are thought to be more slaves of one sort or another than there were when Wilberforce was performing his good works. Should we, or can we, be morally neutral on this? That is surely impossible. But can we, or should we, remain neutral on the fact of slavery in Classical Greece? That is a far more contentious issue, at any rate for those of us who still wish to attribute considerable vitality to the Greek legacy. For if we believe that Greek civilization was in some sense based on slavery—rather than merely acknowledging that Greek societies contained slaves—we shall surely require some remarkably potent antidote to slavery's poison, some extremely powerful toxin to kill the worm in the Greek miracle's bud.

Just such an antidote has been suggested by the Harvard historical sociologist Orlando Patterson, himself a Black West Indian and thus a product of that British enslavement which Wilberforce eventually abolished. No one has done more than Patterson to define cross-culturally the essence of the slave's condition, which he classifies as 'social death' (Patterson 1982). The slave, that is, suffers both natal alienation, having been forcibly ripped from his or her original ties of kin and community, and permanent estrangement in the alien society into which he or she has been forcibly transplanted as a non-assimilable outsider. Although—or rather because—not physically killed at the point of enslavement, the slave must pay for survival indefinitely with a symbolic, living death. Yet, rather as the biblical honey flowed from the carcass of a lion, so, Patterson argues in his recent history of freedom (1991), out of slavery there was born among the ancient Greeks the western world's most cherished value of freedom—personal, sovereignal, and civic. The relation between the two, he further contends, was a causal one, and, moreover, he believes there is an unbroken continuity in the transmission of the value of freedom from the Greeks to us. Hence for him both freedom and slavery, inseparably joined like siamese twins, together constitute a central part of the Greek legacy and the Western cultural tradition.

This is in a way a comforting message. However, not only is it strictly indemonstrable but it may also obscure the precise role and force of slavery in Classical Greek mentality. I prefer therefore to recall how one item in the Greeks' slave-holding legacy was invoked to justify the enslavement of Indians during the Spanish conquest of America. That item was Aristotle's doctrine of 'natural' slavery. Whether or not Aristotle would have approved of this practical application of his doctrine is of course unknowable, but I shall suggest that on his own terms he would have been hard put to it to assert that it was at all legitimate.

Ideology or Philosophy?

One Roman definition of the slave was *instrumentum vocale*, a tool with a voice. A telling definition, from one point of view, since it codifies the dehumanization or depersonalization that is central to the master–slave relationship; but an ironical one, too, in that the slaves of the ancient Greek and Roman world—unlike those of the American Old South—are for us unutterably silent. Hardly a single original word written by an ancient slave while in servitude has come down to us. This is a horrible and tragic fact, given the many hundreds of thousands of slaves that existed at all periods of classical antiquity. However, as with the silence of ancient women (see Chapter 4), this under-representation of slaves in their own write is less of an obstacle for us than it might be for someone attempting to write an economic or social history of the Classical Greeks. For what we are concerned with is the ideology of slavery, the way in which slaves and slavery were represented by, for, and to the literate, slave-holding element of the Greek citizen estate.

A prize specimen of such representation is Aristotle's doctrine of natural slavery, but since this appears within the framework of what is formally a work of political theory, the *Politics*, I shall keep open for the time being the question whether the doctrine should be classed properly as philosophy (within the framework, of course, of Aristotle's own philosophical system) or rather as ideology, that is a doctrine consciously or unconsciously overdetermined by social rather than philosophical imperatives.

The doctrine might at first sight appear to be Aristotle's response to what David Brion Davis (1988: 62) has called 'the inherent contradiction of slavery'. This consists, Davis averred, 'not in its cruelty or economic exploitation, but in the underlying conception of man as a conveyable possession with no more autonomy of will and consciousness than a domestic animal'—an *instrumentum vocale*, in other words. Simone Weil was making a somewhat similar point when she spoke of the 'logical contradiction' in slave-holding between the conception of a person both as a human being and as a thing, adding savagely that 'what is impossible in logic becomes true in life and the contradiction lodged within the soul tears it to shreds' (Weil 1986: 188). However, although Aristotle too defined the slave as a 'tool' (*organon*) and a 'possession' (*ktēma*), he nevertheless did not deny that the slave as well as the slave-holder possessed a 'soul' (*psukhē*). Indeed, he defined the 'natural' slave as precisely an 'animate' or 'ensouled' (*em-psukhon*) tool or possession. What was it, then, about the 'natural' slave's nature that made him or her for Aristotle a slave by nature rather than by mere social (especially legal) convention?

The doctrine is hard to summarize accurately, partly because the *Politics* is not a polished literary production for a wide general readership but rather a set of compressed lecture-notes for his immediate pupils which he would have elaborated at greater length in face-to-face discussion. But it requires more than usually close attention for two main reasons. First, it was Aristotle's announced method to proceed from that which seemed to be the case or to be admirable in the eyes of prudent, practically wise Greeks, that is, from received opinions that he considered to be reputable on matters not susceptible to codification or analysis in terms of mathematical formulae. If, therefore, Aristotle's doctrine of natural slavery was a refined version of such reputable, practical wisdom on slavery, through it we are gaining access to something approaching the standard view of the supposedly rational Greek slave-holder on the nature and justification of slavery. Secondly, and relatedly, although slaves were everywhere in Greek society, not least at Athens, it is a separate question whether that society should be held to have been based on slavery: without the slaves, would Classical Greek civilization have been inevitably and incomparably different? Aristotle's iron commitment to the natural necessity of slaves for the living of the good life in the *polis* by non-slaves may help us answer that vital question.

The initial postulate, that the good life for mankind can be lived only within the framework of the *polis*, is crucial for Aristotle. Opposed as he was almost temperamentally to all merely conventionalist theses, he had little difficulty persuading himself that the *polis* was a natural organism. It was within and for this ideal 'commonwealth' (*koinōnia*) for political man that slavery existed and had to exist. But how were the appropriately 'natural' slaves to be identified? Following the lead of his mentor Plato, he identified them on broadly intellectual grounds, by reason of their lack of the normative kind of intelligence that marked out the truly free, civic human being. The *psukhē* of a natural slave, that is, was for Aristotle irremediably deficient in the ratiocinative element or capacity.

Here, briefly, is the supposed demonstration (the key passage is *Politics* 1253^b–1255^{b}30). Aristotle begins at the level of the *oikos*, the lowest common denominator or minimal constituent of the organic association that is the *polis*. Each and every *oikos*, he asserts, is composed broadly of two mutually exclusive categories of people, free and slave. But that binary analysis in fact masks three paired subcategories of members: master and slave, husband and wife, father and children. The reason for Aristotle's choice of these three and not others (e.g. mistress and slaves, or mother and children) is that he is thinking in practical terms of household-management (*oikonomia*, not to be confused with our 'economy') and therefore in terms of different kinds of hierarchical rule. After mentioning only to dismiss a rival hypothesis that the acquisition of goods through commercial exchange is the whole or the most important part of *oikonomia*, Aristotle proceeds to analyse 'mastership', the rule of a master over slaves, from both a practical and a purely theoretical standpoint.

Again, he begins by mentioning rival views that he will either explicitly or implicitly reject. Most importantly, he takes pains to reject explicitly the view that holding another as a slave is contrary to nature, a matter of mere *nomos* (artificial and arbitrary convention), since by nature the free person and the slave are identical, and slaveholding, because it is based on force, is morally unjust. Clearly Aristotle, who had devoted book 5 of the *Nicomachean Ethics* to defining justice, could not accept that his 'natural' *polis*, of which masters and slaves were 'natural' and necessary parts, was by virtue of that very fact unjust. Hence his ensuing, seven-step argument in favour of his doctrine of natural slavery.

The first step is to assert that property and the art of acquiring it are necessary parts of houshold-management, since both mere existence and the good life for mankind depend on the availability of necessary material goods. The next is to assert that the man skilled in household-management needs tools to perform the necessary work on his property. Thirdly, Aristotle asserts that such tools may be either inanimate or animate, literally without or with a *psukhē*. Fourthly, an article of property is a tool designed with a view to making life possible, and property in general is a mass of such tools, so slaves *qua* tools are animate articles of property. Fifthly, Aristotle distinguishes between making and doing: some tools, such as shuttles, are instruments of production (*poiēsis*), whereas others are instruments of action (*praxis*)—that is, they enable their possessing user to behave in a certain way. Slaves, Aristotle asserts, are such (qualitative) instruments of action, rather than (quantitative) instruments of production. The sixth step is to assert that an article of property is like a part of a whole. The slave, considered as an article of property, is therefore a part of the master, inasmuch as the slave belongs to and is wholly owned by the latter. The seventh and final step is to assert that such a slave is a slave by nature, in that the *oikos* to which the slave belongs and mastership (*despotikē*) are themselves natural phenomena, and the slave serves the master to whom the slave belongs by nature as an instrument of *praxis*.

But if that is what a natural slave is in theory, the question remains whether any in actual fact exist. Sliding from objective to subjective classification, that is, to classification by the slave's individual nature, Aristotle asks first if anyone exists who is by nature of this (servile) kind. Next, he asks whether it is 'better and just' for anyone to be a slave—or is it rather the case, as some of his opponents have alleged, that all slavery is contrary to nature? Happily, for Aristotle, there is no doubt of the right answer to these questions, in both theory and practice. For some things, he claims, are marked out at birth to be ruled, others to rule, and of these two polarized types of things there are (he digresses) many varieties. But before he specifies precisely what it is in virtue of which the 'natural' slave is marked out at birth to be ruled, he prepares the ground with a disquisition on the best natural condition of *psukhē* in man.

Just as the household can be analysed as a set of polarized and hierarchically ordered pairings, so in every living creature (*zōon*) a basic bipartite and hierarchical distinction may be drawn between their *psukhē* (soul, mind, intellect) and body. In man the best natural condition obtains when the best *psukhē* rules the best body, as a master rules a slave; and a human *psukhē* is in the best natural condition when the *nous*, the part of it that contains reason (*logos*), rules over the appetitive and emotional parts, precisely as citizens or kings rule respectively their fellow citizens and subjects. On the other hand, a situation of mutual and equal rule between *nous–logos* and appetite–emotion is harmful in all cases; *a fortiori*, it is harmful when the *nous–logos* is actually ruled by appetite–emotion.

To reinforce this analysis of the ideal soul–body and intra-soul relationship and condition, Aristotle proceeds again by analogy. The rule of the *psukhē* over the body, and of the reasoning part of *psukhē* over the appetitive and emotional parts, is analogous to the rule of humans over animals and of male humans over females, since humans and male humans respectively are relevantly superior by nature and therefore ought to rule—for the benefit of the ruled. With the ground thus elaborately prepared, if also unevenly and slipperily (note especially the prior introduction of the master–slave relation as a comparandum for the soul–body relation), Aristotle can at last (1254^b22-3) reveal what it is about the natural slave, apart from the natural relationship to the master, that makes him or her naturally slavish. It is that, although the natural slave has a share in reason, it is only a partial share: though sufficient to enable the slave to recognize that the master's superior reason ought to be obeyed, it is completely incapable of independent reasoning on its own behalf.

Nor, Aristotle adds for good measure, is the natural slave's inferiority confined to the *psukhē*. It is an inferiority of body too. For the posture of the natural slave is less erect than that of the natural master, so that the former is better suited to performing tasks involving stooping (manual crafts and agriculture), whereas the latter was intended by nature to practise the *politikos bios*, the life of a Greek citizen or actively political member of a *polis* in both war and peace. This latter is, to say the least, a weak, indeed a broken-backed, supporting argument. But the reason why Aristotle adduces it now emerges: whereas it is not so simple to identify securely the nature of a person's *psukhē*, his or her posture is immediately and irrefutably apparent; and as the contemporary Aristotelian tract entitled *Physiognomics* (806^a7-8) puts it (though this work associates upright posture with masculinity rather than freedom), 'permanent bodily signs will indicate permanent mental qualities'. However, even as he adduces it, Aristotle himself exposes its weakness. 'Very often', he confesses, 'the exact opposite is the case.' 'Natural' free men, that is to say, stoop and so have (ser)vile bodies.

That, moreover, is not the only problem that Aristotle, honestly, envisages for his natural slavery doctrine. The very terms 'to be a slave' and 'slave' are, he admits, ambiguous, since—a major concession to his conventionalist opponents— 'there is such a thing as a slave by *nomos* alone'. By that he means to refer to war-captives who, even when not slaves by nature, are slaves both *de facto* and *de iure* (that is, by right of conquest). But Aristotle is careful not to concede any more than this: certainly he would not countenance the extension of the conventionalist thesis to embrace all servitude, without regard to the inner psychic nature of the slaves in question. In any case—and here Aristotle moves triumphantly to the con- clusion of his argument—even those who assert that war- captives are justly slaves in accordance with *nomos* do not in any event mean to refer to Greek war-slaves, but only to barbarians. How much better therefore it would be if these opponents of his would only accept the doctrine of natural slavery in all its rigour. For the latter is entirely consonant with their view of the justice of enslaving barbarians, inasmuch as for natural slaves it is both just and expedient to serve as slaves of a master to whom they belong. Indeed, between such natural slaves and masters there can even exist a limited and conditional kind of instrumental friendship (cf. *Nicomachean Ethics* 1161^{a}35–^{b}5).

Aristotelian Meanness

Aristotle's doctrine, then, hardly constitutes a philosophically adequate demonstration of the naturalness of slavery, either in general terms or in the specific context of the Greek *polis*. It is both ethically retrograde, in comparison to the views of those unnamed opponents who rightly condemned all slavery as based on force and therefore morally wrong, and flawed by its unexamined presuppositions. The question naturally arises, therefore, as to why the giant thinker, the founder of western philosophical logic, should have been on such bad form here. Why was Aristotle so committed to the conclusion that slavery was just and justified, that he made such a hash of the argu- mentative premises?

Two factors, I suggest, overwhelmed his normal moral and intellectual integrity. First, slavery was so embedded in the *phainomena* and the *endoxa*, so much a part of the air that the Greeks breathed (as it had been since time immemorial, or at least since Homer), that apparently not even Aristotle's comparatively enlightened opponents took the step of calling for its abolition: 'everyone was agreed that the institution must be preserved' (Finley 1980: 121–2). Secondly, Aristotle's gloss on the ordinary free Greek's view of slavery could be woven seamlessly into his anti-conventionalist, teleological view of the good life for mankind within the *polis*. For, aside from purely notional automation, he could imagine no alternative to slavery as a means of providing the privileged Greek citizens with the necessary leisure (*skholē*) for their *praxis* of politics and philosophical contemplation. 'No leisure for slaves' went the adage (quoted by Aristotle at *Politics* 1334^{a}20–1), since it was they, rather, who provided the citizens with theirs.

These two reasons received massive reinforcement from an easily observable fact of Greek social life. Most of the many thousands of people held in slavery throughout the Greek world in the third quarter of the fourth century were of barbarian origin (*genos*). As we have seen (Chapter 3), the stereotype of barbarian natural inferiority was well established already by *c*.450 at the latest, thanks largely to the Greek victory over the Persians in 480–479. In so far, therefore, as Greekness was identified with freedom—spiritual and social as well as political—and slavery was equated with being barbarian, Greek civilization, culture, and mentality could be said to have been based, ideologically, on slavery. That dismal conclusion was what Aristotle in his convolutedly philosophical way was in effect acknowledging.

Arguably, however, Aristotle's doctrine of natural slavery was both doing and was intended to do more than merely underpin the existing status quo in Greece. Consistently enough, when Aristotle came to sketch his own version of a perfectly ideal state at the end of the *Politics*, he advocated that the workforce of primary agricultural and manufacturing producers should consist of barbarian slaves, people whom he labelled *perioikoi* ('dwellers round about') to indicate their literally marginal political and social status. But that idea or ideal was not destined to remain confined to the realm of pure theoretical speculation within the Lyceum thinktank. For in the years immediately succeeding the compilation of the *Politics* in the mid-330s, his former pupil Alexander the Great of Macedon effected the conquest of much of the Middle East, a crucial part of which process was the establishment of new Greek cities with labour forces consisting precisely of barbarian *perioikoi* or slaves. Again, as we have seen, in a later epoch of imperialist expansion the Spanish *conquistadores* of the Americas invoked Aristotelian doctrine to justify their enslavement of the Indian populations. But whereas it would of course be unfair to pin the blame for that on Aristotle, his responsibility for the geographical extension of servitude during the post-Classical Hellenistic era is not so easily denied or ignored.

Between Free Men and Slaves

Take away the barbarian slaves, and one would have been left with a very different Classical Greek world, not only materially but mentally and even spiritually. Just how different will become apparent shortly, after looking at the uses to which slaves were put in the Greek world and at the wide metaphorical extension of 'slavish' as an opprobrious epithet. But before leaving the theoretical, definitional discussion of the 'free v. slave' antithesis, I wish to consider first the post-Aristotelian formula 'between free men and slaves', which both demonstrates that the antithesis of free and slave was not in either strict logic or sociological fact a polar antithesis and reflects the increasing sophistication of ancient Greek historiography of slavery.

The formula is preserved in a second-century CE lexicon (Pollux *Onomastikon* 3. 83) but probably goes back to the third-century BCE literary critic Aristophanes of Byzantion: 'Between free men and slaves are the Lakonian Helots, the Thessalian Penestai, the Mariandynian Dorophoroi, the Argive Gymnetes, and the Sikyonian Korynephoroi.' This statement is neither juridically precise nor entirely factually accurate, but the important thing is that, unlike the normative binary classification, it does recognize different degrees and kinds of unfreedom. The various groups of *douloi* in the Greek world had acquired their status in different ways and were held as slaves on different legal and social terms. Some were Greek, most were barbarians, some were collectively enslaved, others individually, some had more privileges than others, more 'elements of freedom' in their lives, and so forth. Moreover, according to this formula, free and slave were being viewed as if they lay along a single continuum of social status, rather than as two mutually exclusive and hierarchically superposed categories. The formula implied, in other words, a 'spectrum of status with the free citizen at one end and the [chattel] slave at the other and with a considerable number of shades of dependence in between' (Finley 1981*i*: 98). Such a conception, I suggest, could not have been entertained widely, let alone normatively, before the Hellenistic period, when the powers and prerogatives of the independent Greek *polis* were so circumscribed that the free Greek citizen had lost his place of honour in the imagination of Greek political philosophers and commentators.

Of the groups mentioned by Pollux, by far the best known, and historically the most significant, were the Helots of Sparta. However precisely one ought to classify them, they alone could have earned the dubious accolade they received in 421 BCE of being included explicitly in the terms of the treaty of alliance sworn between Athens and Sparta after the first, ten-year phase of the great Peloponnesian War: 'if the slave class (*douleia*) should revolt, the Athenians are to come to the aid of the Spartans with all their strength to the limit of their ability' (Thucydides 5. 23. 3). Only the Helots could have been regarded as a collective threat in this way, and the absence of a reciprocal clause binding the Spartans to aid the Athenians in the event of revolt by their *douloi* speaks worlds for the unbridgeable gulf between the Helots—Greek, ethnically homogeneous, collectively owned, self-reproducing, having limited family and property rights—and the heterogeneously multinational (mainly barbarian), individually owned chattel slaves held in Attica.

Fifty years later, however, in the wake of Sparta's defeat by the Theban-led alliance at Leuktra in Boiotia, the Helots of Messenia, the majority population, did revolt (again) from Sparta and did so successfully and permanently. Such was the impact of this mass liberation of a long enslaved portion of Greek humanity that one contemporary Sophist was moved to the proto-abolitionist assertion that 'God has made no man a slave' (Alkidamas, quoted by an ancient commentator on Aristotle *Rhetoric* 1373^{b}).

Greek Historiography of Servitude

About thirty years further on, the Messenians' revolt had a second, no less memorable intellectual fallout, when the dyspeptic historian Theopompos of Khios (*Fragmente der Griechischen Historiker*, ed. F. Jacoby, 115 F 122) became the first writer on record to offer a historical account of the qualitative distinction between what we call 'chattel slavery' (*esclavage marchandise*) and other forms of unfreedom, including what some of us would be prepared to call serfdom. According to Theopompos, his own Khiot ancestors had been the first Greeks to buy slaves individually on the market, the standard Classical mode of acquisition, whereas previously Greeks had acquired them collectively, internally and by military conquest. Whatever the empirical basis for this partly patriotic claim, it was no accident that the distinction was drawn at the same time as Alexander was renewing an older Greek form of slave-procurement by conquering and enslaving the native peoples of the Middle East.

Hitherto the mere fact of slavery had not interested Greek historians; indeed, as we have seen, the naturalness of slavery by dint of timeless historical precedent had occluded the drawing of crucial distinctions. Instead, what did interest them was unusual modes of acquiring slaves, unusually large concentrations of them, and the unusual behaviour or treatment of slaves. For example, an episode such as the abortive conspiracy of Kinadon at Sparta in about 400 captured their imagination because it presented the highly exceptional spectacle of would-be collaboration between free and slave on a political stage.

Aristotle cited the Kinadon episode *exempli gratia* to illustrate how *stasis* might arise within an 'aristocratic' form of political organization 'when a man of high spirit, like Kinadon the leader of the conspiracy against the Spartan peers in the reign of King Agesilaos, is debarred from honours and office' (*Politics* 1306^{b}33–6). But his knowledge of the episode, like ours, comes from Xenophon's remarkably full narrative account (*Hellenica* 3. 3. 4–11), which he in turn had very likely based on information from his patron and friend Agesilaos himself. Like Aristotle, Xenophon is far more interested in the 'Inferior' (i.e. degraded ex-citizen) Kinadon than in the rest of his alleged associates and prospective supporters, and he does not single out the Helots for special emphasis. But he does include them, along with the members of the 'Inferior', Perioikoi and Neodamodeis (ex-Helot), categories, as desiring Homerically to 'eat the Spartiates even raw'. In the event the conspiracy was successfully aborted by the Spartans' efficient counter-insurgency regime, but merely to sketch the possibility of such a combination of sub-citizen categories for revolutionary purposes was an adequate means of illustrating the peculiarity of the Spartan polity by comparison with, above all, Athens.

Equally, in his other two references to non-chattel slaves in the *Hellenica* Xenophon is not interested in them for their own sake but for the light they shed indirectly on his principal objects of concern. The first involves the Penestai of Thessaly, one of those groups classed as 'between free men and slaves' by Pollux (above). According to the speech written by Xenophon for Theramenes in his life-and-death struggle with Kritias in 404, Kritias after the overthrow of the extreme oligarchic regime of the Four Hundred at Athens in 411 had spent part of his exile in Thessaly, supplying arms to the Penestai with a view to establishing democracy there (*Hellenica* 2. 3. 36). The idea of the oligarch Kritias attempting to foment democratic revolution through servile insurrection is so fantastic that the allegation must surely be true. Whatever his motives may have been, the sociologically significant point is that only such slaves as the Penestai, who like the Helots were Greeks and enjoyed certain privileges denied to barbarian chattel slaves, could possibly have been considered suitable for undertaking political activity of this sort.

The other relevant reference in Xenophon concerns those whom Pollux calls the Korynephoroi ('Club-bearers') but who more accurately were known as the Katonakophoroi ('Rough Cloak-wearers'). In the 360s one Euphron succeeded in making himself tyrant of Sikyon. To Xenophon the man was an out-and-out villain. Not only did he betray Sparta but he practised a democratic form of dictatorship. It was therefore only fair that he should have been assassinated (in Thebes). But in order to persuade his readers of the justice of Euphron's fate, Xenophon composed a long speech of self-exculpation for the assassins, which included the following charge: whereas he put to death and confiscated the real property of the Sikyonian upper classes, 'he not only freed slaves but he actually made them citizens' of Sikyon (*Hellenica* 7. 3. 8). Euphron was not the first Greek tyrant to liberate serf-like unfree people and make them citizens: in that he had been anticipated by Dionysios I of Syracuse (405–367 BCE). But Euphron was the first to liberate and enfranchise Greeks belonging to this intermediate category of servitude (the liberated Helots called Neodamodeis were not given the political rights of Spartan citizenship), and the first to do so in the interests of promoting a broadly democratic form of government. In gratitude, therefore, Euphron's own citizens 'brought his body back [from Thebes to Sikyon] and buried it in the *agora*, and they worship him as a founder-hero of the city' (*Hellenica* 7. 3. 12).

Chattel Slaves in Battle

Mass liberation of non-chattel serf-like people was rare enough in Classical Greece. Yet rarer, for the obvious reason that it trespassed on rights of private ownership, was the mass-liberation of chattel slaves who had been purchased on the open market. Nevertheless, it did occasionally occur, most famously in 406, in the dying phase of the great Peloponnesian War.

Athens's empire and international power more generally had rested since the 470s on her fleet of trireme warships. Financed partly by a tax on super-rich Athenian citizens, partly from the revenues of the state-owned silver-mines at Laureion (a 'treasure of the earth', as Aeschylus called them), but more especially from the burdens of tribute and other imposts placed upon Athens's subject-allies in the so-called Delian League, the Athenian fleet ruled the Aegean waves virtually unchecked before 413. In that year, however, the Athenian expedition to Sicily was finally defeated with a huge loss of both manpower and naval *matériel*. The Spartans, aided by Persian subsidy, could at last begin to mount a serious challenge to Athenian supremacy at sea, and in 407, under the admiralship of Lysander, the Spartan alliance finally won a significant naval victory at Notion.

The Athenians' response was typical. Absolutely every available human and material resource was thrown into defending what remained of their empire and revenging themselves on landlubbing, medizing Sparta. The extremity of the situation as perceived by the Athenians is attested above all by the decision of the Assembly to tap slave manpower for service in the fleet. There was nothing new in an Athenian fleet including non-Athenian-citizen rowers. In fact, the fleet had often depended for its full complement of rowers on the hiring of foreign mercenaries, simply because of the numbers required (a large fleet of 200 ships needed 40,000 men, roughly the size of the entire Athenian citizen-body in the third quarter of the fifth century). But these extra hands had hitherto been drawn from free Greek citizen stock, mainly citizens of the states allied to Athens. It would therefore have been a major breach of principle for the Athenians—unlike the Romans, whose galleys were regularly propelled by convict and slave crews—to recruit slave rowers. Hence the compromise adopted in 406 for the Battle of Arginousai: in Xenophon's spare formulation the Athenians 'put aboard these ships all those of military age, slave or free' (*Hellenica* 1. 6. 24). From Aristophanes' *Frogs*, however, staged early in 405, we learn rather more: those slaves who volunteered were granted not just their personal freedom (secured by purchasing them from their owners with state funds) but also Athenian citizenship—a collective passage from servitude to citizenship that was possibly unprecedented (though it may have occurred for Marathon in 490) and certainly not repeated (in the 330s merely to propose such a thing rendered the proposer liable to the death penalty). Many of the new citizens of course lost their lives in the battle, as they knew they probably would, but the desired victory was nevertheless achieved, if a Pyrrhic one.

As at Athens in 406, so on Kerkyra in 427 the ruling democratic regime offered freedom (though not also citizenship) to slaves to fight on its behalf. But whereas the Battle of Arginousai was an interstate conflict, on Kerkyra the slaves were being invited to participate in a civil war. What makes the situation so interesting is that, although the oligarchs made a matching offer of freedom, 'the great majority of the slaves joined the democratic side' (Thucydides 3. 73–4). Interesting, but tantalizing also, because that is precisely all that Thucydides chooses to say. Did the slaves opt for the Kerkyraian democrats because they calculated prudentially that they were the side more likely to win? Or because they thought (as oligarchic propagandists like Theramenes certainly claimed, e.g. Xenophon *Hellenica* 2. 3. 48) that democrats were 'softer' on slaves?

Another state that made use of slaves for fighting in the Peloponnesian War was Theopompos' Khios, the supposed originator of chattel servitude. This we learn, not from Thucydides, but from a contemporary inscription that has been plausibly interpreted as meaning that in the closing phase of the war Khios liberated slaves, quite probably for naval service, and grouped them into 'decads'. What Thucydides does say about slaves on Khios is, however, interesting enough, especially as he makes a direct comparison with Sparta, whose slaves were of a different type: 'There were many slaves (*oiketai*) on Khios —more in fact than in any other single *polis* apart from Sparta; hence, because of their number, they were treated more harshly when they committed offences' (8. 40. 2)—meaning either more harshly than they would have been otherwise by their Khian masters or, in broader perspective, more harshly than deviant slaves typically were in the Greek world as a whole (of which Thucydides' first-hand knowledge extended beyond Athens at least to the Amphipolis region of Thrace, 4. 105).

No Safety in Numbers?

That last numerical statement cannot literally have been true. There were not, and could never have been, absolutely more *oiketai* on the island of Khios (area 858 km^2) than there were in the much larger (2,400 km^2), richer and more populous home territory of Athens. What Thucydides was probably intending to refer to, therefore, was the relative density of the slave populations of Khios and Sparta as a proportion of their respective free citizen populations: David Hume made this inference as long ago as 1742 in his brilliant essay 'Of the Populousness of Ancient Nations'. Absolutely, though, there is no doubt but that Attica contained more (chattel) slaves than Khios, even if not as many as there were Helots in Lakonia and Messenia. However, precisely how many slaves there were at any time in Classical Attica has long been a scholarly battleground, at least since Hume. The problem is that the couple of ancient figures preserved—400,000, allegedly from a census of the late fourth century; and 150,000 adult males, implying something like 400,000 in all including women and subadults—are both fantastic, physically impossible quantities.

Modern estimates or 'guesstimates' have ranged from a low of 20,000, proponents of which claim that only the very richest Athenians and metics owned slaves, to a round 100,000 at the peak of Athens's prosperity in the 430s. The latter in my view is far nearer the truth, but even if this top-of-the-range figure is adopted, it is worth stressing that it would make the slave element no more than about 40 per cent of the total population. That is not wildly out of line with the far better documented modern slave societies of Brazil, the Caribbean, and the American Old South. If, on the other hand, we reduce the maximum figure for slaves at any one time to 60,000–80,000, that would give especial point to the one contemporary figure that has some claim to our credence.

For in the years following the Spartan occupation of Dekeleia within Attica in 413, according to Thucydides (7. 27. 5) 'more than twice ten thousand slaves (*andrapoda*) ran away, and of these the great part were skilled manual craftsmen (*kheirotekhnai*)'. We do not know what Thucydides based this numerical claim upon, though there is a chance that he had access to relevant documentary evidence; but even if it were just an 'educated' guess, the disastrous economic impact of the loss of between a quarter and a third of Attica's total slave population would have been such as Thucydides ascribed to the Dekeleia occupation. Moreover, if many or most of the skilled craftsmen Thucydides singled out had been employed as ancillary workers in the Laureion silver-mines, as is geographically quite plausible, their flight would have had not merely economic but also political and military consequences. For mine-revenue constituted a basic resource for the construction and maintenance of the Athenian fleet.

Man-Footed Creatures

Thucydides, as we have seen, did not only use the most common of the dozen or so current Greek words for 'slaves', namely *douloi*. Speaking of Khios and Sparta, he employed *oiketai*, a term that signified literally 'members of households (*oikoi*)' and could therefore sometimes be applied to free as well as unfree members. But the word he chose to describe the score of thousands of Athenian slaves was an exclusively and unambiguously slave term: *andrapodon*, literally a 'man-footed thing'. This was formed by analogy with a standard Greek word for cattle, *tetrapoda* or 'four-footed things', and so provides as perfect an illustration as could be hoped for of the normative Greek construction of slaves as subhuman creatures. In its more precise application, however (and the Greeks' servile terminology was as a rule anything but precise), *andrapodon* appears to have been the *terminus technicus* for those slaves, typically barbarians, who had been acquired through capture in war (the verb was *andrapodizō*) and sale by slave-dealers (*andrapodistai*) who followed in the train of armies. On this, as on so many other aspects of Greek slaveholding and dealing such as the slaves' places of origin and functions, Herodotus is a peculiarly informative witness.

For the most part, naturally enough, Greek sources are

more interested in barbarians as slaves than in the slaves owned by barbarians, but Herodotus as ever had broader horizons. Eunuchs may well have been, as Xenophon's fictional Cyrus believed (*Cyropaedia* 7. 5. 60), uniquely trustworthy, but in Herodotus' view that end did not in any way justify the 'most unholy' means whereby eunuchs were procured for the real-life Persian court, at least not when the trade was in the hands of Greeks like the man from (we are not now surprised to learn) Khios with the grandiose name of Panionios, 'All-Ionian' (Herodotus 8. 104–6). Another Herodotean passage (1. 114) may imply that the Medes, imperial predecessors of their Persian kinsmen, regularly bred slaves, something the Greeks normally avoided for economic reasons. What the Greeks' normal means of acquiring slaves was emerges through Herodotus' canonical 'mirror' technique. The Scythian kings, he states emphatically, did not buy slaves for cash (4. 72. 1)—by implication, that was precisely what the Greeks usually did.

But sadly for Herodotus, they did not always buy the 'right' kind of slaves in the 'right' way. At some unspecified early date in the island's history Methymna on Lesbos ganged up on the unfortunate Arisba and liquidated it by means of *andrapodismos*, that is the sale into slavery of the surviving inhabitants. The force of Herodotus' moral condemnation is concentrated into the concessive phrase 'although they were related by blood' (1. 151). It is no surprise to find the notion that Greeks should not enslave their fellow Greeks expressed by the author of the famous persuasive definition of Greekness (8. 144. 2) considered in Chapter 3. But the fact that Plato felt obliged to repeat it in the *Republic* (496bc) some forty years later indicates that the ideal was increasingly being honoured only in the breach. Once more, the chief culprit was the long and brutalizing Peloponnesian War. Thucydides' spare descriptions of the fate of Torone (5. 3. 4) and Melos (5. 116. 4) are just two items in a dispiriting catalogue of Greek enslavement of Greek. The standard practice, it would appear, was for the surviving males of a defeated Greek city to be killed and only the women and children to be carted off into servitude abroad, whether in Greece or elsewhere. Such discrimination by gender and age may have served to reinforce free Greek male stereotypes about the naturally slavish quality of those below adult male citizen status.

Barbarian Sources

Typically, though, and normatively, barbarians were the Greeks' preferred source of human servitude, and to judge from Herodotus, backed up by other literary, documentary, and visual evidence, the major country of their origin was Thrace or roughly modern Bulgaria. If in modern English usage Bulgaria has given its name familiarly to homosexual anal copulation ('buggery'), Thrace for the ancient Greeks was apparently almost synonymous with slavery. Poor Thracians, Herodotus (5. 6) was perfectly prepared to believe, habitually sold their surplus children to slave-traders, and all three of Herodotus' individual examples of non-Greek slaves are Thracian by origin.

The individuals in question comprise, first, the Getan Zalmoxis, allegedly (though Herodotus is sceptical) once the slave of Pythagoras the sixth-century Samian mathematician and moral philosopher, to whose school we owe the table of opposites preserved by Aristotle (see Chapter 2, Table 1). 'Whether there was ever really a man of the name, or whether Zalmoxis is nothing but a native god of the Getai, I now bid him farewell' (4. 95–6). Secondly, and probably no less legendarily, there was Aesop, he of the tales, also reputedly the slave of a Samian master. In his case, though, Herodotus, who knew Samos well, provides the added circumstantial detail of the master's name, Iadmon (2. 134). But there is room for doubting the truth of almost everything about Aesop, including his authorship of the tales. Still, even if their author was not in fact this Aesop, there is a peculiar aptness in these fables of veiled resistance, told from the point of view of the oppressed and powerless, being attributed to a slave.

Herodotus' third named Thracian slave, Rhodopis, has an altogether better claim to our credence, even if it is rather too much of a coincidence that she is said to have been a fellow slave of Aesop in the ownership of Iadmon. Whereas 'Aesop' allegedly put his mind to work, it was Rhodopis' body that Iadmon was determined to exploit. For he set her up in business as a prostitute (Rhodopis, 'Rosycheeks', was just her Greek working name) at the Graeco-Egyptian port-of-trade of Naukratis in the Nile Delta. Being sexually very attractive, Herodotus avers, she amassed great wealth—for a person in her condition; the proof of that was a lavish dedication at Delphi seen by Herodotus himself (2. 135). However, it was not for her money, most of which anyway presumably went into the pocket of Iadmon, that Rhodopis' eventual liberator was smitten with her, but for her beauty. In about 600 one Kharaxos son of Skamandronymos and brother of the poet Sappho (small world!) 'redeemed her for a vast sum' and thereby helped to immortalize her name—or at any rate a close approximation of it: with pardonable poetic licence Tennyson celebrated her as Rhodope.

Changing places from fairytale Naukratis at the turn of the sixth century to the mundane world of late fifth-century Athens, we obtain a rare documentary insight into Greek slaveholding from the so-called 'Attic Stelai' recording the official sale by public auction of property confiscated from the fifty or so men convicted of sacrilege for mutilating Herms or profaning the Eleusinian Mysteries in 415/14. One of the records inventories the sixteen slaves confiscated from the metic (not citizen) Kephisodoros. Five of these, three women and two men, were Thracian, constituting the largest national contingent among a cosmopolitan bunch drawn from six nationalities. It was as if Kephisodoros were anticipating in practice the firm injunction of Plato and Aristotle not to hold slaves of the same ethnic origin, an injunction prompted by the Spartans' management problems with their Helots.

A further confirmation of the importance of Thrace as a source of the Athenians' servile population is that Thratta ('Thracian female') was a standard 'stage' name for a female slave, and Getas (from a Thracian people) a male equivalent. But yet more graphic an illustration is an elegant red-figure *hydria* or water jar of *c*.470 that may even have been decorated by a slave painter: it depicts three women collecting water from a fountain, but that they are slave women of Thracian origin is indicated by the elaborate tattoos on their arms, a sort of national stigma (above, pp. 44–6, Plate 6).

Servile Functions

Herodotus' references to servile functions, although by no means exhaustive, and failing characteristically to discriminate between chattel and non-chattel slaves, do cover an adequately broad spectrum, reminding us that in Classical Greece it was not the case that 'a slave is a slave is a slave'. At the top end of the scale was a slave like Sikinnos, the *paidagōgos* or 'tutor' kept by Themistokles to look after his several sons. Through the good offices of his (of course exceptionally influential) master Sikinnos not only gained his personal freedom but was accepted into the citizen body of Thespiai in central Greece (Herodotus 8. 75, 110) which, along with Plataia, was one of the only two cities of the Boiotians, who otherwise 'medized', to have taken the Greek side during the Persian Wars; its citizens fought, for example, shoulder to shoulder with Leonidas' heroic 300 Spartans at Thermopylai. Below Sikinnos came those Greek slaves who at the cost of their manhood achieved high status at the Persian court as eunuchs (above) or, if female, were taken to be concubines of Persian grandees, such as the (unnamed) aristocratic lady from Kos whose father was sufficiently distinguished to be a *xenos* of the Spartan regent Pausanias (9. 76, 81).

Humbler still were the Spartans' Helots, 'between free men and slaves' from one point of view perhaps but nevertheless obliged to carry out their daily tasks as unfree labourers. Most male Helots worked in the fields, but relatively privileged individuals included the royal donkeyman and prison guard mentioned by Herodotus (6. 68, 75), and it was presumably on the whole more tolerable to be a mess attendant (Plutarch *Comparison of Lycurgus and Numa* 2. 7) or, if female, a household servant (Plutarch *Agis* 3. 2) in Sparta than a driven field hand out in the Eurotas or Pamisos valley. On the other hand, if Herodotus' figure of 35,000 (9. 10) is anywhere near correct for the number of Helots enlisted by the Spartans as light-armed soldiers for the Plataia campaign of 479, the supply could not have been confined to the more privileged, Sparta-domiciled Helots.

Among the chattel slave sector, the most privileged were those who worked for themselves as well as for their master or mistress. Rhodopis the prostitute has to stand proxy for this group in Herodotus, but apart from such female (or male) prostitutes the sort of slave who managed best economically was the skilled craftsman set up in business with start-up capital provided by the master and then allowed to keep a portion of the income from sale of his products. Our best evidence for these 'living apart' slaves is furnished by the Attic orators of the fourth century.

As for run-of-the-mill, comparatively unskilled chattel slaves, it is a major modern debate whether they were regularly employed in peasant agriculture in Classical Greece. Herodotus unfortunately provides no directly relevant evidence, although he does mention the agricultural slaves owned by the Hellenized Lydian called Pythios (7. 28). As a rule of thumb, however, it may be assumed that citizens who could afford hoplite armour, roughly the top thirty or forty per cent, would normally aim to have at least one male slave, who would serve his master as a batman on campaign. But a rich, leisured Greek landowner, the counterpart of Pythios, would be expected to maintain a moderately large permanent servile labour force for agricultural purposes, in a social context where fifty slaves was considered a very large number indeed (Plato *Republic* 578de).

A Return to Ideology

In any case, slave-ownership was not a matter simply of economics and practical utility: what better way was there to demonstrate one's own 'natural' freedom than to command the labour power of another human being? In the final sections of this chapter I return therefore to the ideology of Greek slavery, first asking whether there is any pre-echo of Aristotle's 'natural slavery' doctrine to be detected in our selected narrative sources, and then examining the ways in which the 'free v. slave' ideal polarity was intercut with and either reinforced, or was reinforced by, our other four principal polarities, 'Greeks v. barbarians', 'men v. women', 'citizens v. aliens', and—the subject of our next chapter—'gods v. mortals'.

It is Herodotus (4. 1–4), not altogether surprisingly, who provides us with a pre-philosophical, supposedly realistic, instance of 'natural slavery' thinking. The context is Scythian, not Greek, but Scythia here serves Herodotus and his addressee not as Greece's other but as a mirror held up to the nature of slaveownership. The tale is 'paradigmatic, not as history, since it is fictitious from beginning to end, but as ideology' (Finley 1980: 118). The Scythians, so it is told, once invaded Media and stayed on there for a generation, with the result that their wives back home had sex with their blinded but not otherwise incapacitated slaves. This intercourse produced progeny, a whole mixed-blood generation that proved unwilling to yield place when the errant Scythian husbands eventually returned. There ensued a series of conflicts in which the returnees made no headway until one of them observed, 'So long as they [the slaves] see us bearing regular arms in our hands, they think they are our peers in birth and quality (*homoioi ex homoiōn*). But let them see us with horsewhips instead of arms (*hopla*), then they will realize that they are our slaves (*douloi*), and recognizing this will not be able to resist us.'

So indeed it transpired, and the clear contemporary (mid-fifth century) message of this cautionary tale was that slaves are not equal either in birth or in quality of character to their masters, that they are in a word inferior by nature. The context is Scythian, but, as the surely deliberate Spartan reminiscence (*homoios*) was intended to imply, it is no less if differently applicable to Greece than Herodotus' already quoted assertion that Scythian kings do not buy slaves for cash. There are, moreover, similar stories with different outcomes generated for Greek cities, for example that of the so-called 'servile interregnum' at Argos in the early fifth century (6. 83). To cover a temporary shortage of adult male citizens caused by a Spartan massacre, 'the slaves took over everything in government and all management' until the sons of the massacred dead grew to manhood. But the slaves refused to return power quietly to the freeborn citizens and had to be driven out of Argos, and continued to wage war from neighbouring Tiryns 'for a long time, until, with difficulty, the Argives at last won the upper hand'. Not necessarily any more *vero* than the Scythian tale, this story was no less *ben trovato*.

Greeks: Barbarians:: Free: Slave

One of the half-dozen or so most significant passages for Herodotus' own outlook and purpose in writing his *Histories* is the encounter between the medizing Spartan king Damaratos and his new liege lord Xerxes, in which the Greek—despite his formal position of subservient powerlessness—boldly and paradoxically asserts that *nomos*, the rule of law, is the only master (*despotēs*) that the Spartans recognize, whereas Xerxes' subjects know only how to be his slaves. That passage (esp. 7. 104. 4) has been considered fully in our third chapter under the Greek v. Barbarian rubric. But there is a further, comparable passage in book 7 (133–7) which repays attention in the present context.

The dramatic context is some four years earlier than Damaratos' exchange with Xerxes, somewhere around 484, when the Spartans had first got wind of Xerxes' plans for an invasion of Greece. The Spartans were an unusually pious or superstitious people, as Herodotus twice insists (5. 63. 2, 9. 7), so when the entrails of publicly slaughtered sacrificial victims began regularly to convey signs of ill omen in the 480s, they interpreted this as a divine judgement upon their earlier act of impiety in murdering the Persian herald whom King Darius had sent to demand tokens of submission from them in the late 490s. After heated public debate in the Spartan assembly, itself a rare occurrence, they decided that it was both necessary and opportune to make atonement (*poinēn teisein*) to Darius' son Xerxes in a suitably religious way, by sending him two rich and noble Spartans from the hereditary heraldic family of the Talthybiadai as a reciprocal, expiatory sacrifice. *En route* to Susa, however, they were intercepted by Hydarnes, satrap generalissimo in the West of the Persian Empire, and required to attend for interview, probably at Sardis.

Submit to Xerxes, Hydarnes commanded, and Xerxes will do right by you, that is, give you as it were 'most favoured nation' status within the prospective Persian administration of subject Greece. But the Spartans would have no truck with this: 'You know well how to be a slave [to Xerxes] but you have not yet experienced freedom, so you do not know whether it is sweet or not.' Thereupon Hydarnes sent them packing to Susa, where they were ushered into the royal presence. But when the palace guards tried to force them to make the customary obeisance (*proskunēsis*) to Xerxes, the Spartans hotly refused, on the grounds that 'it was not their custom (*nomos*) to do *proskunēsis* to a mere man (*anthrōpos*, rather than *anēr*, which may therefore have borne the further connotation of barbarian man)'.

This nicely illustrates the mutual implication and reinforcement of at least the 'free v. slave' and 'gods v. mortals' polarities, and probably the 'Greek v. Barbarian' polarity as well. Free men, Herodotus' Spartans imply, freely worship only the gods, respecting the unbridgeable status-gap between gods and mortals, whereas slaves like the barbarian Persians, including even the highest-ranking among them, are compelled to worship a mere mortal man. (In actual historical fact, *proskunēsis* was not a religious but a socio-political act of homage, but that of course does not affect the ideological point.) However, for all that Herodotus presumably endorsed this ideological implication, he nevertheless did not choose to draw that moral explicitly here, as he had in the related *nomos despotēs* exchange. Indeed, ever full of surprises, he chooses to turn the tables on the Spartans and allow the barbarian despot Xerxes to emerge with the greater honours.

For Xerxes refused the Spartans' expiatory sacrifice of the two men 'out of greatness of soul' (*megalophrosunē*) and declared that he would not be *homoios* (a pun, once more) to the Spartans, that is, would not sink to their level. For by killing Darius' herald the Spartans had 'broken the *nomima* of all *anthrōpoi*', what are elsewhere (Sophokles *Antigone* 453–7, *Oedipus Tyrannus* 865–70; Thucydides 2. 37. 3) called the 'unwritten' laws held in common by all mankind, barbarian as well as Greek. Moreover, when the sons of the two heralds whom Xerxes had refused to kill were themselves killed some fifty-five years later, through treachery by the semibarbarous Thracians, Herodotus actually crows, 'In my view this was clearly a deed of divine origin (*prēgma theion*).' For him this was a clear instance of the sins of the fathers being visited on the sons, and in his book impiety towards the gods (the killing of heralds who, though barbarian, were by virtue of their office sacrosanct) overrode even the imperative of Greek freedom in the purely human sphere.

Free : Slave :: Men : Women?

The Athenian 'charter' myth for the occupation of Lemnos was considered in Chapter 2 under the 'myth v. history' rubric, but it bears also on the connection, in normative male Greek thought, between women and servility. According to the Herodotean version of the myth, the Athenians' daughters once regularly fetched water from the fountain 'because neither they nor the rest of the Greeks at that time possessed household slaves (*oiketai*)' (6. 137. 3); the same point is made, humorously one hopes, by the comic playwright Pherekrates (Austin and Vidal-Naquet 1977: no. 15). The invention of slavery, that is, was explained as a substitute for female familial labour, but the association of thought between women and slavery went much deeper than that. It was not confined by any means to the retrospective discourse of myth.

In the contemporary, putatively realistic, discourse of history, as we have seen, whereas defeated Greek men were killed by other Greeks, their womenfolk (and children) were regularly enslaved. But perhaps even more suggestively, in the theory of the supposedly objective discourse of Aristotle's *Politics* we find women placed analogously on a par with slaves in relation to their husbands: as slaves are to their masters, so wives are to their husbands. What was natural about Aristotle's 'natural' slave was his or her total deficiency in *nous* or *logos*. In women the deficiency, according to Aristotle, was not total but none the less crucially significant *vis-à-vis* men. Man, in short, must, necessarily, rule Woman. At least Aristotle did not go as far as St Paul, who used precisely the same word (*hupotassesthai*) for the subjection of slave to master as for the (ideal) subjection of wife to husband. For Aristotle, significantly, it was the barbarians who failed to make the necessary distinction between rule over wives and rule over slaves (*Politics* 1252ᵃ30–ᵇ15).

Free : Slave :: Citizen : Alien

On the other hand, Aristotle did claim that in democracies as in tyrannies (Aristotle was no democrat) slaves and women (and children) had a better time of it than they ought to have had if they had been properly supervised by the male citizens (*Politics* 1313ᵇ35, 1319ᵇ30). This unholy coupling of slaves and women under the umbrella of democracy is reminiscent of Thucydides' account of the Kerkyra *stasis*, in which women and slaves anomically joined forces in a public, political context to support the democratic side (3. 73–4). It also brings us to consideration of our final interconnection of polarities, between 'free v. slave' and 'citizen v. alien'.

'Freedom' ultimately came to be understood as the catchword of democracy. The conjunction of democracy with tyranny, as made by Aristotle, could not have been effected by an ideological democrat, at any rate by an Athenian democrat. For him, as we saw from the Tyrannicides myth (Chapter 2), democracy was centrally identified as the antithesis of tyranny. That identification of democracy with anti-tyranny can be traced from Herodotus' ideological celebration of Athenian *isēgoria* (5. 78) to the Athenian law against tyranny passed soon after the defeat of Athens by Philip of Macedon at Khaironeia and the incorporation of Athens in his anti-democratic League of Corinth in 337/6. Since Athenian democracy was held to have originated in emancipation from despotic tyranny, Athenian democrats will have been especially vigorous in upholding the view ascribed by Aristotle to all Greek democrats, that the fundamental principle of democracy was *eleutheria*. That is to say, in order to be a citizen in a democracy, the sole necessary and sufficient criterion was free citizen birth—not aristocratic birth, nor great wealth (Thucydides 2. 37. 2). Moreover, being a citizen in a democracy—as opposed to an oligarchy—connoted having the maximum amount of freedom to do what and to live as one wished, the maximum freedom from dictation by another: that was one of the central messages of Perikles' Funeral Speech as represented by Thucydides (see Chapter 5).

For this strictly ideological construction of freedom by Athenian democrats there was in fact some historical support. In 594, before the introduction of democracy, Solon had made debt-bondage illegal for citizens, and thus helped to define sharply the status-boundary between citizens and aliens in Athens; that law remained on the statute-books under the democracy and probably was not significantly breached until after the democracy was overthrown by Macedon in 322. Aristotle, however, being Aristotle, preferred to caricature the democratic slogan of freedom, misrepresenting it as the near-anarchist claim to live as one wishes no matter what the social consequences might be; indeed, he claimed that an extreme democrat, being an extreme libertarian, considered the obligation to obey the city's laws to be a form of slavery (*Politics* 1310^a25-36). The truth of the matter was the exact converse. In Aristotle's day Athenian democrats were remarkably insistent on the irrefragable sovereignty of the laws and very circumspect about altering them by addition or subtraction. But the Athenian oligarchs in whose name Aristotle was speaking were not going to allow themselves to be confused by the facts.

Among several examples of Athenian anti-democratic propaganda on the record, perhaps pride of place should be awarded to that contained in Xenophon's innocuous-sounding *Memoirs of Socrates* (1. 2. 40–6). The main object of this invented dialogue between the arch-democrat Perikles and his opportunist ward Alkibiades is to get Perikles to concede that democratic majority decision-making, whereby the poor masses of the citizenry compel the propertied minority to endure decisions taken against their interest, is in fact merely a disguised form of tyranny. The point is made characteristically by having the debate turn on the making of laws, supposedly a frivolous and whimsical pastime for democrats. 'You know, Alkibiades,' says an exasperated Perikles, 'when I was your age I was very clever at this sort of thing too.' 'I wish I could have met you when you were at the height of your powers, Perikles,' was the sassy rejoinder of Alkibiades, who is given the last word.

For an ideological oligarch, in other words, democracy was roughly equivalent to 'the dictatorship of the proletariat', and an oligarch who happened to live under a democratic regime really did see himself and his wealthy peers as being enslaved to the poor majority of citizens (Thucydides 4. 86. 2). But there was also another, sociological way in which oligarchs utilized the ideology of slavery as a weapon in the class struggle against their domestic democratic enemies. This was their definition of certain occupations as 'servile', as fitting only for a slave and therefore as degrading their practitioners' character to the condition of a slave, rendering them unfit for the exercise of citizenship. Some oligarchic extremists took this view to the limit and stigmatized all productive labour as servile on the grounds that it deprived the labourer of the total leisure that was the ultimate mark of the truly free man (cf. above). But most oligarchs drew two relevant distinctions: between working for oneself and working for another; and between agriculture and the banausic manual crafts.

Being self-employed, as long as one had to be employed at all, was seen as crucial, because working for another looked uncomfortably like working for the sake of another, and that in turn could so easily shade into working under the constraint of another. Hired employment, in other words, especially if on a long-term basis, could too easily be construed as akin to, little better than, nothing short of outright legal servitude. Fine discriminations like these were all due ultimately to the need to distance oneself as far as possible from real, legal slavery in a society based (ideologically, anyway) on slavery. One of the neatest illustrations may be found again in Xenophon's *Memoirs of Socrates* (2. 8). A certain Eutheros, who had done quite nicely out of the Athenian Empire, had now fallen on hard times after its overthrow in 404; he could barely earn a crust by performing casual, hired manual labour. So 'Socrates' advised him to take up a more comfortable and secure occupation, which he could continue into advancing age, namely to become the manager or agent of a large landed estate. Heaven forfend, was Eutheros' instant reply, for that would be tantamount to slavery. This attitude was partly based on the fact that estate overseers (*epitropoi*) were sometimes actually slaves or more usually ex-slaves, but it was also instinct with the ideological prejudice that being free connoted being under no permanent obligation to any other individual.

So far as the distinction between work in agriculture and work as a craftsman was concerned, most oligarchs took the view that working the land, at any rate as a peasant proprietor, was incommensurably superior and justifiable, the soldier's school. However, the heavy labour involved in clearing land of thorns preparatory to tilling it could still be dismissed as 'toil fitting for a slave' (*ponos douloprepēs*: Herodotus 1. 126. 5), and Aristotle was not speaking only for himself when he advocated that the primary agricultural producers of his ideal state should be barbarian slaves (*Politics* 1330^{a}20). However, if peasant agriculture *per se* normally escaped upper-class condescension, manual craftsmanship by contrast, no matter how skilled, did not: partly because such skilled craftsmen (potters, armourers, shoemakers, and so on) were regularly slaves, their jobs were considered intrinsically incompatible with the freedom of the true citizen.

Herodotus, for example, was not sure whether the Greeks had borrowed their attitude to such *tekhnai* from the Egyptians, as practically all the other barbarians had, but he was quite sure that all Greeks despised skilled manual craftsmen (*kheirotekhnai*), the Spartans doing so the most, the Corinthians the least (2. 167). From that it does not follow necessarily that the craftsmen themselves, if they were Greek and of citizen status, internalized that negative construction; indeed, even Xenophon could find it in him to praise certain forms of skilled manual labour (*Oeconomicus* 4. 20–5). But Aristotle entirely corroborates Herodotus when he makes it a matter for debate whether *banausoi* should be citizens, as though there were an intrinsic contradiction between being a citizen and practising a banausic craft (*Politics* 1277^{b}35). In this case, at least, we may be certain that Aristotle was faithfully representing the ideology of the Greek ruling classes and that the ideas of the ruling classes were Greece's ruling ideas.

Freedom and Independence Externalized

From metaphorical uses of slavery within a *polis* I turn finally to metaphorical slavery in inter-*polis* relations, and so principally to Thucydides (whose information on literal slavery is, by comparison, jejune). By the time the Peloponnesian War broke out in 431, the chief slogans of Greek interstate diplomacy were *autonomia* and *eleutheria*. They were based, obviously enough, on what Greeks took being citizens and having constitutions to mean. Thus *autonomia* denoted literally the right to make and administer one's own *nomoi*, while *eleutheria* primarily denoted external freedom, freedom from outside interference in one's internal affairs of state, sovereignty in that sense. In propagandistic practice, however, the two were used interchangeably, at least if we may trust Thucydides' verbal fidelity. For in 432/1 the Spartans' final ultimatum to the Athenians went, according to him (1. 139. 3), as follows: 'The Spartans wish there to be peace, provided you Athenians leave the Greeks *autonomoi*.' But in his own person Thucydides commented editorially, 'Public opinion by a long way favoured the Spartans, especially as they were proclaiming it as their aim to free (*eleutherousin*) Hellas' (2. 8. 4).

Athens, in other words, was being represented by Sparta as a tyrant city, a doubtless conscious irony in view of Athens's official abhorrence of tyranny at home. This was a view that Thucydides allowed both Perikles and Kleon to endorse (2. 63. 2, 3. 37. 2), and that he allowed himself maximal reflection upon through the medium of the 'Melian Dialogue' (5. 84–116). It was in the light of, and against, this view that Herodotus somewhat hesitantly expressed his own final judgement on Athens's role as 'the saviours of Hellas' in the preceding Persian Wars (7. 139. 1, 5).

Despite the impression Thucydides no doubt intended to convey, it was not all Greeks nor yet the majority, but (as Herodotus implied) many of them, who shared the view of Athens as a tyrant city. For the view was held principally by 'the so-called upper classes' (*kaloikagathoi*) in the states subordinated to Athens in her Delian League alliance, whereas the lower classes of those same states might even envisage democratic Athens as a refuge against their own upper class. Besides, Sparta was itself by no means guiltless of infringing the autonomy of its own allies of the Peloponnesian League, whether by general support given to the upper classes to help them resist democratic takeover from below (Thucydides 1. 19) or by specific and forcible military intervention on the side of the propertied class, as at Mantineia in 385 (Xenophon *Hellenica* 5. 2. 7). Thucydides, in short, spoke with a forked tongue on this issue, his editorializing not always being entirely consonant with his news-columns.

Thucydides, however, was not the only Greek to apply double standards to the interstate sphere. As a general rule jealous preservation of the freedom and sovereignty of one's own state was not found incompatible, in either theory or practice, with depriving another Greek state of its autonomy and independence. On the other hand, for the most ambitious and unscrupulous politicians even the freedom and autonomy of their own state might be willingly sacrificed to the satisfaction of their overriding urge to be in formal control of its organs of power. The *locus classicus* of this syndrome in Thucydides is the behaviour of the oligarchic ultras at Athens in 411. Rapidly losing domestic support for the narrow regime they had instituted by a reign of terror, they turned outside to Sparta. What they wanted above all was preservation of their oligarchic rule, together with control of the Empire, but if the latter was not acceptable to Sparta, then at least they wanted to keep the fleet and the city's fortifications and local self-government (*autonomeisthai*, a euphemism for the maintenance of their oligarchy, which they imagined the pro-oligarchic Spartans might approve). But if that too was unacceptable, then at the very least they trusted that the Spartans would grant them a personal amnesty after they had taken Athens over (8. 91. 3)! Freedom, in fine, was conspicuously divisible in Classical Greece.

7

Knowing Your Place
Gods v. Mortals

No one ever attained excellence without the gods, no
city, no mortal. The all-guileful one is god: for mortals
nothing is free from misery

(Simonides)

The Greeks Did Not Have a Word for It

The Greeks had no one-word equivalent of our 'religion'
(derived from the Latin *ligare* 'to bind', owing to the sense of
binding awe felt by humans in face of supernormal or supernatural phenomena). Nor did they distinguish in quite the
ways we would the 'sacred' from the 'profane' or the 'secular'.
Their vocabulary of sanctity and piety revolved rather around
concepts of appropriateness and order, and depended on
matter and persons being allocated to and remaining in their
proper places.

But perhaps the chief obstacle to comprehending Classical
Greek religion, for those of us brought up within one or other
monotheistic religious culture, is the Greeks' polytheism.
Theirs was a world 'full of gods', as Thales of Miletos (*fl.*
*c.*600) is supposed to have said. Or, as Carlo Levi much more
recently wrote of the incompletely Christianized peasants of
Gagliano in southern Italy, there was no room in their mental
world for religion 'because to them everything participates in
divinity, everything is actually, not symbolically divine' (*Christ*
Stopped at Eboli).

There are of course important continuities as well as discontinuities between Christianity and paganism; not only was
Christianity born within the eastern, Greek-speaking half of

the Roman Empire, but in a crucial sense it could not have been born without it. But the differences between developed Christianity and paganism are far more important, indeed central and essential. In order to bring out this difference of essence, and thus obviate the harm that can be done by interpreting ancient Greek religion in the false light of Christianizing assumptions, it may be helpful to begin this chapter by listing some of the strong contrasts between Christianity (seen as an ideal type, ignoring all doctrinal and sectarian fissures within and between the Christian communions) and Greek paganism.

Christianity, like one of its parents (Judaism), is a spiritual monotheism. It is premissed upon faith in revelation that transcends rational belief and is accompanied by a fervency of emotion. By contrast, the Classical Greeks 'acknowledged', that is paid the due worship to, the gods that their community recognized, so that their faith was chiefly a matter of piety, of performing cult-acts. Christian faith in revelation and the centrality of that faith are anchored to the possession of uniquely sacred texts, a professional priesthood, and a Church (actually, several churches). The Classical Greeks did without sacred books and dogmas for their civic religion, were innocent of the notion of heresy, and had no vocational priesthoods—or priestesshoods (unlike Christians, they not only countenanced the idea of women priests but deemed them indispensable).

Christianity has from the Founder onwards drawn a sharp line between religion and other spheres of social interaction or private experience, most signally between religion and politics ('Render unto Caesar that which is Caesar's, unto God that which is God's') or, as later redefined, between Church and State. This cleavage was to have important historiographical as well as historical consequences (see below). The Classical Greeks, on the other hand, although they were able to distinguish what they called 'the divine' (*to theion*) or 'the things of (the) god(s)' (*ta tou theou/tōn theōn*) from that which was purely or largely human, their *polis* (unlike Augustine's *City of God*) was both a city of gods and a city of men simultaneously: religion and politics (and economics, and war, and so on) were for them inextricably intermingled.

Perhaps the chief reason why Christianity is able to draw such a distinction is that, for a Christian, religion is essentially an individual, personal, and privatized matter, a relation between a particular person's immortal soul and the Almighty. By contrast, the Classical Greeks' religion was typically focused upon relations between men collectively and the gods, and was expressed in collective, official, public rituals, above all festivals. Christianity and paganism, moreover, allot morality a very different place in their respective systems. Whereas Christians claim that their ethical code is Christian in the strong sense that it is grounded directly upon the moral principles laid down by the Founding Fathers, the Classical Greeks had no comparable source of moral authority.

Finally, to quote from the famous fifteenth chapter of Edward Gibbon's *Decline and Fall*, 'The doctrine of a future state was scarcely considered among the devout polytheists of Greece and Rome as a fundamental article of faith', whereas 'the benefits of the Christian communion were those of eternal life'. Although the Greeks did hold afterlife beliefs and many were initiated into mystery religions, what apparently mattered to them most, and most of the time, was the here and now, this regrettably transitory life on earth. One very good reason for this order of priorities was that they, being human, were by definition mortal. By way of polar contrast, according to the usual Greek mode of thinking, it was of the essence of their gods that they were immortal, that is 'forever deathless and ageless', as the poets never tired of repeating.

Greek Religion as a System of Cultural Self-Definition

If Christianity and Classical Greek paganism are so essentially different from and contrary to each other, it might reasonably be asked whether it is helpful to describe the latter as a religion at all. Clifford Geertz's five-point definition of religion (Geertz 1973*b*) would appear to tilt the balance firmly in favour of an affirmative answer, even if one may not wish to adopt it, or at any rate all its phraseology, as a package. For Geertz a religion is a system of symbols that offers 'moods and motivations' predisposing one to act and think in certain ways;

that formulates a conception of a general order of existence (in Greek *kosmos*); that gives these moods, motivations, and orderings a solidary group context; and that binds together disparate features of everyday life into a coherent totality imbued with overarching significance.

Had Herodotus been alive today and cognizant of symbolic anthropology, he might well have agreed that such a definition helps to make sense of an otherwise desperately alien phenomenon. It is, at any rate, congruent with his persuasive definition of Greekness (*to Hellēnikon*, 8. 144. 2), which we have looked at already in connection with the Greek–barbarian polarity (Chapter 3) but bears closer scrutiny in the present context. In winter 480/79 the Persian high command was trying to detach Athens from the small and fragile Hellenic alliance, using their vassal King Alexander I of Macedon as a go-between. To Alexander, according to Herodotus (8. 143), the Athenians delivered an uncompromising retort: 'So long as the sun keeps its present course, we will never make alliance with Xerxes. No, we shall oppose him unceasingly, trusting in as our allies the gods and heroes whom he has slighted by burning their temples (*oikoi*, literally 'homes') and statues (*agalmata*).' For what Alexander was proposing to them was not merely treasonous in the human scale of values, but *athemista*, that is, contrary to divine ordinance, unholy.

After rebuffing the Persians, so Herodotus' account continues, the Athenians made haste to reassure their Spartan allies, who feared that the Athenians might nevertheless be seduced away by Persian gold. Echoing the Callatian Indians of Herodotus' 'custom is king' parable (3. 38), they averred that not all the gold in the world could make them change sides, nor yet the lure of the fairest of territory (even though Attica was by no means such), since to medize would be to 'reduce all Hellas to slavery'—a nice appeal to the equation of Greece with freedom, and the Persian barbarians with servitude. For, they said (8. 144. 2), many and great were the impediments preventing them, above all the following two: (1) specifically, the *agalmata* and *oikēmata* of the gods which Xerxes had impiously burned—these had to be avenged; (2) generally, 'the fact of being Greek', which they further subdivided into three constituents—(*a*) common blood and language, (*b*) common religious ritual of sacrifice (*theōn hidrumata koina kai thusiai*, literally 'common establishments and sacrifices of the gods'), and (*c*) common way of life and outlook (*ēthea homotropa*, partly but not exclusively 'religious'). Here, then, we find religion being given the appropriately central place, sandwiched between and reinforcing their 'racially' and linguistically defined ethnicity and the specific religious obligation derived from the reciprocity principle ('I scratch your back, you scratch mine') that was deemed to govern relations between gods and mortals. The human destruction of sacred sites was always considered by the Greeks to be a self-justifying cause for retaliation and revenge in the name of the gods.

The Origins of the Gods

That neat illustration of the cultural meaning of Classical Greek religion as an explicit ideology is for us only the beginning of our quest to understand the contribution of religion to the making of the Greek mental world. Theoretically armed to the teeth, we may now attempt to advance on three overlapping and not easily separable interpretative fronts into a succession of scholarly battlegrounds: first, the question of origins; secondly, the nature of the Greeks' gods; and lastly, the role of theology in the writing of Greek history.

In the course of his disquisition on Egypt Herodotus boldly asserted that 'the names of nearly all the gods came to Greece from Egypt', this being a particular instance of his general thesis about the direction of origin of all Greek religious customs (*nomaia*), namely from Egypt to Greece and never vice versa (2. 50. 1, 2. 49. 3). For Martin Bernal (1987: 99) this assertion functions straightforwardly as one of the clinching pieces of evidence for his overall 'Black Athena' thesis, that Classical Greek culture as a whole was a direct transplant effected by Egyptian and Phoenician immigrants (see also Chapter 3). But before any such assertion of Herodotus can be used, its implications must first be explicated: what was he meaning to claim about Greek religious origins, and what is the historiographical status of his claim?

Clearly he did not mean that the Greeks borrowed or used Egyptian names for their gods, since he regularly gives the Egyptian name for what he refers to as Greek gods (e.g. 2. 42. 5: the Egyptians call Zeus 'Ammon'). What he must have meant to claim, therefore, is that what came to Greece from Egypt were the gods themselves, or at any rate the concept or idea of them. That inference is confirmed a few chapters later by a famous passage (2. 53. 2): 'Homer and Hesiod were the first to compose theogonies, and give the gods their epithets, to allot them their respective honours (*timai*) and special skills (*tekhnai*), and to describe their forms (*eidea*).' It was not that Homer and Hesiod invented the gods out of whole cloth, but that they so to speak reinvented them for the Greeks, describing and defining them in terms the Greeks could and did comprehend and worship. Put differently, the Egyptians had invented initially the (or a) pantheon, which the Greeks had then much later borrowed and literally transfigured and transformed.

In itself that is a remarkable enough claim, but it is not remarkable in quite the way Bernal supposed. As in most of book 2, Herodotus is here taking special care and a special delight in knocking down Greek ethnocentricity by several pegs. To borrow what Plato was to say explicitly a century later for his own, quite different, purposes (*Timaeus* 22b), Herodotus was as it were telling his Greek addressees that they and their culture were mere children by comparison with the Egyptians, who had been around since time immemorial and had long ago taught the Greeks some of the most basic features of their 'Greek' culture: message—barbarians are not, *ipso facto*, all equally despicable. The truth about the origins of the Greeks' gods, in other words, was not strictly at issue at all, since Herodotus in a sense wanted to have that both ways: the gods both were not and were 'made in Greece'.

This, however, was not Herodotus' only message: he has two hidden agendas, not one, in play simultaneously here. For with 2. 53. 2 we should compare or rather contrast what has sometimes been hailed as the earliest statement of natural religion but is more appropriately understood as the earliest known attempt at a humanistic and rationalistic explanation—

and, in sharp contrast to Herodotus, rejection—of the Greeks' polytheistic pantheon: Xenophanes of Kolophon's theological attacks on both the immorality and the anthropomorphic nature of the gods of traditional religion.

'Homer and Hesiod', ran Xenophanes' hexameter verses as preserved, 'have attributed to the gods everything that is a shame and reproach among men, stealing and committing adultery and deceiving each other' (fragment 166). 'But mortals consider that the gods are born, and that they have clothes and speech and bodies like their own' (fragment 167). 'The Ethiopians say that their gods are snub-nosed and black, the Thracians that theirs have light blue eyes and red hair' (fragment 168). 'If cattle and horses or lions had hands, or were able to draw with their hands and do the works (*erga*) that men can do, horses would draw the forms (*ideai*) of the gods like horses, and cattle like cattle, and they would make their bodies such as each had themselves' (fragment 169).

It may or may not be significant that Herodotus never mentions Xenophanes, but there is no doubt in my mind as to how he would have reacted to his radical relativism—with a horror akin to that of his Callatian Indians when asked to cremate their dead (3. 38). For from Xenophanes' relatively mild protest at the Greeks' projection of their gods as not merely anthropomorphic but human in their manners also it was not too long a theoretical step to outright atheism, that is disbelief in the existence and consequent neglect of the worship of the traditional gods. But so far from being an atheist like his younger contemporary Diagoras of Melos, the believing and pious Herodotus was not prepared to contemplate even the philosophical agnosticism of his reputed friend Protagoras, who wrote: 'Concerning the gods, whether they exist or not, and of what form they are, I cannot speak. The subject is intrinsically obscure and life is too short.' Protagoras was not denying outright the existence of gods (of whatever shape or form or character), but denying that any individual man can discover cosmic truths, so that in his view gods were best banished from rationalistic, humanistic explanatory discourse. If Herodotus shared Protagoras' ethical relativism on the matter of human social customs, including religious ritual practices, he no less firmly rejected anything smacking of doubt in the real independent existence of the traditional Greek gods. Indeed, in addition to his explicit protestations of belief (e.g. in the validity of oracles, 8. 77), his entire work may be seen as an implicit protest against such a radical a-theology. Thus Herodotus' relativism on the difference between the Greek and the Egyptian pantheons posits a cross-cultural continuity of belief in gods as such.

Herodotus' Religious Mirror

Before we turn, or rather return, to the issue of anthropomorphism, therefore, let us explore a little further Herodotus' comparative ethnography of religious customs, to see what light it sheds on the ways in which he manipulated the mirror of his historiography. Two aspects are particularly worthy of our attention: disposal of the dead; and animal sacrifice. As a complement to his book on Herodotus (1988), first published in 1980, Hartog later (1982) devoted a special study to the funeral rites of Scythian kings as described in Herodotus, with a view to illustrating the historian's general comparativist thesis 'Tell me how you die, and I will tell you who you are' (*Dis-moi comme tu meurs, et je te dirai qui tu es*). Hartog's project was to trace a spectrum of barbarian funeral rites, ranging from the most un-Greek to the most Hellenic. He began by quoting from the second-century CE satirist Lucian (*On Mourning* 21): 'the Greek cremates, the Persian inhumes, the Indian places under glass, the Scythian eats, the Egyptian mummifies' the corpse. That statement is not factually accurate—the Greeks did not only cremate but also inhumed; but the attribution of cremation was dictated by the logic of polarized ethnographic discourse, just as in Herodotus' relativist parable of the Greeks and the Callatian Indians (3. 38). Non-Greeks are 'Other', therefore they must dispose of the dead in 'other' ways.

Similarly, it was a matter of complete indifference to Lucian that it was his Scythians who ate their dead, whereas for Herodotus funerary anthropophagy was an Indian rite. How precisely Herodotus' Scythians disposed of their dead kings did, however, matter to Hartog, since he was concerned, first, with the way royal funerals served to mark the relationship of the Scythian people to their territory (*l'espace de la mort*) and, secondly, with their function as a means of comparing and contrasting the Scythian 'others' and the Greeks in the discourse of Herodotus. Among the rituals, predictably enough, we find a classic instance of 'reversed world' othering. In the funeral of a Greek the laying-out (*prothesis*) of the corpse occurred at the home of the deceased, and mourners came there to pay their last respects, before the corpse was laid on a waggon and carried out in procession (*ekphora*) for burial in an extramural cemetery accompanied by a funeral feast. But in a Scythian royal funeral the king's corpse allegedly did the exact opposite— it was laid on a waggon by his nearest kin and taken out and round to all his friends in succession, stopping at each for a feast, over a period of forty days in all, before finally being laid to rest. In case his addressee should miss the point, Herodotus generously spelled it out (4. 76. 1): 'the Scythians have an extreme hatred of all foreign customs, especially those of the Greeks'. That was his cue for telling the sad stories of the deaths of two relatively enlightened, that is Hellenizing, Scythians, who alas were murdered for their assimilationist leanings (4. 76–80).

However, as with the 'usages of women' (Chapter 4), so Herodotus' spectrum of savage barbarian funeral customs is not a case of simple inversion, let alone straightforward opposition of barbarian (and barbarous) Scythians and civilized Greeks. For 'the Greeks' was not itself a homogeneous category, suitable for purposes of simple polarization, as Herodotus to his enormous credit made abundantly plain. To quote Hartog again (1982: 150), 'the grandiose and in many respects unique funeral rites of the Scythian kings invite us, repeatedly, to make comparisons with Sparta'—Sparta, an utterly Greek city from the standpoint of ethnic cleanliness, but one in which hereditary kings were accorded lavish funeral rites that are described in great detail and an ostentatiously ethnographic manner by Herodotus himself (6. 58). Apart from an explicit and general comparative reference to 'what most of the barbarians do', one linguistic trick neatly serves to indicate the un-Greek atmosphere. Instead of the usual *thrēnos*, Herodotus employs for the Spartan women's keening the term *oimōgē*, quite common in Athenian tragedy but otherwise used by Herodotus only of the Persians. In other words, the Spartan royal funeral rites are being represented as not just alien, since they are neither 'republican' nor 'Hellenic', but redolent specifically of oriental despotism.

It is the Persians, too, who provide Herodotus with a basic point of comparison and contrast with the Greeks, here appropriately treated as a unified group, in the fundamental matter of sacrificial ritual (1. 131–2). Again, the comparison is a complex one, the full value of which emerges only when his much more detailed account of Scythian sacrifice (4. 60–3) is brought in as a third term. But since Hartog has done more than justice to the latter (1988: 173–92), I confine myself to the Persian discourse. The Persians, Herodotus observes, 'raise no altars, considering the use of them a sign of folly', although they do make animal sacrifice (*thusiē*) to certain non-anthropomorphic divinities (Sun, Moon, Winds, etc.) 'in the following way: they raise no altars [emphatic repetition], light no fire, pour no libations; there is no sound of the *aulos*, no putting on of wreaths, no consecrated barley-cake'. The point is that, although the Persians did practise animal sacrifice, they practised it in an anti-Hellenic manner. Unlike a Greek sacrifice, for which the sacrificer did not need to be an official priest, no Persian sacrifice was deemed valid unless conducted by a Magus, an expert member of the priesthood (in fact, Median, not Persian, though Herodotus elides the distinction as all Greeks tended to do). There was no distinction made as in a Greek sacrifice between the gods' portion and the portion set aside for human consumption, nor were the innards separated from the rest of the flesh to be roasted, whereas the remainder was boiled. Instead, all the meat was boiled, and it was up to the Magus to do with it what he wished, since he was not under the obligation of his Greek counterpart to distribute some or all to his fellow participants in the sacrifice.

The reason for insisting on the cultural significance of this series of polarized oppositions is hinted at pretty broadly in Herodotus' persuasive definition of Greekness; and if there was one religious ritual that made a Greek conventionally and normatively 'Greek', it was eligibility to participate in a bloody animal sacrifice, which constituted an act of communion in the strict sense. Thus for the full (adult male) citizen of a *polis* it was the very cornerstone of the city, defining precisely what it was to constitute and participate in that peculiar mode of political and social organization. But besides its properly communal meaning, animal sacrifice had also a cosmic, onto-logical function and symbolic significance; it was this ritual above all that situated humankind as a whole somewhere 'between the beasts and the gods' (Vernant 1980*b*). We might therefore add to Hartog's 'tell me how you die' a second, no less determinative, cultural marker of Hellenic identity: 'tell me how (and what) you kill'.

Yet here again 'Greeks' is an insufficiently refined category of distinction, since there were some Greeks, admittedly a tiny minority, who made a virtue of their total abstinence from animal flesh as an essential feature of their religious identity— the members of the Orphic and Pythagorean sects above all. Bloody animal sacrifice, in other words, was not a marker of Greekness simply, or rather not only of Greekness as opposed to barbarianness: it was also a marker of civic status. For those Greeks who were strict vegetarians were also conscientious objectors to full ritual membership in the civic community of the *polis*. Greek religion, one is reminded once more, was essentially a communal, civic affair.

The Debate over Anthropomorphism Renewed

Herodotus was unfortunately born too soon to benefit from the insights into Greek sacrifice of the 'Paris School' of Vernant and Detienne; he was a mere participant observer! But he did, interestingly, venture an explanation as to why the Persians did not sacrifice in the same way as the Greeks. After pointing out, as we saw, that they regarded the erection of altars (and also two other important but not in the same way indispensable items of Greek ritual paraphernalia—statues and temples) as mere 'folly', Herodotus continued (1. 131. 1): 'This comes, so it seems to me, from their not believing the gods to be in the likeness of men, as the Greeks do.' That seemingly uncontroversial opinion in fact plunges us into the heart of the second main issue I wish to tackle in this chapter.

In an influential essay on the Greeks' religious attitudes, A. D. Nock (1972*b*) classified their gods as 'larger Greeks', meaning to imply thereby that Greek anthropomorphism should be taken both literally and seriously by us: for in the eyes of the Greeks, according to Nock, their gods were essentially superhumans, fundamentally like them, but projected as it were on to a huge cosmic-scale screen. Is this view borne out by their historiography? Are the gods of Xenophon, Thucydides, and Herodotus superhuman actors occupying the same stage of dramatic performance? To set the scene, I begin with the more or less conventional reflections and programmes of Aristotle.

All men, according to the Stagirite (*De Caelo* 270^{b}5–10), have some conception of gods, and all those who believe that there are gods agree in allotting to them the highest place on their scale of values. Aristotle himself, although a philosopher, was no atheist, agnostic, or sceptic. He was even prepared to tolerate the propagation of myths, so long as they dealt with the gods (*Metaphysics* 1074^{b}1–14). Perhaps, indeed, that was precisely why he grew fonder of myths the older he got (fragment 668). It was inevitable, therefore, given the congruence of his own views with his society's *phainomena* and *endoxa* regarding the existence and necessity of gods, that the ideal city he began to sketch at the end of the *Politics* should be one of gods as well as men. The 'tribe' of priests, for instance, he regarded as an essential component of the ideal city, since 'it is only right and proper that the gods should be worshipped by the citizens' (1329^{a}27 ff.); the temples of utopia should be sited in conspicuous locations, hard by the communal messes in the town centre (1331^{a}24–31); while over the countryside (*khōra*) there should be scattered shrines in honour of gods and heroes (1331^{b}17–19).

On the other hand, it has to be said that Aristotle does not strive officiously to emphasize the religious element of his ideal polity, and he devotes far more mental energy and space to such mundane matters as the siting of the city, its food supply, educational system, common mess arrangements, sexual practices, marriage regulations, and eugenics. Contrast—and for Aristotle the contrast was surely deliberate—Plato's second best (after the *Republic*) ideal city as constructed in the *Laws*. In direct rejoinder to Protagoras' doctrine, the 'Athenian stranger' (a surrogate for the 80-year-old Plato himself) takes it as axiomatic that, not Man, but 'God is the measure of all things' (*Laws* 716c); or, as a leading modern expert has put it (Burkert 1985: 333), 'in theory the state of the *Laws* is a theocracy'. Which of the two, Plato with his theistic fixation or Aristotle with his temporal preoccupations, was closer to the Hellenic norm?

Not unexpectedly, Aristotle. However, his representation of the normal *polis* religion in the *Politics* is not without ironic overtones. Aristotle, that is, was worldly enough to see how religion could be manipulated for secular, political ends. Also not unexpectedly, but yet more relevant to our concerns, Aristotle's conception of the gods—or 'divinity', 'the divine'— was far more intellectual, spiritualized, and philosophical than that of his *phronimos* (above-averagely intelligent and prudent) man.

Going beyond Herodotus, and echoing Xenophanes, he points out early on in the *Politics* ($1252^b26–8$) that mankind— presumably Greek mankind in particular—conceives the gods anthropomorphically in a twofold sense: not just in terms of their forms (*eidē*) but also in terms of their lifestyles (*bioi*)— here we have Nock's 'larger Greeks' view all right. Aristotle's own opinion, however, differs importantly: as in *On the Universe* ($397^b10–401^b24$), so in the *Politics* (1326^a32) he envisages god as a 'divine power' (*theia dunamis*) that 'holds everything together', as the informing principle of the *kosmos*. Elsewhere, indeed, he gives his conception a specifically intellectualist cast by identifying god with mind (fragment 49). Moreover, in so far as he is prepared to speak of the gods in 'ordinary language' anthropomorphic terms, he emphasizes again and again the qualitative difference between gods and mortals. Perhaps the passage which most graphically expresses their mutual incommensurability and the unbridgeable gulf between them is that in the *Magna Moralia* (1208^b27-31) where he observes that humans cannot be friends with god or love Zeus. For no matter how pious a human being is (in the usual Greek sense of performing ritual actions—making dedications, offering prayers, participating in sacrifices, and so forth), there can be no genuine reciprocity between the two parties, since the inequality between them is too great (cf. *Nicomachean Ethics* 1122^b20-2).

The differences between Aristotle's and the ordinary Greek's anthropomorphic view, however, should not be exaggerated. For example, at the same time as the ritual of animal sacrifice served symbolically as a mode of communication between mortals and the gods, it served also as a marker of the unclosable gap that separated the two parties. The myth of Prometheus as related in Hesiod's *Theogony* and *Works and Days* is emblematic of this separateness. For in order to sacrifice, humankind required the aid of an immortal Titan, Prometheus, but even Prometheus, acting on behalf of humankind, was first obliged to steal fire to enable humans to sacrifice and then had to trick almighty Zeus into accepting the purely olfactory residue of the sacrificed victim as the portion reserved for the gods.

Xenophon, like Aristotle, was clear that men were not really like gods in their physical form, but he could not bring himself to state as much for fear of being tarred with the brush of impiety that had swept away his mentor and idol Socrates— condemned to death and executed in 399 for 'not duly acknowledging the gods the city recognizes and introducing new, unrecognized divinities'. The nearest he comes to an outright denial is in a lengthy Platonic style dialogue in his *Memoirs of Socrates* (4. 3): here his Socrates tells Euthydemos not to hang around 'waiting until you see the gods in physical form' but rather to infer their presence and active intervention in human affairs from their works. The fact of their agency, despite their invisibility, 'Socrates' corroborates with an argument from analogy: like the gods, the human mind is also invisible, yet 'it partakes of divinity if anything else human does [that is, thinking is the nearest humans get to being like gods], and that it is the ruling part of us is evident, but even it cannot be seen'.

As it happens, Xenophon was an uncomplicated believer not only in divine intervention in human affairs, but in divine direction of them in all respects. Human free will or choice was, as the author of the *Hellenica* conceived it, a virtually negligible historical factor. But even if Xenophon's gods or god or 'the divine' (*to daimonion*) were non-human in form and super-human in power, they or it could still experience some remarkably human emotions. After the Thebans have defeated the Spartans at Leuktra (for religious reasons, according to Xenophon—below), Jason tyrant of Thessalian Pherai warns them not to grow overconfident: 'for the god, it seems to me, takes pleasure in raising up the small and bringing down the great' (*Hellenica* 6. 4. 23); the doubtless conscious irony was that the great Jason was himself shortly to be knocked down and out by assassination.

This was not intended by Xenophon as a mere figure of speech. A second example of anthropomorphism in the *Hellenica* demonstrates with particular clarity how even the most pious and god-fearing Greeks found their gods a suitable medium on which to project human values in cases of extreme doubt as to how to act. In 388 King Agesipolis II of Sparta was in charge of operations against Argos during the Corinthian War (*Hellenica* 4. 7). He burned to emulate the great exploits of his senior co-king Agesilaos, and so was not about to be thwarted by Argos' spurious declaration of a sacred truce (*ekekheiria*), a trick they had also pulled in the preceding Peloponnesian War (Thucydides 5. 54). He therefore conducted the prescribed Spartan 'frontier-crossing' sacrifices (*diabatēria*), and finding the entrails propitious, he proceeded northwestwards through Arkadia to Olympia, where there was an oracular shrine of Zeus. Only a dozen or so years previously, the priests of this shrine had forbidden another Spartan king to consult the oracle on the alleged grounds that 'it was an ancient and established principle that Greeks should not consult the oracle with regard to a war waged against Greeks' (*Hellenica* 3. 2. 22). Somehow this principle had been forgotten by 388, and Agesipolis, having duly sacrificed, learned from the god (Zeus) that 'it was right and proper (*hosion*) not to accept a truce that had been offered unjustly'.

However, in order to make doubly sure of his ground, and probably also to leave no room for doubt in the minds of his unusually pious Spartan troops, Agesipolis decided to cross-check by consulting the oracle of Apollo at Delphi. But note his carefully calculated manner of consultation: instead of repeating the question he had put to Zeus at Olympia, he asked Apollo whether on the matter of the sacred truce he was of the same opinion as his father. Since according to the dictates of Greek popular morality (e.g. Lysias 19. 55) filial piety was almost as much a commandment set in tablets of stone as it was for the Jews of the Pentateuch, this was tantamount to leaving Apollo with no choice but to agree.

The sequel shows how wise Agesipolis had been to take out this extra, divine insurance. Just after he had led his army over the border into Argive territory, 'the god shook', another way of saying that there was an earthquake caused by Poseidon. The superstitious Spartans struck up the paean (to Poseidon) to avert further divine wrath and assumed that Agesipolis would at once withdraw. Instead, he chose to interpret the earthquake as a positive omen, since Poseidon had shaken after, not before, their crossing of the Argive frontier. The troops, reluctantly, were persuaded to see things his way, backed as he was by the combined oracular authority of Zeus and Apollo, and they joined in sacrifice to Poseidon. But clearly they, as most Greeks would have done in their place (including apparently Xenophon), had automatically interpreted the earthquake as the hostile act of a 'larger' (and very angry) Greek.

It must be stressed that there was nothing 'unorthodox', let alone irreligious, in the seemingly casuistical behaviour of Agesipolis. Precisely because the gods were made in the image of (larger) men, they were deemed to be amenable to the normal discursive techniques that applied to human inter-

personal relations. However, it did take exceptional confidence
and strength of will, or overmastering worldly ambition, to
handle relations with the divine in quite that way. Far closer
to the Greek norm was Thucydides' Nikias, who—much to the
rationalist historian's evident distaste, not least because of
the disastrous practical consequences of Nikias' addiction—
was 'excessively given to divination (*theiasmos*) and suchlike'
(Thucydides 7. 50. 4). It is very noticeable that the nearest
Thucydides came to making any concession to popular belief
in efficacious divine intervention is in the final speech he
placed in the mouth of Perikles for delivery while the great
plague was at its height: 'the *daimonia* [things sent by *daimones*,
supernatural agencies] we must endure perforce [i.e. because
we can do nothing about them], the things from the enemy we
must endure with manly fortitude' (Thucydides 2. 64. 2). But
even here there is no talk of anthropomorphized intervention,
only of abstract *daimonia*, which for the real Perikles as for
Thucydides himself was very likely a mere figure of speech.

With Herodotus, however, we re-enter the thoughtworld of
Xenophon, a world of anthropomorphized divine intervention.
From a host of possible examples I select just three. First, to
pursue the theme of human illness, there is his account of the
terrible end of Queen Pheretima of Kyrene, who was eaten
alive by intestinally generated maggots. That end, for Herodotus
(4. 205), was intended as a visible proof to mankind that
'violent vengeance earns the envious retribution of the gods'.
My second example is one among the many cultic innovations
prompted by the Greeks' seemingly miraculous victory over
the Persians in 480–479. In 480 the Athenians received an
oracle enjoining them to seek help from their son-in-law,
but who could that be? Study of Athenian myth provided
the answer: Boreas, the personified North Wind, since he
had married the daughter of the founding king of Athens,
Erekhtheus. Herodotus would not commit himself to saying
that it was because the Athenians sacrificed to Boreas that the
north wind 'fell with violence on the barbarians' (7. 189), but
that is precisely what the Athenians did say; and matching
deeds to words, they built a shrine for him on the banks of the

Ilissos river, thereby introducing yet another new god into their official pantheon. It was not only the Persians who sacrificed to winds, even if they did so rather differently.

One final instance of the gods as 'larger Greeks' in Herodotus. Just before the sea-battle of Salamis there was reportedly an earthquake shock felt both on shore and at sea. Such premonitory divine signs tended to cluster around major battles like flies around a honeypot. But much more unusual, exciting, and therefore worthy of Herodotean narrative was another alleged portent, one, moreover, that had unambiguously presaged the Persians' imminent defeat (Herodotus 8. 65). Indeed, so extraordinary was it that Herodotus felt obliged to name his source, a medizing Athenian exile inaptly called Dikaios ('Just')—one of only three such citations in the entire work. A cloud of dust, Dikaios claimed, had risen above the Thriasian plain in western Attica and advanced eastwards towards Athens from Eleusis. Since all Attica had been evacuated, it could not have been any human agency that raised this phantasmagorical dustcloud, yet the noise that emanated from it sounded like the mystic hymn to Iakkhos (Dionysos) sung by initiates in the Eleusinian Mysteries. The inevitable inference, implicitly accepted by Herodotus, was that the gods of Attica themselves (Demeter, Persephone, and Dionysos) had marched to defend their own against the barbarian desecrators of Athens's holy places.

Staying the Hand of God

The third and last aspect of the 'gods v. mortals' polarity that I shall be considering here also raises what is arguably the single most important issue in all Classical Greek historiography. How did Herodotus, Thucydides, and Xenophon construct and construe the role of religion in history? How far, that is, did they believe that it was the gods (or god or the divine) who 'made the difference', who 'caused' human events and processes to turn out a certain way in the sense that, but for their superhuman intervention, they would have turned out otherwise, or not happened at all? By way of background it is worth recalling the lack of any sharp distinction in Classical Greek religious belief and practice between a secular and a sacred sphere, and thus the absence of a theoretical distinction between secular and sacred historiography. That division of the past was a Christian contribution to the western historiographical tradition, and the rift was not healed until Voltaire and Gibbon made its closure central to their Enlightened approach.

I begin with the most straightforwardly theurgical of the Classical historians, Xenophon, and the *locus classicus* of his general approach. The Spartans, by occupying the acropolis of Thebes in peacetime in 382, had indeed broken an oath sworn in the name of the gods to leave the other Greek cities independent and had thus committed manifest perjury on the grand scale. It was precisely for that reason, according to Xenophon, that the Spartans were decisively defeated in battle by the Thebans at Leuktra in 371. This was only one of many instances that 'could be cited from both Greek and non-Greek history to demonstrate that the gods are not indifferent to those who are impious (*asebountes*) or perpetrate unholy (*anosia*) deeds' (*Hellenica* 5. 4. 1).

On a cynical reading one might construe that grand generalization as Xenophon's way of shifting the responsibility away from Sparta's military weakness on to the irresistible might of the gods. But Xenophon of all people would not have done that at the cost of indicting his favourite Spartans for perjury. There is no doubt therefore that Xenophon, himself a man of more than usually demonstrative piety, saw the hand of god everywhere at work in human history, and envisaged it as operating in the strong sense that it made major events happen and happen in a certain way. Indeed, such was Xenophon's piety that he could, and perhaps felt obliged to, explain even civil war (*stasis*) between Greeks who worshipped precisely the same gods in the same way in terms of divine intervention. In 392 opponents of the existing Corinthian oligarchic regime had taken advantage of a religious festival to conduct a slaughter of the innocents (as Xenophon saw them) and effect a political coup. The new regime of Corinth contracted a close union with Argos, prompting Agesilaos to step up the Spartan effort in the Corinthian War. So it came about that during fighting around Corinth's Long Walls 'the god gave them [the Spartans] an achievement (*ergon*) such as they could not even have prayed for', namely a massive counter-slaughter of the anti-Spartan Corinthians. 'How', asks Xenophon rhetorically (*Hellenica* 4. 4. 12), 'could one not consider this a divine dispensation (*theion*)?' Possibly there were those who did not see the massacre as divinely inspired, and this was Xenophon's forceful rejoinder. But far more likely the question was just a particularly vivid way of evoking his and many other Greeks' perception that the gods themselves intervened to punish impiety. From a wider historiographical perspective, however, 'the hand of God is an explanation that dulls the quest for truth' (Cawkwell 1979: 45).

Yet mundane historical truth was not the highest priority for the moralizing Xenophon. In this he was as far from Herodotus as he was from Thucydides. Herodotus, however, agreed with Xenophon in bringing the gods or the divine centrally into his narrative. There is no long stretch in which no reference is made to the gods, or men's attitude and behaviour towards the gods play no role. The question is rather whether Herodotus shared Xenophon's perhaps somewhat simple-minded view of divine intervention and causation: was it chiefly or exclusively the divine factor that for Herodotus explained both the eventuality and the outcome of the Graeco-Persian wars?

There is no doubt that Herodotus did believe that not only oracles (see above) but also prodigies (1. 78. 1), premonitions (6. 27), and dreams (1. 34. 1–2) were divinely sent manifestations genuinely foretelling the future. He was also prepared, as we have seen, to vouch for the gods' direct and efficacious intervention in human affairs, especially to exact due vengeance. Several of his leading characters, for example King Croesus of Lydia (1. 13. 2, 1. 91. 1), are said to be 'bound' to come to a bad end, and to that same Croesus Herodotus makes 'Solon' express the classically anthropomorphized view that 'the divine (*to theion*) is full of jealousy and fond of throwing human affairs into confusion' (1. 32. 1). At one point Herodotus even speaks through 'Croesus' in apparently mechanistic terms of a wheel of human affairs that is in constant motion and never allows people to remain undisturbed in a condition of good fortune (1. 207. 2). Yet for all that, Herodotus remarkably was not—or not only—a fatalist and theurgical determinist whose theology excluded human agency and so historical responsibility altogether. As has been acutely observed (Gould 1989: 80), 'to understand Herodotus' thinking about divinity we need to distinguish between supernatural explanations of specific events which befall specific individuals, and a general theory of historical causation'.

To test that distinction there is no better case than his presentation of Xerxes' decision to invade Greece in 481/0. The factors Herodotus considered relevant to that decision are dramatized, and the improbability of Persian defeat underlined, by way of a series of dreams (7. 12–19). But although divinely sent, the dreams do not by themselves cause the expedition. Rather, Xerxes' dream-vision 'merely stops a plan already conceived from being abandoned', and that plan is conceived in entirely human terms which even we today may find 'a completely satisfactory scheme of causation' (Ste. Croix 1977: 143–5). Herodotus, in summary, could explain major events in history in purely human terms, but his piety made him disinclined to regard such explanations as self-sufficiently satisfactory. What he makes Themistokles say of the Greeks' victory at Salamis—though he contrives to suggest that Themistokles of the many wiles did not necessarily believe it himself— perfectly encapsulates his own view: 'it is not we who achieved this feat but the gods and heroes, who were envious that one man should be lord over both Asia and Europe—a man who besides was impious (*anosios*) and presumptuous (*atasthalos*)' (8. 109. 3).

And so, finally, to Thucydides once more. Whatever precisely he meant by 'the human thing' (*to anthrōpinon*, 1. 22. 4) or 'human nature' (*hē anthrōpōn phusis*, 3. 82. 2), the rhetorical force of these expressions, placed as they are in key explanatory passages, is unmistakable: Thucydides is consciously attempting to explain his Peloponnesian War in human, non-divine terms. That is not to say that for Thucydides men are in complete control of their destiny. Even the supremely provident Perikles could not foresee a stroke of fortune (*tukhē*) such as the great plague of Athens. But although 'Perikles' is made to describe the plague as *daimonion*, that was very far from a Herodotean, let alone a Xenophontic, admission of divine intervention and causation. Nowhere does Perikles, or more importantly Thucydides himself, abandon belief in the possibility of human rationality, even amid the unexpected and unpredictable action of fortune, and notwithstanding the strong tragic colouring of the work as a whole. Moreover, in the Melian Dialogue, where Thucydides makes his Athenian interlocutors strip away the veneer of 'fair names' (*kala onomata*, 5. 89) to reveal the unvarnished truth of human interstate relations, Thucydides comes within a whisker of saying in his own voice that the gods make no difference: 'we believe by repute of the gods (*to theion*), and we know by clear evidence of men (*to anthrōpeion*), that it is a necessity of nature to rule wherever it may be possible' (5. 105. 2). That is the Athenians' cold-blooded response to the Melians' pathetic and unavailing appeal to divine intervention to save them from destruction—the destruction that was shortly to be visited upon them by the Athenians and some of Athens's allies. Even the gods, that is to say, are held to be constrained by this necessity, by this universal 'law' (*nomos*) of nature.

The import and the force of this rejection of the divine by 'the Athenians' in a fictitious dialogue are corroborated by Thucydides' strikingly few references to religion throughout the narrative portions of his work. Moreover, of those few passages there is just one which may, arguably, show Thucydides as less than a completely hardheaded disbeliever in divine intervention for practical historiographical purposes (2. 17. 1–2). In short, Thucydides would surely have agreed with the contemporary author of the Hippokratic medical treatise on epilepsy entitled 'On the Sacred Disease', who laid his intellectual cards on the table at the outset of his tract by denying that there was anything peculiarly divine about the so-called sacred disease, since all diseases were equally sacred—or not; and with another of the Hippokratics who in a treatise on virgins' diseases robustly avowed that the cure for teenage menstrual problems was not making offerings to Artemis but getting married (*Peri Parthenión* 468. 17 ff. ed. E. Littré). The divine element was not for these writers a causally differentiating factor and could therefore be ignored for explanatory purposes. In that sense—but only in that sense—we might want to call Thucydides the father of 'scientific' historiography.

Epilogue

We are all Greeks. Our laws, our literature, our religion,
our arts, have their roots in Greece

(P. B. Shelley, Preface to *Hellas* [1822])

Otherness v. Classicism

It has been no part of my purpose in this book to play down
or belittle what Herodotus would have called 'the great and
wondrous achievements' of the Classical Greeks. In historiography, politics, theatre, philosophy, and so many other fields
of communal intellectual endeavour they stand tall. Nor would
I wish for a moment to deny or diminish the force of the
epithet 'Classical':

In describing the characteristic features of Greek civilisation, it is
customary to invoke the concept of the 'classical'—a model for many,
the attraction of which lay in all that was achieved, experienced and
represented, within the narrow confines of the world of the *polis*, in
terms of accomplishments, of intellectual questions and matching up
to the questioning, of human greatness and commensurability with
events . . . (Meier 1990: 25)

What I would contest are the validity and utility of assuming
or asserting a near-complete cultural self-identification between
'Us' and 'the ancient Greeks'. Greatly though I admire
Shelley, his enthusiasm for the latter led him astray: there is
all the difference in the world between identity, which is to a
significant degree constructed rather than given, and roots.
Indeed, one of my chief aims has been as it were to defamiliarize
Classical Greek civilization, to fracture that beguilingly easy
identification with the ancient Greeks which reached a climax
in post-Enlightenment Germany, Second Empire France, and
Victorian Britain, and which still has its residual adherents
today, partly no doubt for political rather than purely academic reasons.

On the other hand, there is a danger of going to the opposite extreme and overemphasizing the 'otherness' of a culture from which our own has indeed chosen to construct a potent legacy. For, although the human heart is not always the same (as the pioneering sociological historians of the eighteenth-century Enlightenment and, more surprisingly, some modern students of classical antiquity have liked to believe), there is enough of the ancient Greek in our devotion to at any rate the ideology and rhetoric of freedom, equality, and democracy to make the cultural linkage abundantly plain.

However, I do want to insist in conclusion that 'our' mentality, our mindset, as a whole is significantly 'other' than that of the Classical Greeks, and I shall attempt to make that contradictory case on the territory included by Shelley and focused upon more recently by Enoch Powell (a professor of Greek before he entered politics), namely the Athenian theatre. Athens was not of course Greece, though the Athenians themselves were fond of pretending it was, and I have tried to resist 'Athenocentricity' throughout this book. But Athenian drama did consciously aspire to capture the universal in Greek experience and was watched by and to some extent written for non-Athenian Greeks as well as the citizens of Athens. Our contemporary 're-experiencings' (George Steiner's phrase) of Classical Athenian drama, especially tragic drama, arguably encapsulate both the authentic and the mythical aspects of the Greek legacy in about equal proportions.

A Religious Theatre

As the epithet 'Classical' connotes, Athenian drama in its choice of themes and to some extent in its handling of them does somehow transcend cultural barriers. In recent decades, for example, the *Medea* of Euripides and *Lysistrata* of Aristophanes have variously subserved feminist ends, Euripides' *Bacchae* has been presented as a hymn of counter-cultural liberationist rebellion, and Sophokles' *Antigone* (of course) has inspired meditations on both civil war and totalitarianism. In short, Classical Greek (or Athenian) drama does manage still to speak to us today in usable ways. In fact, so apparently familiar and domesticated has it become that it is necessary for the modern stage director no less than for the modern scholar to insist upon its alienness. What does or should make that task easier from the outset is the inescapably central religious dimension of Athenian theatre.

As was stressed in the previous chapter, Classical Greek religion was not, *pace* Shelley's aphorism, either bequeathed to or inherited by us. This was because it was a religion of the city, and the Greek city or *polis* was a culture-bound invention that failed to outlive the Roman conquest of the Greek world and the Christianization of the Roman Empire. Thus the essential religious content and meaning of classical Athenian drama, which originally was always staged within the context of religious festivals organized by the city of Athens in honour of Dionysos, could not possibly have 'travelled' into the alien context of modern stage-theatre. A review of traditional Japanese Kabuki theatre performed at the Royal National Theatre in London was once headlined 'Crash-course in Cultural Otherness'. That would also do very nicely as a subtitle for this concluding chapter.

Not that the religious aspect of Athenian theatre is by any means straightforward. Consider first the apparently paradoxical identity of its divine patron. For despite Dionysos' patronage, Athenian drama, at any rate tragic drama, had very little to do with him. In fact, 'nothing to do with Dionysos' was an ancient phrase meaning roughly 'inapposite'! Those scholars who wish to argue for a strong intrinsic connection between the worship of Dionysos and tragic drama are obliged therefore to make their case in other terms, insisting for instance on the common factor of alienation. In their different ways both the initiates in Dionysiac cults and the performers of drama become 'ecstatic', literally 'standing outside', and so becoming other than their normal selves, aided by such artificial devices as masks. Dionysos' connection with comedy was much more obvious, indeed etymological; *kōmōidia* meant literally song accompanying the quintessentially Dionysiac wine-fuelled *kōmos* or 'revel'. Yet comedy was not formally introduced into the programme of the Great or City Dionysia festival for at least fifteen years after the inclusion there of tragedy.

But even if an intrinsic connection be admitted, the problem of the historical origins of tragedy and comedy, and their combination with satyr drama (the most obviously Dionysiac component of Athenian theatre) into a single religious festival, remains as fraught as ever. So too does that of the representation of Dionysos on the comic stage—at any rate for those not inured to Athenian conventions. Consider Aristophanes' *Frogs*, first performed at the other main Athenian annual drama festival, the Lenaia, in early 405. Here the festival's divine patron is cast as the protagonist of a meta-play about the connection between drama and politics. At a time of deepest crisis for the real city of Athens (on the verge of losing the Peloponnesian War), Dionysos undertakes to make a descent into the Underworld on the city's behalf to bring back to life on earth the greatest of Athens's dead tragic playwrights, so that he can 'save' the city by his excellent advice. The play has two choruses, a subsidiary one of eponymous frogs, and a main chorus composed of Athenians initiated in the Eleusinian Mysteries (selected by Aristophanes because initiates believed that initiation might secure them a happier afterlife in the Underworld). Aristophanes never once makes a joke at the expense of the initiates' chorus. Nor is the idea of the dramatic poet as public teacher ridiculed as intrinsically humorous. By contrast, he never stops making jokes at the expense of Dionysos, who is represented both as a lily-livered effeminate and as grossly ignorant of the finer points of Aeschylean and Euripidean tragic dramaturgy.

Modern scholars have sometimes explained this treatment of Dionysos in terms of the growth of atheism, agnosticism, or more generally rationalism in later fifth-century Athens, associating those with the influence of Sophists like Protagoras (whose influence on the historiography of Herodotus and Thucydides we have already noted). But that explanation hardly squares with the panic terror and ensuing witchhunt provoked by the religious sacrileges at Athens of 415, especially the alleged profanation of the Eleusinian Mysteries, or indeed with Aristophanes' respect for that cult in the *Frogs*. A much better explanation postulates a form of comic licence, in the shape of a strictly delimited privilege to abuse the gods within the context of a religious festival during which the normal priorities and pieties were temporarily suspended or inverted. But that explanation encounters the objection that on at least two occasions legislation was passed to prevent or curtail the comic abuse of humans (contemporary politicians), so why should the gods, especially the festivals' patron god, not have been accorded the same legal protection? In other words, we are dealing here with a deepseated feature of Athenian religion that is not readily amenable to explanation in terms of modern categories of religious understanding.

Another major difficulty for us is to identify and evaluate the contribution made by the three great tragedians to the ordinary Athenians' perception and enactment of their religious beliefs. Through the medium of myths that were set in a putatively historical but distant and usually non-Athenian past, Aeschylus, Sophokles, and Euripides contrived to set in play dramatic debates about the central values of their contemporary Athenian society, honour, justice, and, not least, religious piety. The morality and political implications of endless vendetta in Aeschylus' *Oresteia* trilogy; the contradictory claims of obligation to one's human kin and to the gods in the *Antigone* of Sophokles; the status of women and barbarians in the *Medea* of Euripides—these are just some examples. Moreover, they not only set debates in play, but also thereby put the values at risk, questioning in both the literal and the extended senses of that term their continuing validity.

Among modern scholars it has been standard procedure to place the tragedians' reworkings of myth within a largely artistic or psychological framework of analysis and to underplay their specifically spiritual or ritual aspects. But Athenian religion was not text-based or dogmatic, and the dramatists were as qualified as any other citizens, and moreover were occupationally expected, to teach and to 'preach' on matters affecting the relations between gods and men, including even the advocacy of new religious cults (such as that of the tamed Furies, transformed into the Eumenides or 'Kindly Ones', successfully championed by Aeschylus in his play of that title). We do not look to our admittedly few modern tragedians to perform a similar role, nor can we even imagine Shakespeare as having performed it in Elizabethan and Jacobean England.

A Political Theatre

On the other hand, we do not find the idea of Shakespeare as a political dramatist nearly so rebarbative. In this case, though, it is necessary to distinguish between the strictly official, public, and civic character of Athenian theatre, which was a national theatre in the fullest sense, and Shakespeare's private theatrical enterprise, which did not of its essence bear any contemporary relevance to public political practice. *A fortiori* the gap is infinitely wider between the politics of ancient Athenian drama and of our contemporary theatre.

Some form of tragic and comic drama had been performed at Athens from at least the 530s, the supposed *floruit* of the actor-dramatist Thespis. But it is a recent and persuasive view that the Great or City Dionysia was first organized as a regular city festival of tragic drama only after the institution of democracy in 508/7; specifically, as a religio-political festival of liberation from the actual domestic tyranny of the Peisistratid family (c.545–510) and from the threat of foreign, that is Spartan and Persian, domination. Comedy was certainly not added to the programme until 486, and it can hardly be a coincidence that this was just a year after a change in the method of appointing Arkhons from what was considered the aristocratic mode of election to the peculiarly democratic mode of sortition.

The luminaries of the first generation of Dionysiac tragedy were Phrynikhos and Aeschylus, both of whom essayed explicitly contemporary political themes connected with the resistance against Persia as well as the more conventional reworkings of myth. Phrynikhos, however, was fined for his over-affecting *Capture of Miletos* (Herodotus 6. 21), possibly by a decision taken at the meeting of the Athenian Assembly that at any rate later was regularly held actually in the theatre of Dionysos immediately after the festival. He had strayed too far over the border between representation and reality. This was something Aeschylus was careful to avoid twenty years later by not actually mentioning Themistokles by name in his slightly less immediately contemporary *Persians*, of which he and the battle of Salamis were the heroes. Similarly in the *Supplices* of (probably) 463 and the *Oresteia* trilogy of 458 Aeschylus kept his own political views largely under wraps while intimating for those who needed it a general encouragement of radical changes in Athens's foreign and domestic policy. The pattern for political tragedy was by now set.

Political comedy, however, was a later development, in which the key innovator was apparently Kratinos in the 450s. But if it arrived later, it also went far further than tragedy, the burning political issues of the day providing its plots as well as multiple points of social and ideological reference. Aristophanes for us stands in splendid isolation as the representative of extant Old Comedy, but he had his rivals—notably the older Kratinos and the contemporary Eupolis—and successors. By the time of his death in the 380s, however, the sort of nakedly political and personally abusive comedy represented by his *Knights* (424) and *Wasps* (422) had begun to give way to comedies of situation, which in turn had been replaced by the end of the fourth century by Menander's comedies of manners. It is from these that our own dominant tradition of comedy is derived. Theatre as a whole, though, did not cease to be political, and indeed a central feature of the democracy, in the fourth century. The heated debates in the Assembly over the Theoric Fund (a festival dole to enable the poorest Athenian citizens to pay the small theatre entrance fee) are sufficient testimony to that, as are Plato's contemptuous reference to the 'theatrocracy' of the Athenian masses in the *Laws* (701a) and Demosthenes' huge song-and-dance over being mugged in the theatre by his rival impresario (and political opponent) Meidias.

It is, however, only for the fifth-century Athenian theatre that we are able to situate whole plays in their total political and ceremonial context. This comprised the choice of plays, impresarios, and actors for the year's dramatic festivals by the relevant civic officials; the long period of rehearsals; the prefestival publicity; the initial religious procession to bring the statue of Dionysos back to his shrine adjoining the theatre; the preliminary religious, civic, and imperial rituals immediately before the plays began; the performance of the plays themselves spread over three or more days, and the judging of them by a scratch jury of average citizen playgoers; and the closing Assembly meeting held in the theatre to scrutinize the conduct of the festival as a whole. Not the least merit of this total view is that it enables us to register a dissonance, sometimes even a contradiction, between the discourse of the plays and that of the surrounding civic rituals. Whereas the latter were designed to emphasize civic solidarity, harmony, and unity, 'the tragedies and comedies . . . constitute in some important senses a questioning of the terms of that civic discourse' (Goldhill 1990: 126).

An Open Society?

Here, then, apparently was a truly 'open' society, where speech was genuinely free—surely a model for us to imitate as well as applaud? Sadly, not entirely so. For, to be precise, this Athenian freedom was civic freedom narrowly defined, a precious resource whose value was maintained by rigorous rationing. It was made available only to a small minority of Attica's residents, the privileged descent-group of adult male citizens, who numbered on average some thirty thousand out of perhaps two hundred to two hundred and fifty thousand in all.

It was, moreover, a freedom that was dearly bought—and this applies in varying degrees to all the hundreds of classical Greek communities, not only to Athens—at the expense of others, the excluded many: free foreigners and women (Greek as well as barbarian), but above all slaves (mainly barbarian but also Greek). Indeed, the exclusion of those various 'outgroups', the collective Other, was arguably the very condition and basic premiss of the Classical Greeks' cultural achievements, not least their invention and use of history. If, *pace* Shelley, we are not in fact all Greeks, that may be a just cause of some self-congratulation as well as measured regret.

Afterword to the Second Edition

Origins, motives, and aims

The Greeks: A Portrait of Self and Others in its two English versions so far (originally 1993, corrected and augmented 1997) has sold very well indeed—more than 9,000 copies in all. It has been widely and for the most part favourably reviewed, in all the main western scholarly languages. It has also occasioned a large private correspondence by snail mail and more recently e-mail. Perhaps my most intriguing or disturbing correspondent was an inmate forcibly incarcerated in a State Penitentiary at Ione in California, USA, who had enough time on his hands to undertake an intensive programme of self-education and had developed in the process a special interest in the ancient Greeks. (Was this somehow remotely connected to the experience of Socrates in the Athenian state prison in 399? I hardly dared to ask.) I am therefore delighted to take this welcome opportunity of a second English edition, following on the published German and Japanese translations, to describe very briefly once again the book's origins, motives, and aims.

It is of course presumptuous, almost perhaps hybristic, to call a book *The Greeks*. No one author, obviously, could hope to do anything like full justice to the remarkable achievements of all the ancient Hellenes (as they called themselves), even during the relatively short period of two centuries to which I deliberately confined myself—from *c*.500 to *c*.300 BC. Indeed, it is especially difficult to represent adequately their achievements during those two centuries, since that is the period of ancient Greek history that we in the West have chosen to designate as 'Classical'; we regard it, that is, as in some sense offering a paradigm for our own Western culture or cultures today.

To justify, or at any rate account for, the book's title and contents, let me briefly situate *The Greeks* within the trajectory of my own research, teaching, and publication. The book grew out of a lecture course that I delivered over several years in the late 1980s and early 1990s to final-year undergraduate students in the Faculty of Classics at Cambridge University. It deliberately bears the marks of its origins in a taught course. It is not only quite short but it is also consciously selective. It is intended to open up as many questions as it claims to answer. If it had been conceived and written as a full-scale monograph, it would undoubtedly have turned out very different. Even so, I hope that in its present form the book does make it sufficiently clear that 'the Greeks' more typically serves as an ideal construct than it does as a literal and faithful description of historical reality.

Which Greeks? Whose Greeks?

But which Greeks, exactly, are we talking about—or, rather, *whose* Greeks? The guiding thought behind the book was relatively simple, however much it had been informed or bolstered by appeal to more or less sophisticated theorizing. As a well-known British newspaper pundit put it recently, 'We divide every subject in the world into two, take sides, and then we pretend we know who we are.' My intuition was that the ancient Greeks were the same as us in this respect, only more so. For them, polarity was importantly part of their mentality or mindset, buried deep in their subconscious. From the particles *men* and *de* to . . . Men and Women, or rather Men *versus* Women. It seemed to me therefore that an ideal way to expose their self-perceptions and self-images, which were a vital part of who they (thought they) were, was to explore and analyse a number of key or core polarities.

I was, however, careful to stress throughout that the polarization and polarities of thought that I would be discussing were imaginary, idealized representations rather than supposedly objective or 'scientific' descriptions or classifications. I would add now a strong protest against the unacceptably lax use of the term 'Other' to mean, all too often, no more than different. In my terminology otherness or alterity is definitional, and specifically polar (the two terms of a polar opposition are jointly exhaustive and mutually exclusive). I agree too that, as Robin Osborne has more recently observed, 'the homogeneity of "us" implicit in treating "them" as Other' demands investigation and deconstruction too, though that was not a principal objective of my book. Had I had the space, I would indeed have spent more time than I did on 'internal' Greek Others, such as the Spartans, who were often and especially in Athens regarded as inverting the customary norms of thought and behaviour shared—or claimed to be shared—by almost all other 'normal' Greeks. Further polarities— such as 'Old v. Young' or 'Rich v. Poor'—would have also been treated.

One further lesson that I at any rate have learned very clearly over the past decade or so is that scholars and other people who belong to very different national groupings have, under pressure from their own histories both past and contemporary, both real and imaginary, and both personal and collective, developed very varied and often sharply opposed perceptions of the ancient Greeks' character and achievements. It can also make a huge difference to the way they are interpreted whether the modern interpreter is a Christian or a non-Christian, a man or a woman, a Westerner or an Easterner, and so on. To sum up: 'the Greeks' is to some extent and in some senses a relative concept—inevitably so.

Relativism, for some, is a dirty word. I, however, who do not pretend that my history can be genuinely value-free, find relativism an attractive strategy, so long as it is not interpreted as implying more than the doctrine that principles have only culturally local validity. It is a particularly fruitful way, I find, of trying to understand an ancient culture, that of the Greeks, which is both a foundation stone of our own (Western) civilization and at the same time in key respects a deeply alien phenomenon. What I call 'anthropologization', that is, aiming to act as if I were an anthropologist studying a contemporary alien culture, seems to me a valuable tool for trying to see the mental and spiritual world of the ancient Greeks as far as possible through their own eyes and according to their own values. One consequence of such an approach is that the ancient Greeks as a whole tend to come out looking to me very much less familiar, if no less impressive and influential, than the old 'Glory that was Greece' view—or myth— once standardly made them out to be.

Perhaps I may be allowed to interject here finally my own over-all evaluation of all the polarities of thought and representation that might be considered relevant to the question of Greek or Hellenic identity. I am in no doubt that it was the 'Freedom v. Slavery' polarity that was the most crucial and foundational. Many cultures, including my own British culture, have claimed to value freedom especially highly. But I know no other Western culture that endowed freedom with as many subtle nuances and gave it so central a place in the collective imagination as did Classical Greece. Readers are invited to judge for themselves how far the Greek ideal of freedom corresponded to the realities of life in ancient Greece, and how far it is an ideal that can be—or should be—translated to and implemented in their own society and culture.

Researching otherwise

Since the first English edition of this book appeared in 1993 research has proceeded at an alarming pace on all kinds of areas directly or indirectly relevant to its main concerns. I mention in conclusion just three very recent items, of which the first two are especially relevant to the wider non-Classical readership of histor-ians, historical sociologists, social psychologists, and cultural anthropologists that I have always tried to keep in mind, whereas the third has a more obvious appeal to specialists in Classical Greek culture: P. Otnes, *Other-Wise. Alterity, Materiality, Medi-ation* (Scandinavian University Press, 2000); Chris McManus, *Right Hand, Left Hand* (Weidenfeld & Nicolson, 2001), and Beth Cohen (ed.), *Not the Classical Ideal: Athens and the Construction of the Other in Greek Art* (E. J. Brill, 2000). The latter has served also as a starting-point for the new discussion of a selection of visual images of alterity included as an 'entr'acte' above (pp. 36–50).

October 2001

Further Reading

THESE suggestions for further reading are consciously selective, angled towards recent work in English, especially on Classical Greek historiography (both the writing of history by Greeks and the study of their writing of history).

General

There have of course been many books on 'The (ancient) Greeks', none very recent, in all the main international languages. Dover 1980 ('a by-product of two years' intermittent participation in the making of a set of television programmes on the ancient Greeks for BBC television') begins properly with a chapter on alterity and contrast entitled 'Greeks and Others', but I have sought more firmly and distinctly to 'alienate' and 'anthropologize' the Greeks. Closest to my perspective on the Classical Greeks of the fifth and fourth centuries BCE is Hartog 1988, but this is principally concerned with just one of my main sources, Herodotus, and but one of my polarities, Greeks v. Barbarians. The latter is also the focus of Hall, E. 1989, which concentrates on the distinctively Athenian genre of tragedy but ranges far more widely. On matters historiographical more generally, modern as well as ancient, the late Arnaldo Momigliano can never be lightly ignored, although I—like Woodman 1988—attribute more weight than he would have approved (1981) to the rhetoric and literary artifice of all historiography (not excluding his or my own); cf. White 1973, 1978, 1989; La Capra 1983; Gearhart 1984; and Kramer 1989. Woodman, however, operates with the outmoded, scientific definition of history discredited by Berlin 1980; cf. Atkinson 1978. Recent publications include Georges 1994; Vernant 1995; Cartledge (ed.) (2002).

Prologue

The Genesis of this Book (pp. 1–4)

Ethnicity: Glazer and Moynihan 1975; Degler 1983; Tonkin, McDonald, and Chapman 1989. The latter includes a chapter by the anthropologist-historian Roger Just on ethnicity in modern Greece, a fraught political topic sensitively discussed also from an academic-cultural standpoint by the anthropologist Michael Herzfeld (esp. 1987). On contemporary personal identity in a social-psychological, not philosophical, sense Hoffmann 1989 is a model autobiographical treatment; cf. Geertz's (1985) terrifying roll-call of 'the enormous engines of post-modern self-doubt—Heidegger, Wittgenstein, Gramsci, Sartre, Foucault, Derrida, most recently Bakhtin'. On Levinas and his alterity (not simple difference) see Levinas 1989. Ancient identities: Meyer and Sanders 1982; Schnapp 1988. The heuristic value of 'mentality' (in the '*Annales* School' sense: James 1984: 146–75) is underplayed by Lloyd, G. E. R. 1990. See also Hall, J. M. 1995*a*, 1995*b*; Leontis 1995.

The Greeks and 'Us' (pp. 4–5)

The 'Greek legacy', meaning what we have chosen to appropriate as opposed to what the Greeks had potentially to bequeath: Finley 1981*i*, Thomas, C. G. (ed.) 1988; Easterling 1989; and Taplin 1989. (For the opposite, seriously ethnocentric understanding of 'legacy', see Livingstone 1921.) On the specific issue of freedom and slavery I have developed further my remarks here and in Chapter 6 in Cartledge 1993*a*. Recent works on this subject include Dover (ed.) 1992; Morris, I. (ed.) 1994.

The Savage Greeks (pp. 5–6)

Constant 1988: 307–28 is an English translation with commentary of Benjamin Constant's 1819 address at the Athénée Royal, Paris, 'De la liberté des Anciens comparée à celle des Modernes'. For an intellectual history of the mainly French historical-anthropological tradition of studying the ancient world see now Di Donato 1990. On 'anthropologization' see also Gernet 1968; Nippel 1990; and on the pioneering contribution of Lafitau in particular, Pagden 1986: 198–209. Perhaps the most concentrated exemplar of Lévi-Straussian structuralist analysis is Lévi-Strauss 1976, an earlier translation of which is reproduced and variously discussed in Leach (ed.) 1967. In addition see Thom 1995: ch. 4.

Legacy for Whom? (pp. 6–7)

On democracy ancient and modern see esp. Dunn 1979 and Finley 1985*b*; on the 'emergence of the political' and the 'discovery' or 'invention of politics' in Classical Greece see Meier 1990; Farrar 1988. Rahe 1984 is a controversial plea for the Greeks to be studied from a narrowly political rather than broadly cultural (social, economic, intellectual, mental, and political-cultural) standpoint. See also works cited under 'The Greeks and "Us"', above. Recent publications include Dunn (ed.) 1992, 1993, 1996; Ober and Hedrick 1996.

1. Significant Others: Us v. Them

A Comparativist Perspective (p. 8)

Further discussion of comparativism as a historiographical method and technique: Cartledge 1985*b*. See also Golden 1992.

Greece: Problems of Generalization (pp. 9–11)

Rhodes 1986 gives a good idea of the constitutional diversity of 'the Greek World' (well over 1,000 separate political communities from Georgia on the Black Sea to the Straits of Gibraltar). Ambiguous northern margins of Greece: Hall, E. 1989: 134–9 (Thrace), 164–5 (Macedon). Aristotle as a registered *metoikos* (metic, resident alien) at Athens: Whitehead 1975. Aristotle as natural scientist, primarily: Kullmann 1991; his teleology: Lloyd, G. E. R. 1987: 319–29. His use of 'reputable' and 'received' views: Barnes 1980; Owen 1986. Studies in ancient Greek historiography: besides the voluminous and multifarious works of Momigliano, see briefly Bury 1909; generally Fornara 1983; and, for bibliography chiefly, Meister 1990. The factor of audience-response in generating Greek historiography is stressed by Starr 1968, and is implicit in Hartog's concept of Herodotus' 'Greek addressee'; cf. for Thucydides, Ridley 1981. 'Orality' of Classical Greek culture: Thomas, R. 1989, 1992. In addition to the above see Hornblower (ed.) 1994.

Who Were the Greeks? (pp. 11–13)
Polarity in History (pp. 13–16)

Polarity as an ancient Greek mode of theoretical discourse: Lloyd, G. E. R. 1966; cf. Vidal-Naquet 1986*c*. Subsets of the discourse (right–left, light–dark, white–black): Lloyd, G. E. R. 1973; Vidal-Naquet 1986*b*; Fontaine 1986–7; Radke 1936. *Nomos–phusis*: Heinimann 1945. Dual symbolic classification in anthropology after Robert Hertz: Needham 1973; cf. Arens 1979 (always 'others' who are the cannibals). Interpretative limitations of polarization: Needham 1987; of structuralist polarization in particular: Gellner 1985*b*. Sophists: de Romilly 1992; but note Dodds 1973*c*. Greek irrationality: Dodds 1951.

Interpretative Charity (pp. 16–17)

Problems of intercultural translation: Winch 1987; Geertz 1988;

Ardener 1989. See further Horton and Finnegan 1973. But the work of Geertz himself (1973*a*, 1982, 1987, 1988) equally shows what may be attempted and can be achieved in the way of sympathetic (not empathetic) cross-cultural understanding; cf. Biersack 1989. The Victorians (some) and (their) ancient Greece: Clarke 1989; Knox 1990*b*.

2. Inventing the Past: History v. Myth

History v. Fiction (pp. 18–19)

Definitions (pp. 19–21)

Veyne 1984 is a systematic, if ultimately unpersuasive, assault on the conventional opposition of history and fiction; cf. Veyne 1988. Two good collections of articles representative of the conventional view as applied to ancient historiography: Fondation Hardt 1958; Walbank 1985*a*. For one 'master mind' on another see Syme 1962 on Thucydides; cf. Bowersock 1965. A contradictory view, stressing Thucydidean 'invention', in Woodman 1988: ch 1. Balanced on this issue are Dover 1973, 1988*c*; and Hornblower 1987, both of whom make allowance for Thucydidean literary artistry. Loraux 1980 dismisses Thucydides as 'not a colleague' largely because of his resolutely pre-modernist way with his sources. Influential modern definitions of history at opposite ends of the spectrum: Collingwood 1946/1993 (idealist) and Carr 1986 (materialist); Bloch 1954 is a classic apology for the historian's *métier*; judicious overviews of the pullulent field as a whole in Iggers 1984/5 and Tosh 1991. Definitions and functions of myth: Cohen, P. S. 1969, an anthropologist's overview, is especially helpful; but see also Adair 1986 (myths of popular culture); Griffin 1986 (mainly literary myth); and Samuel and Thompson 1990 for looser constructions. Ackerman 1973 is a historiographical review, embracing Kirk 1970. On ancient Greek myth, see additionally Kirk 1974; Burkert 1979, 1987; Bremmer 1987*a*, 1987*b*; and Edmunds 1990. Recent works on this subject include Gill and Wiseman (eds.) 1993; Hornblower 1994; Buxton 1994.

Myth as History (pp. 21–6)

R. Thomas's work on Greek oral tradition (1989) and ancient orality (1992) is again relevant here; cf. Grote 1873; Goody and Watt 1968; O. Murray 1987; Evans 1991: 89–146. Useful modern comparative data are collected and interpreted by the Africanists Vansina 1973, 1985; and Henige 1982; cf. the tips for anthropological fieldworkers on how to gather and assess oral testimony in Evans-Pritchard 1937; and the experience of oral historians of developed urban communities: Tosh 1991, ch. 10. 'Myth-history' comparatively: Dundes 1985; McNeill 1986. On Herodotus' Alkmaionid digression as a whole see Hart 1982: 1–16; Thomas, R. 1989: 264–72. Particular aspects: How and Wells 1928: appendix 15; McNeal 1985, and Hall, E. 1989: 168–72 (ethnicity of Pelasgians); Rosivach 1987 and Zeitlin 1989 (Athenian autochthony); Vernant and Detienne 1978 (Greek *mētis*); Gould 1980, Walcot 1985, and Lefkowitz 1986 (representation of women in Greek, mainly Athenian, myth). See also Loraux 1993; Steiner 1994.

Myth in History (pp. 26–9)

'Curse' of Alkmaionids: Parker 1983: 16–17; Thomas, R. 1989: 272–81. Spartan religious mentality: Parker 1989. Uses of myth in historiography and tragedy generally: see respectively Wardman 1960 and Knox 1979—though Knox fails to spot the contrast drawn by Herodotus' 'Athenians' at Plataia between different historical times. For the latter distinction see van Leyden 1949–50. It is not accidental that Herodotus claims knowledge of events preserved in oral tradition over three (and not more) generations: Henige 1982: 110–11. See also Vernant and Vidal-Naquet 1988.

Myth versus History (pp. 29–33)

On *muthos* and *logos* see Detienne 1986. On the triumph of reason over myth, apart from Finley 1986c, Starr 1968, and Vernant 1983b, see Wilde 1909, Cook, A. S. 1976, Lloyd, G. E. R. 1979: chs 3 ('The Development of Empirical Research') and 4 ('Greek Science and Greek Society'), and Brillante 1984. But note that there is also a 'reason of myth': Vernant 1980d. On Hekataios: Pearson 1939; van Leyden 1949–50. Herodotus as *logios*: Evans 1991, who also, with Gould 1989, has reaffirmed the coherence and cogency of Herodotus' causal thinking. Athenian Tyrannicides myth: Jacoby 1949: 152–68; Taylor 1981; Day 1985; Thomas, R. 1989: 257–61. (Not everyone, though, agrees with Thucydides that Hipparkhos was not killed *qua* tyrant.) Thucydidean methodology (1. 20–2): Canfora 1977; cf. Howie 1984.

An Archaeological Myth (pp. 33–5)

In addition to Finley 1986c, see Cook, R. M. 1955. Ktesias and the 'Oxyrhynchus Historian': Cartledge 1987: 186, 66–7; Auberger 1991. Aristotle is properly designated an antiquary (Huxley 1973); though unusually historically minded for a philosopher (Weil 1960; Huxley

1972), he favoured poetry over history—wrongly, on his own principles (Ste. Croix 1975a). Poetry v. History generally: Gomme 1954.

Entr'acte

Plate 1 *Myth v. History*

Parthenon frieze: Spivey 1996: ch. 7; Fullerton 2000: 79–88.

Plate 2 *Greeks v. Barbarians I*

Robertson 1992: 146 describes the scene on this vase as 'a masterpiece in his black-comedy mood'. For an acute discussion of other Herakles–Busiris scenes, on Attic red-figure drinking cups signed by the painter Epiktetos (a slave-name meaning literally 'the purchased'), see Lissarrague 1994. One of these, now in the Villa Giulia museum, emphasizes the sympotic, masculine-fantasy aspect by depicting in the tondo a naked woman riding a phallus-bird, what Lissarrague describes as 'a picture of a fantastical hetaira' (23). Developing Athenian attitudes to the Barbarian in the fourth century: Green 1996.

Plate 3 *Greeks v. Barbarians II*

Discussion of Bassai frieze generally: Beard & Henderson 2000: 69, 74–85, 124–5; Rhodes, R. F. 1995: 147–55. Intercutting of Greek v. Barbarian and Men v. Women polarities: Sassi 2001: ch. 3. Arkadian mercenaries: Cartledge 1987: 316–17. Ancient Greek perceptions of ethnicity: Malkin ed. 2001.

Plate 4 *Men v. Women*

For an excellent discussion of all the scenes on the kalyx krater see Osborne 1999. Three of the most incisive recent contributions to the study of Greek femininity as construed by males, in various forms of imaginative and historical literature, are Loraux 1993 (originally 1984), Zeitlin 1996, and Wohl 1998. For an intelligently critical response to, especially, Zeitlin, see Pelling 2000: ch. 10 ('Lysistrata and others: constructing gender'). Images of Amazons: Lissarrague 1992: 226–9.

Plate 5 *Citizens v. Aliens*

The translation of Pl. *Smp.* offered in the text is that of Christopher Rowe, *OMNIBUS* 41 (2001), 31 (emphasis original). 'Between gods and beasts': Detienne 1981; Detienne and Vernant (eds.) 1989. Literary representation of Alkibiades, from Aristophanes and Thucydides through to Plutarch: Gribble 1999 (ch. 4 for Plato). Satyrs: Lissarrague 1990, 1993.

Plate 6 *Free v. Slave*

'Old Oligarch': Ober 1998: ch. 1. Athenian fourth-century lead letter: Jordan 2000 (who also illustrates, figs. 5–7, a late fifth-century imitation black-figure drinking cup from Abai in Lokris, depicting a quite horrifying scene of slave torture). Tattooed Thracian women on pots: cf. Lissarrague 1992: 199. Brygos Painter: Robertson 1992: 93–100.

Plate 7 *Gods v. Mortals I*

On divine worship generally: Schlesier 2000; on dedications: Cartledge 2000.

Plate 8 *Gods v. Mortals II*

Gold stater: Price 1974: 22–3, pl. XI.55, pl. XV. Pausanias and Lysander: Cartledge 1987: esp. 82–6. The Greekness of the Macedonians: Badian 1994; Hall, J. M. 1997: 64. Philip's oriental 'crusade': Griffith 1979: 458–63.

3. Alien Wisdom: Greeks v. Barbarians

General

Besides being an admirable account of its own subject, Hall, E. 1989 contains an extremely useful bibliography; cf. generally Drews 1973; Momigliano 1975; and Browning 1989. Recent publications include Burkert 1992; Morris, S. P. 1992; Georges 1994; Hartog 1996.

Constructing Ethnic Identities (pp. 51–3)

As a political polemicist Bernal (1987–91) has been brilliantly successful; as a historiographer he is not entirely implausible; but as an ancient historian his amateur status (he is a professor of modern Chinese government studies) is palpable—see e.g. the academic responses to Bernal 1987–91: i in Peradotto and Levine 1989, and now Hall, E. 1992. On the Greek vocabulary of 'barbarism' see also Toynbee 1969: 58–63. On the Carian ethnic mix, Hornblower 1982: 11–14; on the ethnic status of Halikarnassos, Hornblower 1982: 10 and n. 48, 14 n. 69.

The Invention of the Barbarian (pp. 53–6)

For the process in general, and the contribution of Aeschylus' *Persians* in particular, see Hall, E. 1989 *passim*; cf. Bacon 1961; Bovon 1963; Weiler 1968; Baslez 1986. 'Orientalism' has become part of current academic parlance thanks chiefly to Edward Said (1978/1995, 1985); cf. Kabbani 1986. 'Nation', by contrast, is a term without an agreed definition (Tonkin,

McDonald, and Chapman 1989), although scholars do agree that the ancient Greeks were not or did not have one: Finley 1986*b*; Walbank 1985*a*: 1–19. The Greek Kroisos (Croesus) and *xenia*: Herman 1987: 19. The Delian League/Athenian Empire: Meiggs 1972. In addition see Gellner 1983; Anderson 1991; Hobsbawm 1992; Ignatieff 1993; Cartledge 1995.

Dissentient Voices (pp. 56–7)

Antiphon 'the Sophist': Hall, E. 1989: 218–21. Antiphon the oligarchic politician (probably one and the same Antiphon): Cartledge 1990*a*.

Pan-Hellenism (pp. 57–60)

Political pan-Hellenism: Perlman 1976. The Macedonian kings and the Olympics: Herodotus 5. 22 (concerning Alexander I nicknamed 'the Philhellene', the carefully chosen internal addressee of 8. 143). Xenophon's career: Anderson 1974; Cawkwell 1972, 1979; Nickel 1979; Cartledge 1987: 57–61. Eleusinian Mysteries initiation (including stress on the 'cultivated' life—English too preserves the etymological ambiguity): Burkert 1985: 285–90. See also Badian 1994.

Some Barbarians More Equal than Others (pp. 60–4)

Greeks as mercenaries in pay of oriental barbarians: Momigliano 1975: 75. Ktesias: Auberger 1991. Agesilaos–Pharnabazus interview: Gray 1989: 52–8. Historical implications of *xenia*: Herman 1987.

A Righteous Barbarian (pp. 64–5)

The *Cyropaedia* as novel: Heiserman 1977; Tatum 1989; cf. generally Due 1989. Wrongly interpreted as fact: Hirsch 1985. Greeks and Jews: Momigliano 1975: 74–96. See also Gera 1993.

Savagery and Civilization (pp. 65–70)

'Shadow' of the Parthenon: Green 1972. Persian Empire: J. M. Cook 1983. Thucydides (not) on Persia: Andrewes 1961. Herodotus' auto-referentiality: Dewald 1987. Thucydides' Thracian connection: Herman 1990: 349–50. Comic Scythians at Athens: Vogt 1974: 8 and n. 21; cf. generally Long 1986.

Holding Up the Mirror (pp. 70–1)

On the mirror metaphor as such, see the reservations of Pocock 1985: 29; on Hartog's (1988) mirror in particular, Dewald 1990. Readership-audience of Herodotus: Momigliano 1978; Flory 1980.

Herodotus' Egyptian Grid (pp. 71–4)

The Egyptian *logos* has provided plenty of grist to the mill of Fehling 1989. For more balanced views see Redfield 1985; Lloyd, A. B. 1990; cf. generally Froidefond 1971; Hartog 1986. Digressions in another, quite Herodotean, ancient historian (Ammianus Marcellinus): Matthews 1989: 462–4. New World comparison: Chiapelli, Benson, and Chiapelli (eds.) 1976.

'Custom is King' (pp. 74–5)

Pindaric reappropriation: Evans 1965. Protagoras' 'Man is the Measure': Farrar 1988: 44–98 (giving the doctrine a democratic spin).

'Herodotus' Law' (of Oriental Despotism) (pp. 75–7)

Momigliano 1979; Cartledge 1990*b*; Evans 1991: 8–40 ('The imperialist impulse'). Herodotus on Scythians: apart from Hartog 1988, see Lloyd, A. B. 1990; cf. on binary opposition of pastoralists and sedentary agriculturalists: Briant 1982: 9–56.

4. Engendering History: Men v. Women

General

Western and other attitudes to Woman: Rosaldo and Lamphere 1974; MacCormack and Strathern 1980; Keuls 1986; Scott 1988. Origins of Western attitude in Greece: Arthur 1984. Also relevant to the chapter as a whole are Pomeroy 1975/6; Lefkowitz 1981; Cameron and Kuhrt (eds.) 1983; Lévy (ed.) 1983; Gallo 1984; Peradotto and Sullivan (eds.) 1984; duBois 1988; Clark, G. 1989; Halperin, Winkler, and Zeitlin (eds.) 1990; Pomeroy (ed.) 1991; Schmitt Pantel (ed.) 1992. Recent publications include Fantham *et al.* 1994; Reeder (ed.) 1995; Doherty 2001.

Genesis as Myth (pp. 78–9)

Laqueur's (1989) attribution of a 'one-sex' view to the Classical Greeks is controversial. Nature v. Culture debate in biological context: Jordanova 1980; cf. Ortner 1974.

The 'Second' Sex (pp. 79–80)

The title and subtitle of Sanday and Goodenough (eds.) 1990 are a tribute to de Beauvoir's influence; cf. Moi 1989; and a special issue of *Yale French Studies* (no. 72, 1987). Women in Christian tradition: Ranke-Heinemann 1990/1.

Male Ordering (pp. 80–1)

Modern Greek anthropology: Dubisch 1986, esp. Du Boulay 1986, Friedl 1986, and Herzfeld 1986; also Du Boulay 1974.

Aristotle's Woman (pp. 81–5)

Clark, S. R. L. 1982 is apropos generally; cf. on the scientific side specifically Horowitz 1979; Lloyd, G. E. R. 1983: 94–105; Saïd 1983; Dean-Jones 1991; Sissa 1992. Hippokratic women: Lloyd, G. E. R. 1983: 62–86; Rousselle 1980; Hanson 1991. Aristotelian teleology: Lloyd, G. E. R. 1987: 319–29. Left–right polarization: Needham 1973; Lloyd, G. E. R. 1973; Vidal-Naquet 1986*b*. The 'feminist' Plato is deconstructed by Zeitlin 1990: 90–6. See also Dean-Jones 1994.

The Silent Women of Thucydides (pp. 85–9)

Aristotle on Spartan women: Cartledge 1981*b*. Thucydidean silence: Wiedemann 1983; Harvey 1985; Loraux 1989*c*; and Cartledge 1993. Women and war: Schaps 1982; Loraux 1989*d*. Herodotus' multiple references to women: Dewald 1981. The translation of Thucydides 2. 45 is by J. S. Rusten. On Thucydides 3. 74. 2 see Loraux 1989*c*. Athenian citizenship law: Davies 1977/8; Loraux 1981; Patterson, C. B. 1981; cf. for various aspects of Athenian women's formal legal position Ste. Croix 1970; Gould 1980; Just 1989. But note Versnel 1987; Cohen, D. 1991 (possibility for 'negotiation' of social roles). Aeschylean 'misogyny': Zeitlin 1984. *Hai Attikai* formula: Patterson, C. B. 1986; cf. Mossé 1985. Non-naming of respectable Athenian women in public: Schaps 1977. In addition see Boegehold 1994.

Dramatic Women (pp. 89–91)

Generally: Winkler and Zeitlin 1990, esp. Zeitlin 1990. Comedy: Gardner 1989; Cartledge 1990*a*: 32–42. Tragedy: Zeitlin 1984; Goldhill 1986: 107–37. Antigones: Steiner, G. 1984; a recent interpretation: Sourvinou-Inwood 1989. *Hubris*: Fisher 1992. See also Taaffe 1993.

An Ethnography of Alterity: Between Myth and Utopia (pp. 91–5)

Herodotean 'usages': Tourraix 1976; Rosellini and Saïd 1978; cf. generally Vidal-Naquet 1986*e*. Lykian matronymy: Pembroke 1965. Amazons as type: Kirk, I. 1987. Amazons in Greek perception: Carlier-Detienne 1980; duBois 1982; Tyrrell 1984, aptly described as 'a general disquisition on the dynamics of the male/female polarity in Greek cultural life'—Marilyn Arthur in *Signs* (Spring 1987), 591. Athenian vase-painting: Lissarrague 1992: 227, fig. 61; generally Harvey 1988*b*; Bérard 1989*b*. Women in Sparta: Redfield 1977/8; Cartledge 1981*b*; Dettenhofer 1994*b*. Spartan 'mirage' generally: Ollier 1933–43; Rawson 1969. Recent work includes Powell and Hodkinson (eds.) 1994.

Sparta through the Looking-Glass (pp. 95–7)

The representation and status of Spartan wives are discussed from different standpoints in Cartledge 1981*b* and Redfield 1977/8.

A Greek Wonderwoman (pp. 97–9)

Artemisia: Weil, R. 1976; Munson 1988. Aeschylean Persians: Hall, E. 1989: 69–100. Greek military code: Loraux 1989*b*; cf. Schaps 1982.

Two Oriental Cautionary Tales (pp. 99–101)

Amestris: Sancisi-Weerdenburg 1983: 27–30; Gray 1989: 15–16. Wife of Kandaules: Gray 1989: 71.

A Modest Proposal (pp. 101–3)

The 'subtle' Xenophon: Higgins 1977. Wife of Iskhomakhos: Harvey 1984; Foucault 1985/7: 152–65. Mania: Gray 1989: 29–32; Cartledge 1993*b*. In addition see Pomeroy 1994.

The Perfect Wife (pp. 103–4)

Pantheia: Tatum 1989; manner of her death: compare and contrast Loraux 1988. I have elaborated my views in Cartledge 1993*b*. See also Oost 1977; cf. North 1977; Murnaghan 1988.

5. In the Club: Citizens v. Aliens

The Primacy of Politics? (pp. 105–8)

Marx and Antiquity: Ste. Croix 1981: 19–30. *Annaliste* response to Marx: e.g. Braudel 1980. Greek political sphere: Vernant 1983*d* (*l'espace civique*); Meier 1990 (*das Politische*). Alkaios' *agora*: Burn 1978: 242. *Politeia* usage: Bordes 1982. See also Hansen (ed.) 1993.

Herodotus and the Tyranny of Nomos (pp. 108–13)

Herodotean power-discourse: Momigliano 1979; Hartog 1988: 322–40; Cartledge 1990*b*. *Nomos* in Herodotus: Giraudeau 1984. Greek invention of 'politics': Finley 1983; Farrar 1988; cf. Dunn 1993. 'Persian

Debate': Lasserre 1976; cf. Dihle 1962; Raaflaub 1989; de Romilly 1992: 219, 221. The 'wise adviser' in Herodotus: Lattimore 1939*b*. In addition see Lateiner 1989.

Thucydides and the Utility of History (pp. 114–17)

'The human thing': Cogan 1981 (though his identification is unpersuasive). Thucydidean utility: Dover 1973: 35–44; Parry 1981: 103–13. A modern view: Ehrenberg 1974*b*: 154–7.

Xenophon and the Privatization of the Political (pp. 117–19)

Greek and oriental historiography contrasted: Momigliano 1991: 1–28. Xenophon's idea of history: Sordi 1950–1; Henry 1967; Cawkwell 1979; Cartledge 1987: 61–5; Gray 1989. Recent work includes Dillery 1995.

Oriental Despotism Revalued (pp. 119–21)

Fourth-century monarchism generally: Ehrenberg 1974*c*. Monarchism in the *Cyropaedia*: Carlier 1978.

Reluctant Mercenaries (pp. 121–2)

The fourth-century mercenary phenomenon: Cartledge 1987: 314–30; Garlan 1989*a*: 143–72. Xenophon's projected colony: Nussbaum 1978.

Aristotle and the Teleological Polis (pp. 122–3)

Mulgan 1977; Keyt and Miller (eds.) 1991; Lord and O'Connor (eds.) 1991. League of Corinth and Greek federalism: Larsen 1968; Harding 1985: no. 101. For a more recent view see Stalley 1995.

Who Was the Greek Citizen? (pp. 123–6)

Aristotelian civism: Mossé 1967; Pečirka 1967; Clark, S. R. L. 1975; Huxley 1979: 40–50; Lévy 1980; Whitehead 1991. Athenian metic status: Whitehead 1977, 1986. Outsiders in the Greek city: Baslez 1984; Whitehead 1984; Lonis 1988.

Stasis, not Stasis (pp. 126–9)

Greek *stasis*: Lintott 1982; Loraux 1991. Aristotelian binarism: Ste. Croix 1981: 69–81. Thucydidean *stasis*: Wassermann 1947; Macleod 1983*b*; Loraux 1986*b*; Connor 1991: 60–5. Xenophontic *stasis*: Gray 1989: 94–106. See also Manopoulos 1991; Berger 1992.

A Discourse of Civic Harmony (pp. 129–32)

On the funeral speech as a genre, see Loraux 1986*a*; on the *Menexenos*, see Coventry 1989. On the values expressed or implied in the funeral speech, see also Walcot 1973 and Loraux 1982.

6. Of Inhuman Bondage: Free v. Slave

General

Relevant to the chapter as a whole are several works by Finley (esp. 1979, 1980) and the two collections he edited (1968, 1987); Wiedemann 1987; Garlan 1988. Comparatively: Cartledge 1985*a*; Archer (ed.) 1988.

Slavery Begins at Home (pp. 133–5)

Twentieth-century slavery: Sawyer 1986. Aristotle and the American Indians: Hanke 1959; Huxley 1980; Pagden 1986: 27–56.

Ideology or Philosophy? (pp. 135–41)

Roman slavery: Buckland 1908. Ancient ideology of slavery: Schlaifer 1968; Ste. Croix 1975*b*; Finley 1980; Ste. Croix 1981: 409–52; Clark, S. R. L. 1985; Just 1985; Garnsey 1996. Aristotelian doctrine: weak defence by Fortenbaugh 1977; Schofield 1990 is better but overstresses Aristotle's philosophical anti-conventionalism; Schlaifer 1968: 130–2 and Smith 1991 expose the logical flaws; cf. briefly Lloyd, G. E. R. 1991*b*: 365–6 for relationship of science and morality in Aristotle. In addition to the above see Bradley 1994.

Aristotelian Meanness (pp. 141–3)

Aristotle's contemporary opponents: Cambiano 1987. Necessity of leisure: Stocks 1936; cf. Aymard 1967*b*. Greek ideas of freedom: Finley 1981*d*, Raaflaub 1985; de Romilly 1989; Patterson, O. 1991.

Between Free Men and Slaves (pp. 143–5)

Formula: Finley 1981*b*; cf. Lotze 1959. The translation of Pollux 3. 83 is from Cartledge 1979: 352. 'Elements of freedom': Westermann 1968*b*. Helots: Cartledge 1979: ch. 10; Cartledge 1987: ch. 10; Ducat 1990 (with caution).

Greek Historiography of Servitude (pp. 145–7)

Generally Vidal-Naquet 1986*d*. The 'serfdom' debate: Ste. Croix 1981: 147–62; *contra* Garlan 1988: 93–102. Kritias and the Penestai: Lintott 1982: 269–70. Recent work includes Ducat 1994; Hunt, P. 1998.

Chattel Slaves in Battle (pp. 147–9)

Generally: Welwei 1974–7; Hunt, P. 1998. Arginousai: Garlan 1988: 164–6. Kerkyra: Loraux 1989c. Khios: Garlan 1988: 171 and n. 70.

No Safety in Numbers? (pp. 150–1)

Athens: Westermann 1968b is balanced. Figures for modern slave-societies: Patterson, O. 1982: appendix C. Thucydides' 'more than twice ten thousand': Parke 1932.

Man-Footed Creatures (pp. 151–3)

Herodotus on slaves: Harvey 1988a; cf. Wiesen 1980. Enslavement of war-captives: Pritchett 1991: 223–45.

Barbarian Sources (pp. 153–5)

Thrace as source: Finley 1981f. 'Attic Stelai': Austin and Vidal-Naquet 1977: no. 75. Recommendation of ethnic mix of slaves: Ste. Croix 1981: 146. 'Thratta': Ehrenberg 1962: 172. Visual representation: Lissarrague 1992: 198, fig. 37.

Servile Functions (pp. 155–6)

Debate over slaves in agriculture: Jameson 1977/8 and Ste. Croix 1981: 505–9 v. Wood 1988. Garlan 1989b is decisive in favour of their use by large landowners. See also Jameson 1994.

A Return to Ideology (pp. 156–8)

Servile interregnum at Argos: Garlan 1988: 99.

Greeks:Barbarians::Free:Slave (pp. 158–60)

'Unwritten laws': Ostwald 1986: 130, 252.

Free:Slave::Men:Women? (pp. 160–1)

Greek ideas of self-control: North 1977; Most 1989. Slaves as 'children': Golden 1985. Aristotle and the feminine psyche: Clark, S. R. L. 1982; Just 1985 (confessedly indebted to Dover 1974 for collection of evidence and commentary); Vidal-Naquet 1986e: 207. St Paul: Ste. Croix 1981: 104–5.

Free:Slave::Citizen:Alien (pp. 161–5)

Slavery and citizenship: Finley 1981d; Raaflaub 1983; Clark, S. R. L. 1985; cf. for an American comparison Morgan 1975. Democratic respect for sovereignty of laws: Ostwald 1986. Critics of democracy: Jones, A. H. M. 1957: 41–72; Finley 1985*b*; Ober 1998; Roberts 1994. 'Servile' occupations and attitudes to labour: Schlaifer 1968: 99–104; cf. Aymard 1948, 1967*b*; Vernant 1983*c*.

Freedom and Independence Externalized (pp. 165–6)

autonomia/eleutheria slogans: Ostwald 1982; cf. Ste. Croix 1954/5. Athenian imperial 'tyranny': Tuplin 1985. Spartan intervention at Mantineia: Cartledge 1987: 257–62. Obstacles to interstate freedom: Larsen 1962.

7. Knowing your Place: Gods v. Mortals

General

Of general relevance are Gernet and Boulanger 1932; Fondation Hardt 1952; Rudhardt 1958; Nock 1972*a*, Gordon (ed.) 1981; Rudhardt 1981*a*; Burkert 1985; Easterling and Muir (eds.) 1985; Vernant 1991*a*; Bruit Zaidman and Schmitt Pantel 1992. Recent work on this subject includes Bremmer 1994.

The Greeks Did Not Have a Word for It (pp. 167–9)

Derivation of 'religion': Ste. Croix 1972*b*. Polytheism: Rudhardt 1966. Continuities between paganism and Christianity: Lane Fox 1986; discontinuities: Price 1984: 11–15. (Rightly, there is no chapter on religion in Finley 1981*j*.) Greek religious festivals: Cartledge 1985*a*.

Greek Religion as a System of Cultural Self-Definition (pp. 169–71)

Discussion of Geertz: Helgeland 1986. 'Making sense' of Greek religion: Rudhardt 1981*b*; Gould 1985; cf. Vernant 1991*d*; and on Vernant, Segal 1982.

The Origins of the Gods (pp. 171–4)

Herodotus on names of gods: Linforth 1926, 1928; Lattimore 1939*a*; Burkert 1982. Xenophanes on nature of gods: Kirk, Raven, and Schofield 1983: 168–9; cf. Dover 1988*b*: 152–3. Diagoras: Dover 1988*b*: 137–8; cf. generally Fahr 1969. Protagoras' agnosticism: Müller 1967; Farrar 1988: 50–3.

Herodotus' Religious Mirror (pp. 174–7)

Ancient death and burial generally: Gnoli and Vernant (eds.) 1982. Scythian royal burials: Hartog 1982. Spartan royal burials: Cartledge 1987: 331–43. Greek animal blood-sacrifice: compare and contrast Kirk, G. S. 1981 with Vernant 1991c (both in Fondation Hardt 1981); also Burkert 1983 with Detienne and Vernant 1989.

The Debate over Anthropomorphism Renewed (pp. 177–84)

Aristotle's gods: Verdenius 1960. Myth of Prometheus: Bruit Zaidman and Schmitt Pantel 1992: 164–9. Sokrates' condemnation: Garland 1992: 136–51. Filial piety: Dover 1974: 274–5. The Athenian plague as *daimonion*: Mikalson 1984. Athenian introduction of Boreas: Garland 1992: 71, 163. 'God-making' comparatively: Haldane 1985. See also Wallace 1994.

Staying the Hand of God (pp. 184–9)

Religion in history—Xenophon: Gray 1989: 157; Herodotus: Waters 1985: 96–118; Gould 1989: 67–76. Thucydides: Stahl 1966; Oost 1975; Marinatos 1981a; Chambers 1991; Hornblower 1992. Thucydides 2. 17. 1–2: Marinatos 1981b v. Dover 1988d.

8. Epilogue

Otherness v. Classicism (pp. 191–2)

See works cited under Prologue, 'The Greeks and "Us"'.

A Religious Theatre (pp. 192–6)

Generally: Goldhill 1986; Winkler and Zeitlin (eds.) 1990. Festivals: Cartledge 1985a, 1990a: 1–10. Athenian self-representation: Segal 1986; Zeitlin 1986b, 1989. Alleged religious crisis of Sophistic 'enlightenment': Burkert 1985: 311–17; cf. Fahr 1969. Religious theatre: Mikalson 1991.

A Political Theatre (pp. 196–8)

Democratic origins of tragedy: Connor 1990. Democratic sortition: Headlam 1933. Demosthenes' mugging and his democratic response: Wilson 1991. Recent works include Segal 1995; Easterling (ed.) (1997).

An Open Society? (p. 198)

On Greek civic freedom (and its limitations) see esp. Finley 1981*d* and Patterson, O. 1991.

Afterword

Origins, motives, and aims (pp. 199–200)

A German translation, under the title *Die Griechen und Wir*, by Drs Reinhard Brenneke and Barbara von Reibnitz, was published by the Metzler Verlag in 1998; a Japanese translation by Dr Y. Hashiba appeared in 2001. To these three translators I am indebted for their patient and skilful work.

On 'classic' status, see the quotation from Christian Meier reproduced at the beginning of the Epilogue above, p. 191.

Which Greeks? Whose Greeks? (pp. 200–2)

Quotation from Osborne 2000: 23. I cannot resist citing, as an egregious instance of laxity of usage, McNiven 1995. Also unacceptably loose is Barkan 1995: 73, a discussion of Victorian 'Othering' of the Classical (Greek) nude. See also, e.g., Dover (ed.) 1992, which begins with Roman perceptions; or Hölscher (ed.) 2000, which has a section entitled 'Von der Antike in die Neuzeit und Zurück'. On cultural relativism see recently Barry 2001, though he merely asserts, rather than justifies, the distinction he draws between locally varying conventional norms and universally, cross-culturally valid principles.

Researching otherwise (p. 202)

See further Cartledge 1998 and my contributions to Cartledge (ed.) 2002. Sargisson 2000: ch. 5, in a book concerned with 'the politics of transgression', has a discussion of 'Self/Other Relations' within a framework of 'green political thought'.

Bibliography

THIS selective Bibliography mainly lists those works cited by author-name and date in either the main text or the Further Reading section above. But I have also included a number of works, especially historiographical, which I have not had occasion to cite specifically. Abbreviations of journals are those used in the classicists' research yearbook *L'Année philologique*.

ACKERMAN, R. (1973), 'Writing about Writing about Myth', *JHI* 34: 147–55.

ADAIR, G. (1986), *Myths & Memories* (London).

AMPOLO, C. (1997), *Storie greche: La formazione della moderna storiografia sugli antichi Greci* (Turin).

ANDERSON, B. (1991), *Imagined Communities* (London).

ANDERSON, J. K. (1974), *Xenophon* (London).

ANDREWES, A. (1961), 'Thucydides and the Persians', *Historia* 10: 1–18.

ARCHER, L. J. (1988) (ed.), *Slavery and Other Forms of Unfree Labour* (London).

ARDENER, E. (1989), 'Comprehending Others' (1977), in M. Chapman (ed.), *The Voice of Prophecy and Other Essays* (Oxford): 159–85.

ARENS, W. (1979), *The Man-Eating Myth: Anthropology and Anthropophagy* (New York).

ARTHUR, M. B. (1984), 'The Origins of the Western Attitude to Women' (1973), in Peradotto and Sullivan (1984): 7–58.

ASSMANN, J. (1992), *Das kulturelle Gedächtnis: Schrift, Erinnerung und politische Identität in frühen Hochkulturen* (Munich).

—— and HÖLSCHER, T. (eds.) (1988), *Kultur und Gedächtnis* (Frankfurt-am-Main).

ATKINSON, R. F. (1978), *Knowledge and Explanation in History: An Introduction to the Philosophy of History* (London).

AUBERGER, J. (1991) (ed.), *Ctésias: Histoires de l'Orient* (Paris).

AUSTIN, M. M., and VIDAL-NAQUET, P. (1977), *Economic and Social History of Ancient Greece: An Introduction* (London).

AYMARD, A. (1948), 'L'Idée de travail dans la Grèce archaïque', *Journal de Psychologie* 41: 29–50.

—— (1967a), *Études d'histoire ancienne* (Paris).

—— (1967b), 'Hiérarchie de travail et autarcie individuelle dans la Grèce archaïque' (1943), in Aymard (1967a): 316–33.

BACKHAUS, W. (1976), 'Der Hellenen-Barbaren Gegensatz und die hippokratische Schrift *peri Aëron Hydaton Topon*', *Historia* 25: 170–85.

BACON, H. (1961), *Barbarians in Greek Tragedy* (New Haven, CT).

BADIAN, E. (1994), 'Herodotus on Alexander I of Macedon: A Study in some Subtle Silences', in Hornblower (1994): 107–30.

BALDRY, H. C. (1965), *The Unity of Mankind in Greek Thought* (Cambridge).

BARKAN, E. (1995), 'Victorian Promiscuity: Greek Ethics and Primitive Exemplars', in E. Barkan and R. Bush (eds.), *Prehistories of the Future: The Primitivist Project and the Culture of Modernism* (Stanford, CA), 56–92.

BARKER, F. (1985) (ed.), *Europe and its Others: Proceedings of the Essex Conference on the Sociology of Literature*, 2 vols. (Colchester).

BARNES, J. (1980), 'Aristotle and the Methods of Ethics', *Revue internationale de philosophie* 34: 490–511.

——, SCHOFIELD, M., and SORABJI, R. (1977) (eds.), *Articles on Aristotle*, ii: *Ethics and Politics* (London).

BARRY, B. (2001), *Culture and Equality: An Egalitarian Critique of Multiculturalism* (Cambridge: Polity).

BASLEZ, M.-F. (1984), *L'Étranger dans la Grèce antique* (Paris).

—— (1986), 'Le Péril barbare, une invention des Grecs?', in Mossé (1986): 284–99.

BEARD, M., and HENDERSON, J. (2000), *Classics: A Very Short Introduction* (Oxford) [revised reissue of 1995 original.]

BEAUVOIR, S. DE (1953), *The Second Sex* (London) (pub. in French Paris, 1949).

BENTLEY, M. (1997) (ed.), *The Routledge Companion to Historiography* (London).

BERARD, C. (1989a) (ed.), *A City of Images: Iconography and Society in Ancient Greece* (Princeton, NJ) (1st pub. in French, Lausanne, 1984).

—— (1989b), 'The Order of Women', in Berard (1989a): 89–108.

BERGER, S. (1992), *Revolution and Society in Greek Sicily and Southern Italy* (Stuttgart).

BERLIN, I. (1980), 'The Concept of Scientific History' (1960), in id., *Concepts and Categories* (Oxford): 103–42.

BERNAL, M. (1987–91), *Black Athena: The Afroasiatic Roots of Classical Civilization*, 2 vols (London).

BICKERMAN, E. J. (1952), 'Origines Gentium', *CP* 47: 65–81.

BIERSACK, A. (1989), 'Local Knowledge, Local History: Geertz and Beyond', in Hunt (1989): 72–96.

BINDER, G., and EFFE, B. (1990) (eds.), *Mythos: Erzählende Weltdeutung im Spannungsfeld von Ritual, Geschichte und Rationalität* (Trier).

BLEICKEN, J. (1995), *Die athenische Demokratie*, 4th edn. (Paderborn).

BLOCH, M. (1954), *The Historian's Craft* (Manchester).

BOEGEHOLD, A. L. (1994), 'Perikles' citizenship law of 451/50 B.C.', in Boegehold and Scafuro (1994): 57–66.

—— and SCAFURO, A. C. (1994) (eds.), *Athenian Identity and Civic Ideology* (Baltimore).

BORDES, J. (1982), *'Politeia' dans la pensée grecque jusqu'à Aristote* (Paris).

BOVON, A. (1963), 'La Représentation des guerres perses et la notion de barbare dans la Iʳᵉ moitié du Vᵉ siècle', *BCH* 87: 579–602.

BOWERSOCK, G. W. (1965), 'The Personality of Thucydides', *Antioch Review* 25: 135–46.

BRADLEY, K. R. (1994), *Slavery and Society at Rome* (Cambridge).

BRAUDEL, F. (1980), *On History* (London) (1st pub. in French, Paris, 1969).

BREMMER, J. (1987a) (ed.), *Interpretations of Greek Mythology* (London).

—— (1987b), 'What Is a Greek Myth?' in Bremmer (1987a): 1–9.

—— (1996), *Götter, Mythen und Heiligtümer im antiken Griechenland* (Darmstadt).

BRIANT, P. (1982), *État et pasteurs au Moyen-Orient ancien* (Cambridge).

BRILLANTE, C. (1984), 'Fra storia e mito', *QUCC* 16: 175–87.

BROWNING, R. (1989), 'Greeks and Others: From Antiquity to the Renaissance', in id., *History, Language and Literacy in the Byzantine World*, ch. 2 (Northampton).

BRUIT ZAIDMAN, L., and SCHMITT PANTEL, P. (1992), *Religion in the Ancient Greek City* (Cambridge) (1st pub. in French, Paris, 1989).

BRYCE, T. R. (1986), *The Lycians I* (Copenhagen).

BUCKLAND, W. W. (1908), *The Roman Law of Slavery* (Cambridge).

BURKERT, W. (1979), *Structure and History in Greek Mythology and Ritual* (Berkeley, Calif.).

—— (1982), 'Herodot über die Namen der Götter: Polytheismus als historisches Problem', *MH* 39: 121–32.

—— (1983), *Homo Necans: The Anthropology of Ancient Greek Sacrificial Ritual and Myth* (Berkeley, CA) (1st pub. in German, Berlin, 1972).

—— (1985), *Greek Religion: Archaic and Classical* (Oxford).

—— (1987), 'Oriental and Greek Mythology: The Meeting of Parallels', in Bremmer (1987a): 10–40.

—— (1992), *The Orientalizing Revolution: Near Eastern Influence on Greek Culture in the Early Archaic Age* (Cambridge, Mass.) (1st pub. in German, Heidelberg, 1984).

BURN, A. R. (1978), *The Lyric Age of Greece* (1st pub. 1960, repr. with bibliographical add. London).

BURY, J. B. (1909), *The Ancient Greek Historians* (London).

BUXTON, R. G. A. (1980), 'Blindness and Limits: Sophokles and the Logic of Myth?, *JHS* 100: 22–37.

—— (1994), *Imaginary Greece: The Contexts of Mythology* (Cambridge).

CAMBIANO, G. (1987), 'Aristotle and the Anonymous Opponents of Slavery', in Finley (1987): 22–41.

CAMERON, A., and KUHRT, A. (1983) (eds.), *Images of Women in Antiquity* (London) (repr. with add. 1993).

CANARY, R. H., and KOZICKI, H. (1978) (eds.), *The Writing of History: Literary Form and Historical Understanding* (Madison, WI).

CANFORA, L. (1977), 'La Préface de Thucydide et la critique de la raison historique', *REG* 90: 455–61.

CARLIER, P. (1978), 'L'Idée de monarchie impériale dans la Cyropédie de Xénophon', *Ktema* 3: 133–63.

CARLIER-DETIENNE, J. (1980), 'Les Amazones font la guerre et l'amour', *Ethnographie* 76: 11–33.

CARR, E. H. (1986), *What is History?* (2nd edn., London), (new edn., 2002).

CARTLEDGE, P. A. (1979), *Sparta and Lakonia. A Regional History 1300–362 BC* (London), (new edn., 2001).

—— (1981a), 'The Politics of Spartan Pederasty', *PCPS* 27: 17–36 (repr. with add. in Siems (1988): 385–415).

—— (1981b), 'Spartan Wives: Liberation or Licence?', *CQ* 31: 84–105.

—— (1985a), 'The Greek Religious Festivals', in Easterling and Muir (1985): 98–127.

—— (1985b), 'Rebels and Sambos in Classical Greece: A Comparative View', in Cartledge and Harvey (1985): 16–46.

—— (1987), *Agesilaos and the Crisis of Sparta* (London).

—— (1990a), *Aristophanes and his Theatre of the Absurd* (Bristol) (new edn. 1999).

—— (1990b), 'Herodotus and "the Other": A Meditation on Empire', *EMC/CV* 9: 27–40.

—— (1990c), 'Fowl Play: A Curious Lawsuit in Classical Athens

(Antiphon XVI, fr. 27–9 Thalheim)', in Cartledge, Millett, and Todd (1990): 41–61.

CARTLEDGE, P. A. (1993), 'The Silent Women of Thucydides: 2, 45, 2 Re-Viewed', in R. M. Rosen and J. Farrell (eds.), *Nomodeiktes: Festschrift M. Ostwald*, 125–32 (Ann Arbor, MI).

—— (1993a), '"Like a Worm i' the Bud"? A Heterology of Greek Slavery', in *G&R* 40/2: 163–80.

—— (1993b), 'Xenophon's Women: A Touch of the Other', in H. D. Jocelyn and H. Hurt (eds.), *Tria Lustra: Festschrift J. Pinsent* (Liverpool): 5–14.

—— (1995), '"We are all Greeks"?: Ancient (especially Herodotean) and modern contestations of Hellenism', *BICS* 40: 75–82.

—— (1996), 'La Politica', in Settis (1996): 39–72.

—— (1997a) '"Deep plays": theatre as process in Greek civic life', in Easterling (1997): 3–35.

—— (1997b) 'Historiography and ancient Greek self-definition', in Bentley (1997): 23–42.

—— (1998), 'Classics: From Discipline in Crisis to (Multi)cultural Capital?', in Y. L. Too and N. Livingstone (eds.), *Pedagogy and Power: Rhetorics of Classical Learning* (Cambridge): 16–28.

—— (2000), '"To Poseidon the Driver": An Arkado-Lakonian Ram Dedication', in G. R. Tsetskhladze, A. J. N. W. Prag, and A. M. Snodgrass (eds.), *Periplous: Papers on Classical Art and Archaeology presented to Sir John Boardman* (London): 60–7.

—— (2001) *Spartan Reflections* (London, Berkeley and Los Angeles).

—— (2002) (ed.), *The Cambridge Illustrated History of Ancient Greece*, 2nd edn. (Cambridge).

—— and HARVEY, F. D. (1985) (eds.), *CRUX: Essays in Greek History Presented to G. E. M. de Ste. Croix on his 75th birthday* (Exeter).

—— MILLETT, P. C., and TODD, S. C. (1990) (eds.), *NOMOS: Essays in Athenian Law, Society and Politics* (Cambridge).

CAWKWELL, G. L. (1972) (ed.), *Xenophon: 'The Persian Expedition'* (Harmondsworth).

—— (1979) (ed.), *Xenophon: 'A History of My Times'* (Harmondsworth).

CHAMBERS, M. H. (1991), 'Cornford's Thucydides Mythistoricus', in W. M. Calder III (ed.), *The Cambridge Ritualists Reconsidered* (*ICS* Suppl. 2; Atlanta, GA): 61–77.

CHIAPELLI, A., BENSON, M. J. B., and CHIAPELLI, R. L. F. (1976) (eds.), *First Images of America: The Impact of the New World on the Old* (Berkeley, CA).

CHRISTIANSEN, J., and MELANDER, T. (1988) (eds.), *Proceedings of the 3rd Symposium on Ancient Greek and Related Pottery* (Copenhagen).

CLARK, G. (1989), *Women in Antiquity* (*G&R* New Surveys in the Classics, 21; Oxford).

CLARK, S. R. L. (1975), *Aristotle's Man: Speculations upon Aristotelian Anthropology* (Oxford).

—— (1982), 'Aristotle's Woman', *HPT* 3: 71–91.

—— (1985), 'Slaves and Citizens', *Philosophy* 60: 27–46.

CLARKE, G. W. (1989) (ed.), *Rediscovering Hellenism: The Hellenic Inheritance and the English Imagination* (Cambridge).

COGAN, M. (1981), *The Human Thing: The Speeches and Principles of Thucydides's History* (Chicago).

COHEN, B. (2000) (ed.), *Not the Classical Ideal: Athens and the Construction of the Other in Greek Art* (Leiden).

COHEN, D. (1991), *Law, Society and Sexuality: The Enforcement of Morals in Classical Athens* (Cambridge).

COHEN, P. S. (1969), 'Theories of Myth', *Man*, NS 4: 337–53.

COLLINGWOOD, R. G. (1946), *The Idea of History* (Oxford).

—— (1993), *The Idea of History*, rev. edn. of Collingwood 1946 (Oxford).

CONNOR, W. R. (1977), 'A Post-Modernist Thucydides?', *CJ* 72: 289–98.

—— (1984), *Thucydides* (Princeton, NJ).

—— (1990), 'City Dionysia and Athenian Democracy', in J. R. Fears (ed.), *Aspects of Athenian Democracy* (*CetM* Diss. XI, Copenhagen): 7–32.

—— (1991), 'Polarization in Thucydides', in Lebow and Strauss (1991): 53–69.

CONSTANT, B. (1988), *Political Writings*, ed. B. Fontana (Cambridge).

COOK, A. S. (1976), 'Herodotus: The Act of Inquiry as a Liberation from Myth', *Helios* 3: 23–66.

—— (1988), *History/Writing: The Theory and Practice of History in Antiquity and in Modern Times* (Cambridge).

COOK, J. M. (1983), *The Persian Empire* (London).

COOK, R. M. (1955), 'Thucydides as Archaeologist', *ABSA* 50: 266–70.

CORNFORD, F. M. (1907), *Thucydides Mythistoricus* (London).

COVENTRY, L. J. (1989), 'Philosophy and Rhetoric in the Menexenus', *JHS* 109: 1–15.

DAVIES, J. K. (1977/8), 'Athenian Citizenship: The Descent-Group and the Alternatives', *CJ* 73: 105–21.

DAVIS, D. B. (1984), *Slavery and Human Progress* (New York).

—— (1988), *The Problem of Slavery in Western Culture* (rev. edn., New York).

DAY, J. W. (1985), 'Epigrams and History: The Athenian Tyrannicides, a Case in Point', in Jameson (1985): 25–46.

DEAN-JONES, L. (1991), 'The Cultural Construct of the Female Body in Classical Greek Science', in Pomeroy (1991): 111–37.

—— (1994), *Women's Bodies in Classical Greek Science* (Oxford).

DEGLER, C. N. (1983), 'Can the American People be Put Together Again?', *History Today* (Aug.): 3–4.

DETIENNE, M. (1981), 'Between Beasts and Gods' (1972), in Gordon (1981): 215–28.

—— (1986), *The Creation of Mythology* (Chicago) (1st pub. in French, Paris, 1981).

—— and VERNANT, J. P. (1989) (eds.), *The Cuisine of Sacrifice among the Greeks* (Chicago) (1st pub. in French, Paris, 1979).

DETTENHOFER, M. H. (1994*a*) (ed.), *Reine Männersache? Frauen in Männerdomänen der antiken Welt* (Cologne).

—— (1994*b*), 'Die Frauen von Sparta: Ökonomische Kompetenz und politische Relevanz', in Dettenhofer (1994): 15–40.

DEWALD, C. (1981), 'Women and Culture in Herodotus' Histories', in Foley (1981): 91–125.

—— (1987), 'Narrative Surface and Authorial Voice in Herodotus' Histories', *Arethusa* 20: 147–70.

—— (1990), rev. of Hartog (1988), in *CP* 85: 217–24.

—— and MARINCOLA, J. (1987), 'A Selective Introduction to Herodotean Studies', *Arethusa* 20: 9–40.

DI DONATO, R. (1990), *Per una antropologia storica del mondo antico* (Pisa).

DIHLE, A. (1962), 'Herodot und die Sophistik', *Philologus* 106: 207–20.

DILLER, A. (1937), *Race Mixture among the Greeks before Alexander* (Urbana, IL).

DILLERY, J. (1995), *Xenophon and the History of his Times* (London).

DODDS, E. R. (1951), *The Greeks and the Irrational* (Berkeley, CA).

—— (1973*a*), *The Ancient Concept of Progress and Other Essays* (Oxford).

—— (1973*b*), 'The Religion of the Ordinary Man in Classical Greece', in Dodds (1973*a*): 140–55.

—— (1973*c*), 'The Sophistic Movement and the Failure of Greek Liberalism' (1937), in Dodds (1973*a*): 92–105.

DOHERTY, L. (2001), *Gender and the Interpretation of Classical Myth* (London).

DOVER, K. J. (1973), *Thucydides* (*G&R* New Surveys in the Classics, 7; Oxford).

—— (1974), *Greek Popular Morality in the time of Plato and Aristotle* (Oxford).

—— (1980), *The Greeks* (Oxford).

—— (1988a), *The Greeks and their Legacy: Collected Papers, II* (Oxford).

—— (1988b), 'The Freedom of the Intellectual in Greek Society' (1976), in Dover (1988a): 135–58.

—— (1988c), 'Thucydides "as History" and Thucydides "as Literature"' (1983), in Dover (1988a): 53–64.

—— (1988d), 'Thucydides on Oracles' (1987), in Dover (1988a): 65–73.

—— (1992) (ed.), *Perceptions of the Ancient Greeks* (Oxford: Blackwell).

DREWS, R. (1973), *The Greek Accounts of Eastern History* (Washington, DC).

DUBISCH, J. (1986) (ed.), *Gender and Power in Rural Greece* (Princeton).

DUBOIS, P. (1982), *Centaurs and Amazons* (Chicago).

—— (1988), *Sowing the Body: Psychoanalysis and Ancient Representations of Women* (Chicago).

DU BOULAY, J. (1974), *Portrait of a Greek Mountain Village* (Oxford).

—— (1986), 'Women—Images of their Nature and Destiny in Rural Greece', in Dubisch (1986): 139–68.

DUCAT, J. (1990), *Les Hilotes* (*BCH* Suppl. 20, Paris).

—— (1994), *Les Pénestes de Thessalie* (Paris).

DUE, B. (1989), *The 'Cyropaedia': A Study of Xenophon's Aims and Methods* (Aarhus).

DUNDES, A. (1985), 'Nationalistic Inferiority Complexes and the Fabrication of Fakelore: A Reconsideration of Ossian, the Kinder- und Hausmärchen, the Kalevala, and Paul Bunyan', *Journal of Folklore Research* 22: 5–18.

DUNN, J. (1993), *Western Political Theory in the Face of the Future*, 2nd edn. (Cambridge).

—— (1992) (ed.), *Democracy: The Unfinished Journey 508 BC to AD 1993* (Oxford).

—— (1996), *History of Political Theory* (Cambridge).

EASTERLING, P. E. (1989), *The Survival of Greek* (London) (1988 Inaugural Lecture, University College London).

—— (1997) (ed.), *The Cambridge Companion to Greek Tragedy* (Cambridge).

—— and MUIR, J. V. (1985) (eds.), *Greek Religion and Society* (Cambridge).

EDER, W., and HÖLKESKAMP, K.-J. (1997) (eds.), *Volk und Verfassung im vorhellenistischen Griechenland* (Stuttgart).

EDMUNDS, L. (1990) (ed.), *Approaches to Greek Myth* (Baltimore).

EHRENBERG, V. (1962), *The People of Aristophanes: A Sociology of Old Attic Comedy*, 3rd edn. (New York).

—— (1974a), *Man, State and Deity: Essays in Ancient History* (London).

—— (1974b), 'Remarks on the Meaning of History', in Ehrenberg (1974a): 143–82.

—— (1974c), 'Some Aspects of the Transition from the Classical to the Hellenistic Age', in Ehrenberg (1974a): 52–63.

EUBEN, J. P. (1997), *Corrupting Youth: Political Education, Democratic Culture and Political Theory* (Princeton).

EVANS, J. A. S. (1965), 'Despotes Nomos', *Athenaeum* 43: 142–53.

—— (1969), 'Father of History or Father of Lies: The Reputation of Herodotus', *CJ* 64: 11–17.

—— (1991), *Herodotus Explorer of the Past: Three Essays* (Princeton, NJ).

EVANS-PRITCHARD, E. E. (1937), *Witchcraft, Oracles and Magic among the Azande* (Oxford) (shortened repr. 1976).

—— (1965), *Theories of Primitive Religion* (Oxford).

FAHR, W. (1969), '*Theous nomizein*': *Zum Problem der Anfänge des Atheismus bei den Griechen* (Hildesheim).

FANTHAM, E., *et al.* (1994), *Women in the Classical World* (New York).

FARRAR, C. (1988), *The Origins of Democratic Thinking: The Invention of Politics in Classical Athens* (Cambridge).

FEHLING, D. (1989), *Herodotus and his 'Sources': Citation, Invention and Narrative Art* (Leeds) (1st pub. in Germany, Berlin, 1971).

FINLEY, M. I. (1968) (ed.), *Slavery in Classical Antiquity*, 2nd edn. (Cambridge).

—— (1979), 'Slavery and the Historians', *Histoire sociale/Social History* 12: 247–61.

—— (1980), *Ancient Slavery and Modern Ideology* (London).

—— (1981a), *Economy and Society in Ancient Greece*, ed. B. D. Shaw and R. P. Saller (London).

—— (1981b) 'Between Slavery and Freedom' (1964), in Finley (1981a): 116–32.

—— (1981c), 'Debt-Bondage and the Problem of Slavery' (1965), in Finley (1981a): 150–66.

—— (1981d), 'The Freedom of the Citizen in the Greek World' (1976), in Finley (1981a): 77–95.

—— (1981e), 'The Servile Statuses of Ancient Greece' (1960), in Finley (1981a): 133–49.

—— (1981*f*), 'The Slave Trade in Antiquity: The Black Sea and Danubian Regions' (1962), in Finley (1981*a*): 167–75.

—— (1981*g*), 'Sparta and Spartan Society' (1968), in Finley (1981*a*): 24–40.

—— (1981*h*), 'Technical Innovation and Economic Progress in the Ancient World' (1965), in Finley (1981*a*): 176–95.

—— (1981*i*), 'Was Greek Civilization based on Slave Labour?' (1959), in Finley (1981*a*): 97–115.

—— (1981*j*) (ed.), *The Legacy of Greece: A New Appraisal* (Oxford).

—— (1982), 'Problems of Slave Society: Some Reflections on the Debate', *OPVS* I: 201–11.

—— (1983), *Politics in the Ancient World* (Cambridge).

—— (1985*a*), *The Ancient Economy*, 2nd edn. (London).

—— (1985*b*), *Democracy Ancient and Modern*, 2nd edn. (London; 1st pub. 1973).

—— (1986*a*), *The Use and Abuse of History*, 2nd edn. (London).

—— (1986*b*), 'The Ancient Greeks and their Nation' (1954), in Finley (1986*a*): 120–33, 233–6.

—— (1986*c*), 'Myth, Memory and History' (1965), in Finley (1986*a*): 11–33, 215–17.

—— (1987) (ed.), *Classical Slavery* (London), (repr. 1999).

FISHER, N. R. E. (1992), *Hybris* (Warminster).

FLORY, S. (1980), 'Who Read Herodotus's Histories?', *AJP* 101: 12–28.

FOLEY, H. P. (1981) (ed.), *Reflections of Women in Antiquity* (New York).

FONDATION HARDT (1952), *La Notion du divin depuis Homère jusqu'à Platon* (Entretiens Hardt 1, Vandœuvres-Geneva).

—— (1958), *Histoire et historiens dans l'Antiquité* (Entretiens Hardt 4, Vandœuvres-Geneva).

—— (1962), *Grecs et Barbares* (Entretiens Hardt 8, Vandœuvres-Geneva).

—— (1964), *La 'Politique' d'Aristote* (Entretiens Hardt 11, Vandœuvres-Geneva).

—— (1981), *Le Sacrifice dans l'Antiquité* (Entretiens Hardt 27, Vandœuvres-Geneva).

—— (1990), *Hérodote et les peuples non-Grecs* (Entretiens Hardt 35, Vandœuvres-Geneva).

FONTAINE, P. F. M. (1986–7), *The Light and the Dark: A Cultural History of Dualism*, 2 vols. (Leiden).

FORNARA, C. W. (1971), *Herodotus: An Interpretative Essay* (Oxford).

FORNARA, C. W., (1983), *The Nature of History in Ancient Greece and Rome* (Berkeley, CA).

FORTENBAUGH, W. W. (1977), 'Aristotle on Slaves and Women', in Barnes, Schofield, and Sorabji (1977): 135–9.

FOUCAULT, M. (1985/7), *The History of Sexuality, II. The Use of Pleasure* (New York) (1st pub. in French, Paris, 1984).

FRIEDL, E. (1986), 'The Position of Women: Appearance and Reality' (1967), in Dubisch (1986): 42–52.

FRITZ, K. VON (1936), 'Herodotus and the Growth of Greek Historiography', *TAPA* 67: 315–40.

FROIDEFOND, C. (1971), *Le Mirage égyptien dans la littérature grecque d'Homère à Aristote* (Paris).

FULLERTON, M. (2000), *Greek Art* (Cambridge).

GALLO, L. (1984), 'La donna greca e la marginalità', *QUCC* 18: 1–51.

GARDNER, J. F. (1989), 'Aristophanes and Male Anxiety: The Defence of the oikos', *G&R* 36: 51–62.

GARLAN, Y. (1988), *Slavery in Ancient Greece* (Ithaca, NY) (1st pub. in French, Paris, 1982).

—— (1989*a*), *Guerre et économie en Grèce ancienne* (Paris).

—— (1989*b*), 'A propos des esclaves dans l'Économique de Xenophon', in *Mélanges P. Lévêque*, ii. 237–43 (Besançon).

GARLAND, R. (1992), *Introducing New Gods: The Politics of Athenian Religion* (London).

GARNSEY, P. (1996), *Ideas of Slavery from Aristotle to Augustine* (Cambridge).

GEARHART, S. (1984), *The Open Boundary of History and Fiction: A Critical Approach to the French Enlightenment* (Princeton, NJ).

GEERTZ, C. (1973*a*), *The Interpretation of Cultures: Selected Essays* (New York).

—— (1973*b*), 'Religion as a Cultural System' (1966), in Geertz (1973*a*): 87–125.

—— (1983), *Local Knowledge: Further Essays in Interpretative Anthropology* (New York).

—— (1985), 'Waddling In', *TLS* (7 June): 623–4.

—— (1987), '"From the Native's Point of View": On the Nature of Anthropological Understanding' (1974), in Gibbons (1987): 133–47.

—— (1988), *Works and Lives: The Anthropologist as Author* (Oxford)

GEHRKE, H.-J. (1985), *Stasis: Untersuchungen zu den inneren Kriegen in den griechischen Staaten des 5. u. 4. Jahrhunderts* (Munich).

—— (1987), 'Die Griechen und die Rache: Ein Versuch in historischer Psychologie', *Saeculum* 38: 121–49.

—— (1994), 'Mythos, Geschichte, Politik—antik und modern', *Saeculum* 45: 239–64.

—— (1994) (ed.) *Rechtskodifizierung und soziale Normen im interkulturellen Vergleich* (Tübingen).

GELLNER, E. (1983), *Nations and Nationalism* (Oxford).

—— (1985*a*), *Relativism and the Social Sciences* (Cambridge).

—— (1985*b*), "What is Structuralisme?" (1982), in Gellner (1985*a*): 128–57.

GEORGES, P. (1994), *Barbarian Asia and the Greek Experience: From the Archaic Period to the Age of Xenophon* (Baltimore).

GERA, D. L. (1993), *Xenophon's Cyropaedia* (Oxford).

GERNET, L. (1968), *Anthropologie de la Grèce antique*, ed. J.-P. Vernant (Paris).

—— and BOULANGER, A. (1932), *Le Génie grec dans la religion* (Paris) (repr. 1970).

GIBBONS, M. T. (1987) (ed.), *Interpreting Politics* (Oxford).

GILL, C., and WISEMAN, T. P. (1993) (eds.), *Lies and Fiction in the Ancient World* (Exeter).

GIRAUDEAU, M. (1984), *Les Notions juridiques et sociales chez Hérodote: Études sur le vocabulaire* (Paris).

GLAZER, N., and MOYNIHAN, D. P. (1975) (eds.), *Ethnicity: Theory and Experience* (Cambridge, Mass.).

GNOLI, G., and VERNANT, J.-P. (1982) (eds.), *La Mort, les morts dans les sociétés anciennes* (Cambridge).

GOLDEN, M. (1984), 'Slavery and Homosexuality at Athens', *Phoenix* 38: 308–24.

—— (1985), ' "Pais", "Child" and "Slave" ', *AC* 65: 91–104.

—— (1992), 'The Uses of Cross-cultural Comparison in Ancient Social History', *ECM/CV* NS 11: 309–31.

GOLDHILL, S. (1986), *Reading Greek Tragedy* (Cambridge) (corrected impression 1988).

—— (1990), 'The Great Dionysia and Civic Ideology', in Winkler and Zeitlin (1990): 97–129.

GOMME, A. W. (1954), *The Greek Attitude to Poetry and History* (Berkeley, CA).

——, ANDREWES, A., and DOVER, K. J. (1945–56, 1970–81), *A Historical Commentary on Thucydides*, 5 vols. (Oxford).

GOODY, J., and WATT, I. (1968), 'The Consequences of Literacy' (1962/3), in J. Goody (ed.), *Literacy in Traditional Societies* (Cambridge): 27–68.

GORDON, R. L. (1981) (ed.), *Myth, Religion and Society: Structuralist Essays by M. Detienne, L. Gernet, J.-P. Vernant and P. Vidal-Naquet* (Cambridge).

GOULD, J. P. A. (1980), 'Law, Custom and Myth: Aspects of the Social Position of Women in Classical Athens', *JHS* 100: 38–59.

GOULD, J. P. A. (1985), 'On Making Sense of Greek Religion', in Easterling and Muir (1985): 1–33.

—— (1989), *Herodotus* (London).

GRAY, V. J. (1989), *The Character of Xenophon's 'Hellenica'* (London).

GREEN, P. (1972), *The Shadow of the Parthenon* (London).

—— (1996), 'The Metamorphosis of the Barbarian: Athenian Panhellenism in a Changing World', in R. W. Wallace and E. M. Harris (eds.), *Transitions to Empire: Essays in Greco-Roman History, 360–146 B.C., in honor of E. Badian* (Norman, OK): 5–36.

GREEN, T. (1989), 'Black Athena and Classical Historiography', in Peradotto and Levine (1989): 55–65.

GRIBBLE, D. (1999), *Alcibiades and Athens: A Study of Literary Presentation* (Oxford).

GRIFFIN, J. (1986), *The Mirror of Myth: Classical Themes and Variations* (London).

GRIFFITH, G. T. (1979), in N. G. L. Hammond and G. T. Griffith, *A History of Macedonia*, vol. ii: *559–336 B.C.* (Oxford).

GROTE, G. (1873), 'Grecian Legends and Early History', in id., *Minor Works*, ed. A. Bain, 73–134 (London).

—— (1888), *A History of Greece*, 10 vols. (London).

GUTHRIE, W. K. C. (1950), *The Greeks and their Gods* (London).

HALDANE, J. B. S. (1985), 'God-Makers' (1932), in id., *On Being the Right Size and Other Essays*, ed. J. Maynard Smith, 85–100 (Oxford).

HALL, E. (1989), *Inventing the Barbarian: Greek Self-Definition through Tragedy* (Oxford).

—— (1992), 'When is a Myth not a Myth? Bernal's "Ancient Model"', *Arethusa* 25: 181–200.

HALL, J. M. (1995*a*), 'How Argive was the "Argive" Heraion? The Political and Cultic Geography of the Argive Plain, 900–400 BC', *AJA* 99: 577–613.

—— (1995*b*), 'The role of language in Greek ethnicities', *PCPS* 41: 83–100.

—— (1997), *Ethnic Identity in Greek Antiquity* (Cambridge).

HALPERIN, D. M., WINKLER, J. J., and ZEITLIN, F. I. (1990) (eds.), *Before Sexuality: The Construction of Erotic Experience in the Ancient Greek World* (Princeton, NJ).

HANKE, L. (1959), *Aristotle and the American Indians: A Study in Race Prejudice in the Modern World* (Bloomington, IL).

HANSEN, M. H. (1993) (ed.), *The Ancient Greek City-State* (Copenhagen).

HANSON, A. E. (1991), 'Continuity and Change: Three Case Studies in Hippocratic Gynecological Therapy and Theory', in Pomeroy (1991): 73–110.

HARDING, P. (1985) (ed.), *From the End of the Peloponnesian War to the Battle of Ipsus* (Cambridge).

HARMATTA, J. (1990), 'Herodotus, Historian of the Cimmerians and the Scythians', in Fondation Hardt (1990): 115–30.

HART, J. (1982), *Herodotus and Greek History* (London).

HARTOG, F. (1982), 'La Mort et l'Autre: Les funérailles des rois Scythes', in Gnoli and Vernant (1982): 143–52.

—— (1986), 'Les Grecs égyptologues', *Annales (ESC)* 41: 953–67.

—— (1988), *The Mirror of Herodotus: The Representation of the Other in the Writing of History* (Berkeley, CA) (1st pub. in French, Paris, 1980; rev. edn. 1992, 2001).

—— (1996), *Mémoire d'Ulysse: Récits sur la frontière en Grèce ancienne* (Paris). (English trans., Edinburgh, 2001.)

HARVEY, F. D. (1984), 'The Wicked Wife of Ischomachos', *EMC/CV* 3: 68–70.

—— (1985), 'Women in Thucydides', *Arethusa* 18: 67–90.

—— (1988a), 'Herodotus and the Man-Footed Creature', in Archer (1988): 42–52.

—— (1988b), 'Painted Ladies: Past, Fiction and Fantasy', in Christiansen and Melander (1988): 242–54.

HEADLAM, J. W. (1933), *Election by Lot at Athens*, 2nd edn. (Cambridge).

HEINIMANN, F. (1945), *Nomos und Physis: Herkunft und Bedeutung einer Antithese im griechischen Denken des 5. Jahrhunderts* (Basle; repr. Darmstadt, 1980).

HEISERMAN, A. J. (1977), *The Novel before the Novel* (Chicago).

HELGELAND, J. (1986), 'Their World and Ours: Ancient and Modern', *Helios* 13/1: 3–15.

HENIGE, D. P. (1982), *Oral Historiography* (London).

HENRY, W. P. (1967), *Greek Historical Writing: A Historiographical Essay based on Xenophon's 'Hellenica'* (Chicago).

HERMAN, G. (1987), *Ritualised Friendship and the Greek City* (Cambridge).

—— (1990), 'Patterns of Name Diffusion within the Greek World and Beyond', *CQ* 40: 349–63.

HERZFELD, M. (1986), 'Within and Without: The Category of "Female" in the Ethnography of Modern Greece', in Dubisch (1986): 215–33.

—— (1987), *Anthropology through the Looking Glass: Critical Ethnography in the Margins of Europe* (Cambridge).

HIGGINS, W. E. (1977), *Xenophon the Athenian: The Problem of the Individual and the Society of the Polis* (Albany, NY).

HIRSCH, S. W. (1985), *The Friendship of the Barbarians: Xenophon and the Persian Empire* (Hanover).

HOBSBAWM, E. J. (1992), *Nations and Nationalism since 1870*, 2nd edn. (Cambridge).

HOFFMANN, E. (1989), *Lost in Translation: Life in a New Language* (New York).

HÖLSCHER, T. (1973), *Griechische Historienbilder des 5. und 4. Jht. v. Chr.* (Würzburg).

—— (1988), 'Tradition und Geschichte: Zwei Typen der Vergangenheit am Beispiel der griechischen Kunst', in Assmann and Hölscher (1988): 115–49.

—— (2000) (ed.), *Gegenwelten zu den Kulturen Griechenlands und Roms in der Antike* (Munich).

HORNBLOWER, S. (1982), *Mausolus* (Oxford).

—— (1987), *Thucydides* (London).

—— (1992), 'The Religious Dimension to the Peloponnesian War or, What Thucydides Does Not Tell us', *HSCP* 94: 160–97.

—— (1994) (ed.), *Greek Historiography* (Oxford).

—— (1994a), 'Narratology and Narrative Techniques in Thucydides', in Hornblower (1994): 131–66.

HOROWITZ, M. C. (1979), 'Aristotle and Woman', *Journal of the History of Biology* 9: 183–213.

HORTON, R., and FINNEGAN, R. (eds.) (1973), *Modes of Thought: Essays on Thinking in Western and Non-western Societies* (London).

HOW, W. W., and WELLS, J. (1928), *A Commentary on Herodotus*, 2 vols. (Oxford).

HOWIE, J. G. (1984), 'Thukydides' Einstellung zur Vergangenheit: Zuhörerschaft und Wissenschaft in der "Archäologie"', *Klio* 66: 502–32.

HUNT, L. (1989) (ed.), *The New Cultural History* (Berkeley, CA).

HUNT, P. (1998) *Slaves, Warfare, and Ideology in the Greek Historians* (Cambridge).

HUXLEY, G. L. (1972), 'On Aristotle's Historical Methods', *GRBS* 13: 157–69.

—— (1973), 'Aristotle as Antiquary', *GRBS* 14: 271–86.

—— (1979), *On Aristotle and Greek Society* (Belfast).

—— (1980), 'Aristotle, Las Casas and the American Indians', *PRIA* 80C: 57–68.

IGGERS, G. (1984/5), *New Directions in European Historiography*, rev. edn. (Middletown, CT; 1st pub. 1975).

IGNATIEFF, M. (1993), *Blood and Belonging: Journeys into the New Nationalism* (London).

IMMERWAHR, H. R. (1966), *Form and Thought in Herodotus* (Cleveland).

IRWIN, T. H. (1989), *Classical Thought* (Oxford).

JACOBY, F. (1949), *Atthis: The Local Chronicles of Ancient Athens* (Oxford).

JAMES, S. (1984), *The Content of Social Explanation* (Cambridge).

JAMESON, M. H. (1977/8), 'Agriculture and Slavery in Classical Athens', *CJ* 73: 122–45.

—— (1985) (ed.), *The Greek Historians: Literature and History: Papers Presented to A. E. Raubitschek* (Saratoga, Calif.).

—— (1994), 'Class in the ancient Greek countryside', in P. N. Doukellis and L. G. Mendoni (eds.), *Structures rurales et sociétés antiques* (Paris): 55–63.

JONES, A. H. M. (1957), 'The Athenian Democracy and its Critics' (1953), in id., *Athenian Democracy* (Oxford): 41–72.

JONES, J. (1962), *On Aristotle and Greek Tragedy* (London).

JORDAN, D. P. (2000), 'A Personal Letter Found in the Athenian Agora', *Hesperia* 69: 91–103.

JORDANOVA, L. (1980), 'Natural Facts: A Historical Perspective on Science and Sexuality', in MacCormack and Strathern (1980): 42–69.

JUST, R. (1973), 'Conceptions of Women in Classical Athens', *Journal of the Anthropological Society of Oxford* 6: 153–70.

—— (1985), 'Freedom, Slavery and the Female Psyche', in Cartledge and Harvey (1985): 169–88.

—— (1989), *Women in Athenian Law and Life* (London).

KABBANI, R. (1996), *Europe's Myths of Orient: Devise and Rule* (Basingstoke).

KEULS, E. (1985), *The Reign of the Phallus: Sexual Politics in Ancient Athens* (New York).

—— (1986), 'History without Women: Necessity or Illusion?', *DHA* 12: 125–45.

KEYT, D., and MILLER, F. D. (1991) (eds.), *A Companion to Aristotle's 'Politics'* (Oxford).

KIRK, G. S. (1970), *Myth: Its Meaning and Functions in Ancient and Other Cultures* (Cambridge).

—— (1972), 'Greek Mythology: Some New Perspectives', *JHS* 92: 74–85.

—— (1974), *The Nature of Greek Myths* (Harmondsworth).

—— (1981), 'Some Methodological Pitfalls in the Study of Ancient Greek Sacrifice (in particular)', in Fondation Hardt (1981): 41–80.

—— RAVEN, J. E., and SCHOFIELD, M. (1983) (eds.), *The Presocratic Philosophers*, 2nd edn. (Cambridge).

KIRK, I. (1987), 'Images of Amazons: Marriage and Matriarchy', in S. MacDonald (ed.), *Images of Women in Peace and War: Cross-Cultural and Historical Perspectives* (London): 27–39.

KNOX, B. M. W. (1979), 'Myth and Attic Tragedy', in *Word and Action: Essays on the Ancient Theater* (Baltimore): 3–24.

—— (1990*a*), *Essays Ancient and Modern* (Baltimore).

—— (1990*b*), 'The Greek Conquest of Britain' (1981), in Knox (1990*a*): 149–61.

KRAMER, L. S. (1989), 'Literature, Criticism and Historical Imagination: The Literary Challenge of Hayden White and Dominick La Capra', in Hunt (1989): 97–128.

KULLMANN, W. (1991), 'Aristotle as a Natural Scientist', *Acta Classica* 34: 137–50.

LA CAPRA, D. (1983), *Rethinking Intellectual History: Texts, Contexts, Language* (Ithaca, NY).

LACHENAUD, G. (1978), 'Mythologies, religion et philosophie de l'histoire dans Hérodote' (Diss. Lille).

LANE FOX, R. (1986), *Pagans and Christians in the Mediterranean World from the Second Century AD to the Conversion of Constantine* (New York).

LANZA, D. (1979), *Lingua e discorso nell'Atene delle professioni* (Naples).

LAQUEUR, T. (1989), *Making Sex: Body and Gender from the Greeks to Freud* (Cambridge, MA).

LARSEN, J. A. O. (1962), 'Freedom and its Obstacles in Ancient Greece', *CP* 57: 230–34.

—— (1968), *Greek Federal States: Their Institutions and History* (Oxford).

LASSERRE, F. (1976), 'Hérodote et Protagoras: Le débat sur les constitutions', *MH* 33: 65–84.

LATEINER, D. W. (1989), *The Historical Method of Herodotus* (Toronto).

LATTIMORE, R. (1939*a*), 'Herodotus and the Names of Egyptian Gods', *CP* 34: 357–65.

—— (1939*b*), 'The Wise Adviser in Herodotus', *CP* 34: 24–35.

LEACH, E. R. (1967) (ed.), *The Structural Study of Myth and Totemism* (London).

—— (1969), *Genesis as Myth and Other Essays* (London).

LEBOW, R. N., and STRAUSS, B. S. (1991) (eds.), *Hegemonic Rivalry: From Thucydides to the Nuclear Age* (Boulder, CO).

LEFKOWITZ, M. (1981), *Heroines and Hysteries* (London).

—— (1986), *Women in Greek Myth* (London).

LEONTIS, A. (1995), *Topographies of Hellenism* (Princeton, NJ).

LEVINAS, E. (1989), *A Levinas Reader*, ed. S. Hand (Oxford).

LÉVI-STRAUSS, C. (1964–71), *Mythologiques*, i–iv (Paris).

—— (1976), 'The Story of Asdiwal' (1958), repr. with postscript, in id.,

Structural Anthropology, ii. 146–97 (New York) (1st pub. in French, Paris, 1973).

Lévy, E. (1980), 'Cité et citoyen dans la *Politique* d'Aristote', *Ktema* 5: 228–39.

—— (1983) (ed.), *La Femme dans les sociétés anciennes* (Strasbourg).

Leyden, W. van (1949–50), 'Spatium historicum: The Historical Past as Viewed by Hecataeus, Herodotus and Thucydides', *DHJ* 11: 89–104.

Linforth, I. M. (1926), 'Greek Gods and Foreign Gods in Herodotus', *University of California Publications in Classical Philology* 7: 1–25.

—— (1928), 'Named and Unnamed Gods in Herodotus', *University of California Publications in Classical Philology* 9: 201–43.

Lintott, A. W. (1982), *Violence, Civil Strife and Revolution in the Classical City* (London).

Lissarrague, F. (1990), 'Why Satyrs are Good to Represent', in Winkler and Zeitlin (1990): 228–36.

—— (1992), 'Figures of Women', in Schmitt Pantel (1992): 139–229.

—— (1993), 'On the Wildness of Satyrs', in T. Carpenter and C. Faraone (eds.), *Masks of Dionysus* (Ithaca, NY): 207–20.

—— (1994), '*Epiktetos egraphsen*: The Writing on the Cup', in S. Goldhill and R. G. Osborne (eds.), *Art and Text in Ancient Greek Culture* (Cambridge): 12–27.

Livingstone, R. (1921) (ed.), *The Legacy of Greece* (Oxford).

Lloyd, A. B. (1990), 'Herodotus on Egyptians and Libyans', in Fondation Hardt (1990): 215–44.

Lloyd, G. E. R. (1966), *Polarity and Analogy: Two Types of Argumentation in Early Greek Thought* (Cambridge) (repr. Bristol 1987).

—— (1968), *Aristotle: The Growth and Structure of his Thought* (Cambridge).

—— (1973), 'Right and Left in Greek Philosophy' (1962), in Needham (1973): 167–86; also in G. E. R. Lloyd (1991a): 27–48.

—— (1979), *Magic, Reason and Experience: Studies in the Origins and Development of Greek Science* (Cambridge).

—— (1983), *Science, Folklore and Ideology: Studies in the Life Sciences in Ancient Greece* (Cambridge).

—— (1987), *The Revolutions of Wisdom: Studies in the Claims and Practice of Ancient Greek Science* (Berkeley, CA).

—— (1990), *Demystifying Mentalities* (Cambridge).

—— (1991a), *Methods and Problems in Greek Science: Selected Papers* (Cambridge).

LLOYD, G. E. R. (1991*b*), 'Science and Morality in Greco-Roman Antiquity' (1985), in G. E. R. Lloyd (1991*a*): 352–71.

LONG, T. (1986), *Barbarians in Greek Comedy* (Carbondale, IL).

LONIS, R. (1988) (ed.), *L'Étranger dans le monde grec* (Besançon).

LORAUX, N. (1980), 'Thucydide n'est pas un collègue', *QS* 12: 55–81.

—— (1981), *Les Enfants d'Athéna: Idées athéniennes sur la citoyenneté et la division des sexes* (Paris) (new edn., 1984).

—— (1982), 'Mourir devant Troie, tomber pour Athènes', in Gnoli and Vernant (1982): 27–43.

—— (1986*a*), *The Invention of Athens: The Funeral Oration in the Classical City* (Cambridge, MA) (1st pub. in French, Paris, 1981).

—— (1986*b*), 'Thucydide et la sédition dans les mots', *QS* 23: 95–134.

—— (1988), *Tragic Ways of Killing a Woman* (Cambridge, MA) (1st pub. in French, Paris, 1985).

—— (1989*a*), *Les Expériences de Tirésias: Le féminin et l'homme grec* (Paris).

—— (1989*b*), 'La "Belle Mort" spartiate' (1977), in Loraux (1989*a*): 77–91.

—— (1989*c*) 'Le Naturel féminin dans l'histoire', in Loraux (1989*a*): 273–300.

—— (1989*d*) 'Le Lit, la guerre' (1981), in Loraux (1989*a*): 29–53.

—— (1991), 'Reflections of the Greek City on Unity and Division', in Molho, Raaflaub and Emlen (1991): 33–51.

—— (1993 [1984]), *The Children of Athena: Athenian ideas about citizenship and the division between the sexes* (Princeton, NJ) (trans. of Loraux (1984)).

—— (1995), *The Experiences of Tiresias: The Feminine and the Greek Man* (Chicago) (trans. of Loraux (1989*a*)).

—— (1997) *La Cité divisée: L'oubli dans la mémoire d'Athènes* (Paris).

LORD, C., and O'CONNOR, D. K. (1991) (eds.), *Essays on the Aristotelian Foundations of Political Science* (Berkeley, CA).

LOTZE, D. (1959), *Metaxy eleutheron kai doulon: Studien zur Rechtsstellung unfreier Landbevölkerungen in Griechenland im 4. Jahrhundert v. Chr.* (Berlin).

LOUDEN, R. B., and SCHOLLMEIER, P. (1997) (eds.), *The Greeks and Us: Essays in honor of Arthur W. H. Adkins* (Chicago).

LOVEJOY, A. O., and BOAS, G. (1935), *Primitivism and Related Ideas in Antiquity* (Baltimore).

MACCORMACK, C. P., and STRATHERN, M. (1980) (eds.), *Nature, Culture and Gender* (Cambridge).

MACLEOD, C. W. (1983*a*), *Collected Essays* (Oxford).

—— (1983*b*), 'Thucydides on Faction (3. 82–3)' (1978), in Macleod (1983*a*): 123–39.

McMANUS, C. (2001), *Right Hand, Left Hand* (London).

McNEAL, R. A. (1985), 'How Did Pelasgians Become Hellenes?', *ICS* 10: 11–21.

McNEILL, W. H. (1986), *Mythistory and Other Essays* (Chicago).

McNIVEN, T. J. (1995), 'The Unheroic Penis: Otherness Exposed', in *Source: Notes in the History of Art* 15: 10–16.

MALKIN, I. (2001) (ed.), *Ancient Perceptions of Greek Ethnicity* (Washington, DC).

MANOPOULOS, L. (1991), *Stasis–Epanastasis, Neoterismos–Kinesis* (Thessaloniki).

MARANDA, P. (1972) (ed.), *Mythology* (Harmondsworth).

MARINATOS, N. (1981*a*), *Thucydides and Religion* (Königstein).

—— (1981*b*), 'Thucydides and Oracles', *JHS* 101: 138–41.

MASON, P. G. (1984), *The City of Men: Ideology, Sexual Politics and Social Formation* (Göttingen).

—— (1990), *Deconstructing America: Representations of the Other* (London).

MATTHEWS, J. F. (1989), *The Roman Empire of Ammianus* (London).

MEIER, C. (1988), *Die politische Kunst der griechischen Tragödie* (Munich).

—— (1990), 'The Greek Discovery of Politics' (Cambridge, MA) (1st pub. in German, Frankfurt-am-Main, 1980).

MEIGGS, R. (1972), *The Athenian Empire* (Oxford).

MEISTER, K. (1990), *Die griechische Geschichtsschreibung* (Stuttgart).

MELEZE-MODRZEJEWSKI, J. (1975), 'Hommes libres et bêtes dans les droits antiques', in Poliakov (1975): 75–102.

MEYER, B. F., and SANDERS, E. P. (1982) (eds.), *Jewish and Christian Self-Definition*, iii: *Self-Definition in the Graeco-Roman World* (London).

MIKALSON, J. D. (1983), *Athenian Popular Religion* (Chapel Hill, NC).

—— (1984), 'Religion and the Plague in Athens 431–423 B.C.', *Festschrift Sterling Dow*, ed. K. J. Rigsby (*GRBS* Monograph 10) (Durham, NC): 217–25.

—— (1991), *Honor Thy Gods: Popular Religion in Greek Tragedy* (Chapel Hill, NC).

MOI, T. (1985), *Sexual/Textual Politics* (London).

—— (1989), *Feminist Theory and Simone de Beauvoir* (Oxford).

MILLENDER, E. G. (forthcoming), 'The Teacher of Hellas: Athenian Democratic Ideology and the "Barbarization" of Sparta in Fifth-Century Greek Thought' (Diss. Pennsylvania).

MILLER, M. C. (1997), *Athens and Persia in the Fifth Century B.C: A Study in Cultural Receptivity* (Cambridge).

MOLHO, A., RAAFLAUB, K., and EMLEN, J. (1991) (eds.), *City States in Classical Antiquity and Medieval Italy* (Stuttgart).

MOLYNEAUX, B. L. (1997) (ed.), *The Cultural Life of Images: Visual Representation in Archaeology* (London).

MOMIGLIANO, A. D. (1966a), *Studies in Historiography* (London).

—— (1966b), 'The Place of Herodotus in the History of Historiography' (1958), in Momigliano (1966a): 127–42.

—— (1975), *Alien Wisdom: The Limits of Hellenization* (Cambridge).

—— (1977), *Essays in Ancient and Modern Historiography* (Oxford).

—— (1978), 'The Historians of the Classical World and their Audience Some Suggestions', *ASNP* (3) 8: 59–75.

—— (1979), 'Persian Empire and Greek Freedom', in A. Ryan (ed.), *The Idea of Freedom, Festschrift I. Berlin* (Oxford): 139–51.

—— (1980), 'The Place of Ancient Historiography in Modern Historiography', in W. Den Boer (ed.), *Les Études classiques aux XIXᵉ et XXᵉ siècle: Leur place dans l'histoire des idées* (Entretiens Hardt 26, Vandœuvres-Geneva): 127–53.

—— (1981), 'The Rhetoric of History and the History of Rhetoric: On Hayden White's Tropes', *Comparative Criticism: A Year Book*, iii, ed. E. S. Shaffer (Cambridge): 259–68.

—— (1990), *The Classical Foundations of Modern Historiography* (Berkeley, CA).

—— (1998), *Ausgewählte Schriften zur Geschichte und Geschichtsschreibung*, ed. G. Most, vol. i (ed. W. Nippel) (Stuttgart).

MORGAN, E. S. (1975), *American Slavery, American Freedom* (New York).

MORRIS, I. (1994) (ed.), *Classical Greece: Ancient Histories and Modern Archaeologies* (Cambridge).

MORRIS, S. P. (1992), *Daidalos and the Origins of Greek Art* (Princeton NJ).

MOSSE, C. (1967), 'La Conception du citoyen dans la Politique d'Aristote', *Eirene* 6: 17–21.

—— (1985), '"Aste kai politis": La dénomination de la femme athénienne dans les plaidoyers demosthéniens', *Ktema* 10: 77–9.

—— (1986) (ed.), *La Grèce ancienne* (Paris).

MOST, G. W. (1989), 'The Stranger's Stratagem: Self-Disclosure and Self-Sufficiency in Greek Culture', *JHS* 109: 114–33.

MULGAN, R. R. (1977), *Aristotle's Political Theory: An Introduction for Students of Political Theory* (Oxford).

MÜLLER, C. W. (1967), 'Protagoras über die Götter', *Hermes* 95: 140–59.

MUNSON, R. V. (1988), 'Artemisia in Herodotus', *CA* 7: 91–106.

MURNAGHAN, S. (1988), 'How a Woman can be more like a Man: The Dialogue between Ischomachus and his Wife in Xenophon's *Œconomicus*', *Helios* 15: 9–18.

MURRAY, G. (1921), 'The Value of Greece to the Future of the World', in Livingstone (1921): 1–23.

MURRAY, O. (1987), 'Herodotus and Oral History', in Sancisi-Weerdenburg and Kuhrt (1987): ii. 93–115.

—— (1988), 'The Ionian Revolt', *CAH*(2), iv. 461–90.

MYRES, J. L. (1953), *Herodotus: The Father of History* (Oxford).

NEEDHAM, R. (1973) (ed.), *Right and Left: Essays on Dual Symbolic Classification* (Chicago).

—— (1987), *Counterpoints* (Berkeley, CA).

NICKEL, R. (1979), *Xenophon* (Darmstadt).

NILSSON, M. P. (1940), *Greek Popular Religion* (New York).

—— (1948), *Greek Piety* (Oxford).

—— (1951), *Cults, Myths, Oracles and Politics in Ancient Greece* (Lund) (repr. Göteborg, 1986).

NIPPEL, W. (1990), *Griechen, Barbaren und 'Wilde': Alte Geschichte und Sozialanthropologie* (Frankfurt-am-Main).

—— (1996) 'La costruzione dell' "Altro"', in Settis (1996): 165–96.

NOCK, A. D. (1972a), *Essays on Religion and the Ancient World*, ed. Z. Stewart, 2 vols. (Oxford).

—— (1972b), 'The Cult of Heroes' (1944), in Nock (1972a): ii. 575–602.

—— (1972c), 'Religious Attitudes of the Ancient Greeks' (1942), in Nock (1972a), ii, 534–50.

NORTH, H. F. (1977), 'The Mare, the Vixen and the Bee: Sophrosyne as the Virtue of Women in Antiquity', *ICS* 2: 35–49.

NUSSBAUM, G. B. (1978), 'Plato and Xenophon—Political Theory and Political Experiment', *LCM* 3: 279–84.

OBER, J. (1998), *Political Dissent in Classical Athens: Intellectual Critics of Popular Rule* (Princeton).

OBER, J., and HEDRICK, C. W. (1996) (eds.), *Demokratia: A Conversation on Democracies, Ancient and Modern* (Princeton, NJ).

OLLIER, F. (1933–43), *Le Mirage spartiate: Étude sur l'idéalisation de Sparte dans l'Antiquité grecque*, 2 vols. (Paris).

OOST, S. I. (1975), 'Thucydides and the Irrational: Sundry Passages', *CP* 70: 186–96.

—— (1977), 'Xenophon's Attitude toward Women', *CW* 71: 225–36.

ORTNER, S. (1974), 'Is Female to Male as Nature is to Culture?', in Rosaldo and Lamphere (1974): 67–87.

—— (2000), 'An Other View: An Essay in Political History', in B. Cohen 2000: 23–42.

OSBORNE, R. G. (1999), 'Representing Pandora', *OMNIBUS* 37: 13–14.

OSTWALD, M. (1982), *Autonomia: Its Genesis and Early History* (Chico, CA).

—— (1986), *From Popular Sovereignty to the Sovereignty of the Law: Law, Society and Politics in Fifth-Century Athens* (Berkeley, CA).

OTNES, P. (2000), *Other-Wise: Alterity, Materiality, Mediation* (Scandinavian University Press).

OWEN, G. E. L. (1986), '*Tithenai ta phainomena*' (1961), in id., *Logic, Science and Dialectics*, ed. M. Nussbaum (London): 239–51.

PAGDEN, A. (1986), *The Fall of Natural Man: The American Indian and the Origins of Comparative Ethnography* (2nd edn., Cambridge).

PARKE, H. W. (1932), 'The Tithe of Apollo and the Harmost at Decelea, 413 to 404 B.C.', *JHS* 52: 42–6.

PARKER, R. (1983), *Miasma: Pollution and Purification in Early Greek Religion* (Oxford).

—— (1989), 'Spartan Religion', in A. Powell (ed.), *Classical Sparta: Techniques behind her Success* (London): 142–72.

PARRY, A. (1981), *Logos and Ergon in Thucydides* (New York) (Diss. Harvard, 1957).

PATTERSON, C. B. (1981), *Perikles' Citizenship Law of 451–450 B.C.* (New York).

—— (1986), '*Hai Attikai*: The Other Athenians', *Helios* 13/2: 49–68.

PATTERSON, O. (1982), *Slavery and Social Death: A Comparative Study* (Cambridge, Mass.).

—— (1991), *Freedom in the Making of Western Culture* (London).

PEARSON, L. (1939), *Early Ionian Historians* (Oxford).

PECIRKA, J. (1967), 'A Note on Aristotle's Definition of Citizenship', *Eirene* 6: 23–6.

PELLING, C. B. R. (2000), *Literary Texts and the Greek Historian* (London).

PEMBROKE, S. G. (1965), 'Last of the Matriarchs: A Study in the Inscriptions of Lycia', *Journal of the Economic and Social History of the Orient* 8: 217–47.

—— (1967), 'Women in Charge: The Function of Alternatives in Early Greek Tradition and the Ancient Idea of Matriarchy', *JWCI* 30: 1–35.

PERADOTTO, J., and LEVINE, M. M. (1989) (eds.), *The Challenge of 'Black Athena'* (Arethusa Special Issue) (Buffalo).

—— and SULLIVAN, J. P. (1984) (eds.), *Women in the Ancient World: The Arethusa Papers* (Buffalo).

PERLMAN, S. (1976), 'Panhellenism, the Polis and Imperialism', *Historia* 25: 1–30.

POCOCK, J. G. A. (1985), *Virtue, Commerce, and History: Essays on Political Thought and History, chiefly in the Eighteenth Century* (Cambridge).

POLIAKOV, L. (1975) (ed.), *Hommes et bêtes: Entretiens sur le racisme* (Paris).

POMEROY, S. B. (1975/6), *Goddesses, Whores, Wives and Slaves: Women in Classical Antiquity* (New York).

—— (1991) (ed.), *Women's History and Ancient History* (Chapel Hill, NC).

—— (1994), *Xenophon, Oeconomicus: A Social and Historical Commentary* (Oxford).

POWELL, A., and HODKINSON, S. J. (1994) (eds.), *The Shadow of Sparta* (Cardiff).

PRICE, M. (1974), *Coins of the Macedonians* (London).

PRICE, S. R. F. (1984), *Rituals and Power: The Roman Imperial Cult in Asia Minor* (Cambridge).

PRITCHETT, W. K. (1991), *The Greek State at War* (Berkeley, CA), v.

RAAFLAUB, K. (1983), 'Democracy, Oligarchy and the Concept of the Free Citizen in Late Fifth-Century Athens', *Political Theory* 11: 517–44.

—— (1985), *Die Entdeckung der Freiheit: Zur historischen Semantik und Gesellschaftsgeschichte eines politischen Grundbegriffes der Griechen* (Munich).

—— (1987), 'Herodotus, Political Thought and the Meaning of History', *Arethusa* 20: 221–48.

—— (1993) (ed.), *Anfänge des politischen Denkens in der Antike* (Munich).

RADKE, G. (1936), 'Die Bedeutung der weissen und schwarzen Farbe im Kult und Brauch der Griechen' (Diss. Berlin).

RAHE, P. A. (1984), 'The Primacy of Politics in Classical Greece', *AHR* 89: 265–93.

RANKE-HEINEMANN, U. (1990/1), *Eunuchs for the Kingdom of Heaven: The Catholic Church and Sexuality* (New York) (1st pub. in German, Hamburg, 1988).

RAPHAEL, F. (1997), *The Necessity of Anti-Semitism* (Manchester).

RAWSON, E. (1969), *The Spartan Tradition in European Thought* (Oxford; repr. 1991).

REDFIELD, J. M. (1977/8), 'The Women of Sparta', *CJ* 73: 146–61.

—— (1985), 'Herodotus the Tourist', *CP* 80: 97–118.

REEDER, E. D. (1995) (ed.), *Pandora: Women in Classical Greece* (Baltimore).

RHODES, P. J. (1986), *The Greek City-States: A Source Book* (London).

RHODES, R. F. (1995), *Architecture and Meaning on the Athenian Acropolis* (Cambridge).

RIDLEY, R. T. (1981), 'Exegesis and Audience in Thucydides', *Hermes* 109: 23–46.

ROBERTS, J. T. (1994), *Athens on Trial: The Anti-democratic Tradition in Western Thought* (Princeton).

ROBERTSON, C. M. (1992), *The Art of Vase-painting in Classical Athens* (Cambridge).

ROHDE, E. (1974), *Psyche: Seelencult und Unsterblichkeitsglaube der Griechen* (Darmstadt, repr. of the 2nd edn. 1898).

ROMILLY, J. DE (1989), *La Grèce antique à la découverte de la liberté* (Paris).

—— (1992), *The Great Sophists in Periclean Athens* (Oxford) (1st pub. in French, Paris, 1988).

ROSALDO, M. Z., and LAMPHERE, L. (1974) (eds.), *Woman, Culture and Society* (Stanford, CA).

ROSELLINI, M., and SAÏD, S. (1978), 'Usages des femmes et autres *nomoi* chez les "sauvages" d'Hérodote', *ASNP* (3) 8: 949–1005.

ROSIVACH, V. J. (1987), 'Autochthony and the Athenians', *CQ* 37: 294–306.

ROUSSELLE, A. (1980), 'Observation féminine et idéologie masculine: Le corps de la femme d'après les médecins grecs', *Annales (ESC)* 35: 1089–115.

RUDHARDT, J. (1958), *Notions fondamentales de la pensée religieuse et actes constitutifs du culte dans la Grèce ancienne* (Geneva).

—— (1966), 'Considérations sur le polythéisme', *Revue Théologique et Philologique* 99: 353–64.

—— (1981*a*), *Du mythe, de la religion grecque et de la compréhension d'autrui* (Geneva).

—— (1981*b*), 'Sur la possibilité de comprendre une religion étrangère' (1964), in Rudhardt (1981*a*): 13–32.

SAID, E. (1978), *Orientalism* (London).

—— (1985), 'Orientalism Reconsidered', in Barker (1985): i. 14–27.

—— (1995), *Orientalism*, new edn. with 'Afterword' (Harmondsworth).

SAÏD, S. (1983), 'Féminin, femme et femelle dans les grands traités biologiques d'Aristote', in Lévy (1983): 93–123.

STE. CROIX, G. E. M. DE (1954/5), 'The Character of the Athenian Empire', *Historia* 3: 1–41.

—— (1970), 'Some Observations on the Property Rights of Athenian Women', *CR* 20: 273–8.

—— (1972a), *The Origins of the Peloponnesian War* (London).

—— (1972b), 'The Religion of the Roman World', *Didaskalos* 4: 61–74.

—— (1975a), 'Aristotle on History and Poetry (*Poetics* 9, 1451a36-b11)', in B. Levick (ed.), *The Ancient Historian and his Materials (Festschrift C. E. Stevens)* (Farnborough): 45–58.

—— (1975b) 'Early Christian Attitudes to Property and Slavery', *Studies in Church History* 12: 1–38.

—— (1977), 'Herodotus', *G&R* 24: 130–48.

—— (1981), *The Class Struggle in the Ancient Greek World: From the Archaic Age to the Arab Conquests* (London) (corr. impr. 1983).

SAMUEL, R., and THOMPSON, P. (1990) (eds.), *Myths We Live By* (London).

SANCISI-WEERDENBURG, H. (1983), 'Exit Atossa: Images of Women in Greek Historiography on Persia', in Cameron and Kuhrt (1983): 20–33.

—— and KUHRT, A. (1987) (eds.), *Achaemenid History*, 3 vols. (Leiden).

SANDAY, P. G., and GOODENOUGH, R. G. (1990) (eds.), *Beyond the Second Sex: New Directions in the Anthropology of Gender* (Philadelphia).

SARGISSON, L. (2000), *Utopian Bodies and the Politics of Transgression* (London).

SASSI, M. M. (2001), *The Science of Man in Ancient Greece* (Chicago) (1st pub. in Italian, 1988).

SAWYER, R. (1986), *Slavery in the Twentieth Century* (London).

SCHAPS, D. (1977), 'The Woman Least Mentioned: Etiquette and Women's Names', *CQ* 27: 323–30.

—— (1982), 'The Women of Greece in Wartime', *CP* 77: 193–213.

SCHLAIFER, R. (1968), 'Greek Theories of Slavery from Homer to Aristotle' (1936), in Finley (1968): 93–132.

SCHLESIER, R. (2000), 'Menschen und Götter unterwegs: Rituale und Reise in der griechische Antike', in Hölscher (2000): 129–57.

SCHMITT PANTEL, P. (1992) (ed.), *A History of Women in the West*, i: *From Ancient Goddesses to Christian Saints* (Cambridge, MA) (1st pub. in Italian, Rome, 1990).

SCHNAPP, A. (1988), 'Why Did the Greeks Need Images?', in Christiansen and Melander (1988): 568–74.

—— (2000), 'Pourquoi les Barbares n'ont-ils point d'images?', in Hölscher (2000): 205–16.

SCHNEIDER, R. M. (1992), 'Barbar II (ikonographisch)', *Reallexikon für Antike und Christentum*, Supp. Bd. I: coll. 895–962.

SCHOFIELD, M. (1990), 'Ideology and Philosophy in Aristotle's Theory of Slavery', in G. Patzig (ed.), *Aristoteles' 'Politik': Akten des XI. Symposium Aristotelicum* (Göttingen): 1–27.

SCOTT, J. WALLACH (1988), *Gender and the Politics of History* (New York).

SEGAL, C. P. (1982), 'Afterword: J.-P. Vernant and the Study of Ancient Greece', *Arethusa* 15: 221–34.

—— (1986), 'Greek Tragedy: Writing, Truth and the Representation of the Self', in id., *Interpreting Greek Tragedy: Myth, Poetry, Text* (Ithaca, NY): 75–109.

—— (1995), 'Spectator and Listener', in Vernant (1995): 184–217.

SETTIS, S. (1996) (ed.), *I Greci I. Noi e I Greci* (Turin).

SIEMS, A. K. (1988) (ed.), *Sexualität und Erotik in der Antike* (Darmstadt).

SISSA, G. (1990), 'Maidenhood without Maidenhead: The Female Body in Ancient Greece' (1984/7), in Halperin, Winkler, and Zeitlin (1990): 339–64.

—— (1992), 'The Sexual Philosophies of Plato and Aristotle', in Schmitt Pantel (1992): 46–81.

SKINNER, Q. R. D. (1997), *Liberty before Liberalism* (Cambridge).

SMITH, N. D. (1991), 'Aristotle's Theory of Natural Slavery' (1983), corr. repr. in Keyt and Miller (1991): 142–55.

SNOWDEN, F. M., jun. (1970), *Blacks in Antiquity: Ethiopians in Greco-Roman Experience* (Cambridge, MA).

—— (1983), *Before Color Prejudice* (Cambridge, MA).

SORDI, M. (1950/1), 'I caratteri dell'opera storiografica di Senofonte nelle Elleniche', *Athenaeum* 28–9: 3–53, 273–348.

SOURVINOU-INWOOD, C. (1988), *Studies in Girls' Transitions: Aspects of the 'Arkteia' and Age Representation in Attic Iconography* (Athens).

—— (1989), 'Assumptions and the Creation of Meaning: Reading Sophocles' *Antigone*', *JHS* 109: 134–48.

SPARKES, B. A. (1997), 'Some Greek Images of Others', in Molyneaux (1997): 130–58.

SPIVEY, N. J. (1996), *Understanding Greek Sculpture: Ancient Meanings, Modern Readings* (London).

—— (1997), *Greek Art* (London).

STAHL, H.-P. (1966), *Thukydides: Die Stellung des Menschen im geschichtlichen Prozess* (Munich).

STAHL, M. (1987), *Aristokraten und Tyrannen im archäischen Athen:*

Untersuchungen zur Überlieferung, zur Sozialstruktur und zur Entstehung des Staates (Stuttgart).

—— (1997), 'Antike und moderne Demokratie: Probleme und Zukunftsperspektiven der westlichen Demokratie im Spiegel des griechischen Bürgerstaates', in Eder and Hölkeskamp (1997): 227–45.

STALLEY, R. F. (1995) (ed.), *Aristotle Politics*, trans. E. Barker (Oxford).

STAMPP, K. M. (1956), *The Peculiar Institution: Slavery in the Ante-Bellum South* (New York).

STARR, C. G. (1968), *The Awakening of the Greek Historical Spirit* (New York).

STEDMAN JONES, G. (1972), 'History: The Poverty of Empiricism', in R. Blackburn (ed.), *Ideology in Social Science: Readings in Critical Social Theory* (London): 96–115.

STEIN-HÖLKESKAMP, E. (1989), *Adelskultur und Polisgesellschaft: Studien zum griechischen Adel in archäischer und klassischer Zeit* (Stuttgart).

STEINER, D. T. (1994), *The Tyrant's Writ: Myths and Images of Writing in Ancient Greece* (Princeton, NJ).

STEINER, G. (1984), *Antigones* (Oxford).

STEWART, A. (1997), *Art, Desire, and the Body in Ancient Greece* (Cambridge).

STOCKS, J. L. (1936), 'Skhole', *CQ* 30: 177–87.

SYME, R. (1962), 'Thucydides', *PBA* 48: 39–56.

TAAFFE, L. K. (1993), *Aristophanes and Women* (London).

TAPLIN, O. (1989), *Greek Fire* (London).

TARN, W. W., and GRIFFITH, G. T. (1952), *Hellenistic Civilisation*, 3rd edn. (London).

TATUM, J. (1989), *Xenophon's Imperial Fiction* (Princeton, NJ).

TAYLOR, M. W. (1981), *The Tyrant Slayers: The Heroic Image in Fifth-Century BC Athenian Art* (New York) (Diss. Harvard 1975).

THOM, M. (1995), *Republics, Nations and Tribes* (London).

THOMAS, C. G. (1988) (ed.), *Paths from Ancient Greece* (Leiden).

THOMAS, R. (1989), *Oral Tradition and Written Record in Classical Athens* (Cambridge).

—— (1992), *Literacy and Orality in Ancient Greece* (Cambridge).

THOMMEN, L. (1996*a*), *Lakedaimonion Politeia: Die Entstehung der spartanischen Verfassung* (Stuttgart).

—— (1996*b*), 'Nacktheit und Zivilisationsprozess in Griechenland', in *Historische Anthropologie, Kultur, Gesellschaft, Alltag* 43: 438–58.

THOMPSON, N. S. (1996), *Herodotus and the Origins of the Political Community: Arion's Leap* (New-Haven).

THOMSON, J. A. K. (1935), *The Art of the Logos* (London).

TONKIN, E., McDONALD, M., and CHAPMAN, M. (1989) (eds.), *History and Ethnicity* (London).

TOSH, J. (1991), *The Pursuit of History*, 2nd edn. (London).

TOURRAIX, A. (1976), 'La Femme et le pouvoir chez Hérodote', *DHA* 2: 369–86.

TOYNBEE, A. J. (1969), *Some Problems of Greek History* (Oxford).

TUPLIN, C. J. (1985), 'Imperial Tyranny: Some Reflections on a Classical Greek Political Metaphor', in Cartledge and Harvey (1985): 348–75.

TYRRELL, W. B. (1984), *Amazons: A Study of Athenian Mythmaking* (Baltimore).

ULF, C. (1996), *Wege zur Genese griechischer Identität: Die Bedeutung der früharchäischen Zeit* (Berlin).

—— (1997), 'Überlegungen zur Funktion überregionaler Feste in der frühgriechischen Staatenwelt', in Eder and Hölkeskamp (1997): 37–62.

VANSINA, J. (1973), *Oral Tradition: A Study in Historical Methodology*, 2nd edn. (Harmondsworth).

—— (1985), *Oral Tradition as History* (London).

VEESER, H. ARAM (1989) (ed.), *The New Historicism* (London).

VERDENIUS, W. J. (1960), 'Traditional and Personal Elements in Aristotle's Religion', *Phronesis* 5: 56–70.

VERNANT, J.-P. (1980a), *Myth and Society in Ancient Greece* (London) (1st pub. in French, Paris, 1974).

—— (1980b), 'Between the Beasts and the Gods' (1972), in Vernant (1980a): 130–67.

—— (1980c), 'Marriage' (1973), in Vernant (1980a): 45–70.

—— (1980d), 'The Reason of Myth' (1974), in Vernant (1980a): 186–242.

—— (1983a), *Myth and Thought among the Greeks* (London) (1st pub. in French, Paris, 1965).

—— (1983b), 'From Myth to Reason: The Formation of Positivist Thought in Archaic Greece' (1st pub. in French, 1957), in Vernant (1983a): 343–74.

—— (1983c), 'Some Psychological Aspects of Work in Ancient Greece' (1st pub. in French, 1953), in Vernant (1983a): 271–8.

—— (1983d), 'Space and Political Organization in Ancient Greece' (1st pub. in French, 1965), in Vernant (1983a): 212–34.

—— (1991a), *Mortals and Immortals: Collected Essays*, ed. F. I. Zeitlin (Princeton, NJ).

—— (1991b), 'The Birth of Images' (1st pub. in French, 1975), in Vernant (1991a): 164–85.

—— (1991c), 'A General Theory of Sacrifice and the Slaying of the

Victims in the Greek "thusia"' (1st pub. in French in Fondation Hardt 1981), in Vernant (1991*a*): 290–302.

—— (1991*d*), 'Greek Religion, Ancient Religions' (1st pub. in French, 1975) in Vernant (1991*a*): 269–89.

—— (1995) (ed.), *The Greeks* (Chicago) (1st pub. in Italian, Rome, 1991).

—— and DETIENNE, M. (1978), *Cunning Intelligence in Greek Culture and Society* (Hassocks) (1st pub. in French, Paris, 1974).

—— and VIDAL-NAQUET, P. (1988), *Myth and Tragedy in Ancient Greece*, 2 vols. (in 1) (Cambridge, MA) (1st pub. in French, Paris, 1972–86).

VERSNEL, H. S. (1987), 'Wife and Helpmate: Women of Ancient Athens in Anthropological Perspective', in J. Blok and P. Mason (eds.), *Sexual Asymmetry: Studies in Ancient Society* (Leiden): 59–86.

VEYNE, P. (1984), *Writing History: Essay on Epistemology* (Manchester) (1st pub. in French, Paris 1971).

—— (1988), *Did the Greeks Believe in their Myths? An Essay on the Constitutive Imagination* (Chicago) (1st pub. in French, Paris, 1983).

VIDAL-NAQUET, P. (1975), 'Bêtes, hommes et dieux chez les Grecs', in Poliakov (1975): 129–42.

—— (1986*a*), *The Black Hunter: Forms of Thought and Forms of Society in the Greek World* (Cambridge, MA) (1st pub. in French, Paris, 1981).

—— (1986*b*), 'Epaminondas the Pythagorean, or the Tactical Problem of Right and Left' (with P. Lévêque, 1960), in Vidal-Naquet (1986*a*): 61–82.

—— (1986*c*), 'Greek Rationality and the City' (1967), in Vidal-Naquet (1986*a*): 249–62.

—— (1986*d*), 'Reflections on Greek Historical Writing about Slavery' (1973), in Vidal-Naquet (1986*a*): 168–88.

—— (1986*e*), 'Slavery and the Rule of Women in Tradition, Myth, and Utopia' (1st pub. In French 1970; rev. 1979), in Vidal-Naquet (1986*a*): 205–23.

VLASTOS, G. (1968), 'Slavery in Plato's Thought' (1940), repr. with add. in Finley (1968): 133–49.

VOGT, J. (1974), *Ancient Slavery and the Ideal of Man* (Oxford) (1st pub. in German, Wiesbaden, 1972).

WALBANK, F. W. (1985*a*), *Selected Papers on Greek and Roman History and Historiography* (Cambridge).

—— (1985*b*), 'The Problem of Greek Nationality' (1951), in Walbank (1985*a*): 1–19.

WALCOT, P. (1973), 'The Funeral Speech: A Study of Values', *G&R* 20: 111–21.

WALCOT, P. (1985), 'Greek Attitudes towards Women: The Mythological Evidence', *G&R* 31: 37–47.

WALLACE, R. W. (1994), 'Private Lives and Public Enemies: Freedom of Thought in Classical Athens', in Boegehold and Scafuro (1994): 127–55.

WALSER, G. (1984), *Hellas und Iran: Studien zu den griechisch-persischen Beziehungen vor Alexander* (Darmstadt).

WALTER, U. (1993), *An der Polis teilhaben: Bürgerstaat und Zugehörigkeit im Archäischen Griechenland* (Stuttgart).

WARDMAN, A. E. (1960), 'Myth in Greek Historiography', *Historia* 9: 403–13.

WASSERMANN, F. M. (1947), 'Thucydides and the Disintegration of the polis', *TAPA* 78: 18–36.

WATERFIELD, R., and CARTLEDGE, P. (1997) (eds.), *Xenophon: Hiero the Tyrant and other Treatises* (London).

WATERS, K. H. (1985), *Herodotus the Historian: His Problems, Methods and Originality* (London).

WEIL, R. (1960), *Aristote et l'histoire: Essai sur la 'Politique'* (Paris).

—— (1976), 'Artémise, ou le monde à l'envers', in *Recueil A. Plassart* (Paris): 215–24.

WEIL, S. (1986), 'The *Iliad* or the Poem of Force' (1st pub. in French, 1940–1), repr. in Simone Weil, *An Anthology*, ed. S. Miles (London): 182–215.

WEILER, I. (1968), 'The Greek and Non-Greek World in the Archaic Period', *GRBS* 9: 21–9.

—— (1974), 'Von "Wesen", "Geist" und "Eigenart" der Völker der Alten Welt: Eine Anthologie altertumswissenschaftlicher Typisierungskunst', in 'Kritische und vergleichende Studien zur Alten Geschichte und Universalgeschichte', in *Innsbrucker Beiträge zur Kulturwissenschaft* 18: 243–91.

—— (1996), review of Cartledge, *The Greeks* (1st edn.), in *Gnomon* 68: 385–89.

WELWEI, K.-W. (1974–7), *Unfreie im antiken Kriegsdienst*, 2 vols. (Mainz).

—— (1990), 'Die Staatswerdung Athens: Mythos und Geschichte', in Binder and Effe (1990): 162–87.

WEST, M. L. (1997), *The East Face of Helicon: West Asian elements in Greek poetry and myth* (Oxford).

WESTERMANN, W. L. (1968a), *Athenaeus and the Slaves of Athens* (1941), in Finley (1968): 73–92.

—— (1968b), 'Slavery and the Elements of Freedom' (1943), in Finley (1968): 17–32.

WHITE, H. (1973), *Metahistory: The Historical Imagination in Nineteenth-Century Europe* (Baltimore).

—— (1978), 'The Historical Text as Literary Artifact', in Canary and Kozicki (1978): 41–72.

—— (1989), *The Content of the Form: Narrative Discourse and Historical Representation* (Baltimore).

WHITEHEAD, D. (1975), 'Aristotle the Metic', *PCPS* 21: 94–9.

—— (1977), *The Ideology of the Athenian Metic* (Cambridge).

—— (1980), 'Thucydides: Fact-Grubber or Philosopher?', *G&R* 27: 158–65.

—— (1984), 'Immigrant Communities in the Classical Polis: Some Principles for a Synoptic Treatment', *AC* 53: 47–59.

—— (1986), 'The Ideology of the Athenian Metic: Some Pendants and a Reappraisal', *PCPS* 32: 145–58.

—— (1991), 'Norms of Citizenship in Ancient Greece', in Molho, Raaflaub, and Emlen (1991): 135–54.

WIEDEMANN, T. (1983), 'Thucydides, Women and the Limits of Rational Analysis', *G&R* 30: 163–70.

—— (1987), *Slavery* (*G&R* New Surveys in the Classics 19; Oxford).

WIESEN, D. (1980), 'Herodotus and the Modern Debate over Race and Slavery', *AncW* 3: 3–14.

WILDE, O. (1909), 'The Rise of Historical Criticism' (1879), in *Essays and Lectures* (London): 1–108.

—— (1954), 'The Decay of Lying: An Observation' (1889), also in id., *'De Profundis' and Other Writings*, ed. H. Pearson (Harmondsworth): 55–87.

WILSON, P. J. (1991), 'Demosthenes 21 (Against Meidias): Democratic Abuse', *PCPS* 37: 164–95.

—— (1999), 'The Aulos in Athens', in S. Goldhill and R. Osborne (eds.), *Performance Culture and Athenian Democracy* (Cambridge), 58–95.

—— (2001), *The Athenian Institution of the Khoregia: The Chorus, the City and the Stage* (Cambridge).

WINCH, P. B. (1987), 'Understanding a Primitive Society' (1964), in Gibbons (1987): 32–63.

WINKLER, J. J. (1990), *The Constraints of Desire: The Anthropology of Sex and Gender in Ancient Greece* (London).

—— and ZEITLIN, F. I. (1990) (eds.), *Nothing to Do with Dionysos? Athenian Drama in its Social Context* (Princeton, NJ).

WOHL, V. (1998), *Intimate Commerce: Exchange, Gender and Subjectivity in Greek Tragedy* (Austin).

WOOD, E. M. (1988), *Peasant-Citizen and Slave: The Foundations of Athenian Democracy* (London).

WOODMAN, A. J. (1988), *Rhetoric in Classical Historiography* (London).

ZAICEV, A. (1993), *Das griechische Wunder: Die Entstehung der griechischen Zivilisation* (Konstanz).

ZEITLIN, F. I. (1984), 'The Dynamics of Misogyny: Myth and Myth-making in the "Oresteia"' (1978), in Peradotto and Sullivan (1984): 159–94.

—— (1986a), 'Configuration of Rape in Greek Myth', in S. Tomaselli and R. Porter (eds.), *Rape* (London): 122–51.

—— (1986b), 'Thebes: Theater of Self and Society in Athenian Drama', in J. P. Burian (ed.), *Greek Tragedy and Political Theory* (Berkeley, CA): 101–41.

—— (1989), 'Mysteries of Identity and Designs of the Self in Euripides' *Ion*', *PCPS* 35: 144–97.

—— (1990), 'Playing the Other: Theater, Theatricality and the Feminine in Greek Drama' (1985), in Winkler and Zeitlin (1990): 63–96.

—— (1996), *Playing the Other: Gender and Society in Classical Greek Literature* (Chicago).

Index

Bold type indicates main entries